SOME KṢATRIYA TRIBES OF ANCIENT INDIA

SOME KṢATRIYA TRIBES OF ANCIENT INDIA

Bimala Charan Law

BKP

BHARATIYA KALA PRAKASHAN
DELHI (INDIA)

First Edition : 1923
Revised Edition : 2009

Published by **C.P. Gautam**
BHARATIYA KALA PRAKASHAN
3421-A, IInd Floor Narang Colony, Tri Nagar,
Delhi-110035. Ph. : 32967505, Telefax : 01127393083
E-mail : 3241bkp@yahoo.co.in
Website : www.bkpbooks.com

ISBN : 978-81-8090-229-1

Printed By :
Laxmi Offset Process, Delhi.

To

THE SACRED MEMORY OF MY GRANDFATHER.

THE LATE BABU JAYGOBINDA LAW, C.I.E.,

AS A

TOKEN OF PROFOUND REVERENCE
AND ADMIRATION

CONTENTS

FOREWORD

Ancient India, though she passed through many vicissitudes of fortune, has left us no historian of her national life. Brahmins and Buddhists alike, intent on the satisfaction of the desire to attain that insight which delivers from the burden of empirical existence, could see nothing of sufficient value in the passing events of life to render them willing to record them or to seek to interpret their significance, while princes and their followers found an adequate substitute for historic narrations in the famous legends of the epics. Hence it follows that, if with the curiosity of the modern world we seek to reconstruct the history of India in the centuries immediately preceding and following the Christian era, we are compelled to build up a structure by the careful collection and fitting together of every available fragment of evidence. Much has indeed already been accomplished, but what has been achieved has only brought into greater prominence the innumerable lacunae in our information, and the necessity of persistent and detailed work before it will be possible to feel any assurance as to the soundness of our reconstruction of early Indian history.

The most pressing need at the present day is the detailed investigation of carefully chosen aspects of Indian history, and it was a happy thought of Dr. Bimala Charan Law to select for investigation the history of certain Kṣatriya tribes of ancient India. Careful collections of facts, such as are contained in this work, form the only sound basis of further research, and the future historian of India will find his task substantially furthered both by the wide knowledge and by the sound judgment of the author. Many things are obscure in the history of these tribes, and it is of special value to have the whole of the facts regarding them set out, without *parti pris,* in a spirit of scientific research.

There is much here recorded that is of direct historical interest; it is a striking instance of the continuity of Indian history that the great Emperor Samudragupta should boast himself son of a daughter of Licchavis, a tribe famous in the Buddha's time, nine centuries earlier. But there is also material which appeals to the student of Indian politics and of social development. The legendary origin of the Licchavis as of the Śākyas presents us with the marriage of brother and sister, seen also in the Jātaka version of the tale of Rāma and Sītā. We are, of course, here brought into contact with a problem which is debated in the hymn of Yama and Yamī in the Ṛgveda, while in the Aitareya Brāhmaṇa the wise Nārada insists that the need of offspring may justify incest; that real facts lie at the back of the legends is attested by the custom of sister marriage enjoined, if not by Zoroaster, at any rate in the later Avesta. It is curious that Buddhism appears to have found the practice less repellent than the priestly authors of the Ṛgveda. Another relic of primitive practice is found in the usage of the Licchavis to expose their dead; the late Dr. Vincent Smith deduced hence that they were of Tibetan origin, and from this it is an easy step to claim that the Buddha and his doctrine are un-Aryan; a similar, but independent, train of reasoning in the case of Iran has stigmatised the Magi as aboriginal because they approved a like practice. But we must doubtless, with Dr. Law, disabuse ourselves of any over-estimation of the civilisation of the primitive Aryans, and accept the patent fact that they brought with them to Iran and. India habits in no way superior to those of other nomad tribes.

—A. Berriedale Keith

PREFACE

The present treatise was submitted as a thesis for the degree of Doctor of Philosophy of the University of Calcutta. A year ago I wrote a work on "Kṣatriya Clans in Buddhist India" which has been well received by scholars. This treatise is an improvement of the first and I have added four new chapters to it. The object of the entire volume is to present a narrative of the history, manners, customs, etc., of some Kṣatriya tribes of ancient India. Scholars like Rhys Davids, Hoernle, Macdonell, Keith, Cunningham and others have no doubt from time to time supplied valuable information regarding some of these tribes but a comprehensive and systematic account of the Kṣatriya tribes who play such an important part in the history of Pre-Mauryan India is, I believe, presented for the first time in the following pages. I venture to think that I have collected all available information from the works of my predecessors but this forms only an infinitesimal part of my work. The major portion of the present volume embodies—the results of my own researches. I have utilised original works, Sanskrit, Pāli, and Prākṛt such as the Vedas, the Upaniṣads, the Mahābhārata, the Rāmāyaṇa, the Purāṇas, the Nikāyas, the Jātakas, the Pāli commentaries, the Kalpa Sūtra, the Sūtrakṛtāṅga, etc. The portions for which I am indebted to previous writers have carefully been indicated in the footnotes. The rest constitutes my original work. For instance, in the first section of the first chapter the discussion regarding the name, Licchavi, and its significance, is entirely new and original. In the second section of the first chapter a full and systematic account of the capital of the Licchavis is given for the first time. Buddhaghoṣa's knowledge of the Mahāvana has first been pointed out by me. The third section of the first chapter treats of the manners and customs of the Licchavis. In it I have pointed out for the first time that they were not vegetarians; they were fond of manly pastimes; they had a passion for hunting, regard for elders, and love of education. They knew something about construction of palaces and shrines, etc. I have described their matrimonial rites which have not been noticed by anybody else. The fourth section of the same chapter is entirely new and original and the major portion of the remaining chapters also may claim the same merit.

In a work of the kind that I have undertaken, one has got to rely mainly, if not entirely, on literary tradition. I have spared no pains to make full use of the materials that may be gathered from our ancient literature; at the same time I have not overlooked the fact that much of this tradition is late and of little value for historical purposes. I have tried to separate legends from authentic history and have noticed the difference between the two in the marginal notes. But the task is beset with difficulties and it is not always easy to draw the dividing line. It must not, however, be thought that my work is based wholly on literary evidence. I have made use of coins and inscriptions so far as they are useful for my purpose.

For some of the photographs and the map and for kind permission to reproduce them in this volume, my thanks are due to the Director-General of Archology of India, Lionel Heath Esqr., Curator, Central Museum, Lahore, Mr. Ramaprasad Chanda, B.A., F.A.S.B., Superintendent, Archaeological Section, Indian Museum, Calcutta, and the Superintendent of the Archaeological Survey, Frontier Circle. I shall be failing in my duty if I do not acknowledge my indebtedness to my friend, Babu Puran Chand Nahar, M.A., B.L., Vakil, High Court, Calcutta, for the photograph of Varddhamāna Mahāvīra so kindly lent to me for reproduction in this volume.

I find no word to express my deep gratitude to the late

lamented Sir Asutosh Mookerjee whose encouragement was a source of inspiration to me in my literary endeavours, particularly in the field of Ancient Indian history.

Dr. A. Berriedale Keith, D.C.L., D. Lit., Barrister-at-Law, Regius Professor of Sanskrit and Comparative Philology, University of Edinburgh, has laid me under a great debt of obligation by writing a foreword to my humble treatise.

—Bimala Charan Law

LIST OF ILLUSTRATIONS

MAP

CHAPTER 1

THE LICCHAVIS

I. NAME AND ORIGIN

Introductory

The Licchavis were a great and powerful people in Eastern India in the sixth century before Christ. Their peculiar form of government, their free institutions, their manners and customs, their religious views and practices, afford us glimpses of India of the transition period, when the ancient Vedic culture was making a fresh development and undergoing a novel transformation under the influence of that speculative activity out of which emerged the two great religions of Jainism and Buddhism. Fortunately for us, Buddhist literature, and to a less extent the Jaina sacred books, have preserved for us facts and comments which, though in bits and fragments, are yet sufficient to hold up before our eyes a living picture of this interesting people. From the account of their political institutions that can be gleaned from the Pāli Buddhist Canon, we get an insight into the democratic ideas of statecraft and government that prevailed among the majority of the Aryan clans that peopled northern India before the imperialistic policy of the Mauryas grew and developed, as we have it on the authority of the great Brahmin statesman whose policy and activity were responsible, in no little measure, for the foundation of the Maurya Empire. This great people who were one of the earliest and most devoted followers of Jainism and Buddhism, whose high character, unity, power of organisation, and religious devotion were held up by Śākyamuni himself as a model for the Buddhist congregation to follow, deserve to be studied with as much care and attention as the materials at our command will require or permit. Such a close study will, we think, well repay the trouble bestowed upon it and with this hope we proceed to piece together the bits and scraps that lie scattered in literature, and to a smaller extent, in epigraphs and coins.

The Name and its Ṣignificance

We find in Indian literature the name of this great people in slightly varying forms—Licchavi, Licchivi, Lecchavi, Lecchaī and so on. Throughout the Pāli Canon, the name invariably occurs in the form "Licchavi" In some of the Buddhist Sanskrit texts, *e.g.*, the Divyāvadāna[1], the name is found in the same form, *i.e.*, "Licchavi," but in others, for example, the Mahāvastu Avadāna, the usual form is Lecchavi.[2] In the Chinese translations of the Buddhist sacred books, the name occurs in both forms, Licchavi and Lecchavi,[3] and this is what may be expected, as these translations are based on the Sanskrit Buddhist texts. The Mahāvastu form, Lecchavi, answers very well to the Prākṛt form, Lecchaī, as we find it in another set of works that claim to be contemporaneous in origin with the Buddhist Canon, namely the Jaina sacred literature which, according to some scholars, began to be composed perhaps by the direct disciples of Mahāvīra in the first century after his death, or at the latest, in the next century, by the time of Candragupta Maurya when the first council of the Jainas was held at Pāṭaliputra.[4]

In the Sūtrakṛtāṅga, one of the earliest works of the Jaina sacred literature, we meet with the name Lecchaī[5] and the same form ocuurs in the Kalpasūtra attributed to Bhadravāhu who is considered to have been, a contemporary of the great Maurya Emperor, Candragupta. The Jaina commentators equate the Prākṛt Lecchaī with the Sanskrit Lecchakī,[6] and according to the laws of phonetic transformation, the Sanskrit Lecchavi and Lecchakī would both lead to Lecchaī in Prākṛt. In the form Lecchakī, however, the name does never occur in Sanskrit literature in which the earliest mention, so far as we have been able to ascertain, of this powerful people is in Kauṭilya's Arthaśāstra, where they are called Licchivis, and we read that "the corporations of Licchivika, Vṛjika, Mallaka, Madraka, Kukura, Kuru, Pāñcāla and others live by the title of rājā"[7]. We next find them mentioned in the Mānava Dharmaśāstra (x. 22). Here, of course, there are some *varioe lectiones;* the anonymous Kashmirian comment on the Mānava Dharmaśāstra reads *Lichavi* which approximates very closely to the Buddhistic form and Medhātithi and Govindarāja, the two earliest commentators of the Mānava Dharmaśāstra, read *Licchivi* and this reading tallies exactly with the name as given by Kauṭilya; this form, therefore, represents the earliest spelling of this word in the Brāhmanic Sanskrit literature. It is only Kullūka Bhaṭṭa, the Bengali commentator, who eads *Nicchivi* in this verse of Manu; Rāghavānanda, another commentator, follows Kullūka, in this as in other matters, both in spelling as well as in interpretation, and the ordinary printed editions of the Manusaṁhitā, that implicitly follow Kullūka, have adopted this reading.[8] Both Jolly and Bühler, the two great authorities on Manu, have accepted the form *Licchivi* which is without doubt the correct reading. Kullūka who wrote apparently in the fifteenth century and was thus younger by about six hundred years than Medhātithi and by about three hundred years than Govindarāja, was evidently misled by the similarity of the letters 'N' and 'L' as they were written in Bengali in the fifteenth century, and as they are still found to be written even in modern Bengali manuscripts.

Already in the early years of the eleventh century, the Bengali forms of *Na* and *La* had developed almost completely from the eastern variety of the north Indian alphabet as we find from the Kṛṣṇa Dwārika temple inscription of the fifteenth year of Nayapāla; but a little later on, towards the end of the century, we find in the Deopārā inscription of Vijaya Sena that "*La* has a peculiar form, resembling *La* which is still found in some cases in modern Bengali manuscripts where *La* is denoted by a dot placed under *Na*"[9]. Coming down still later, nearer the time of Kullūka, we observe that "the Kamauli grant shows the use of the peculiar twelfth century form of *la* which is also found in the Deopārā *Praśasti* and the Tetrawan image inscription of the second year of Rāmapāla. The form of this letter is the same as the *Ta* of the modern Nāgarī"[10] and this peculiar *Ta*-shaped form also occurs in many other inscriptions of a later date, and Mr. R.D. Banerji from whom we have quoted above, observes that "the *Ta*-shaped form of *la* still survives in Bengali where a dot is put under *na.* to denote *la*"[11] This dot, however, was often omitted by scribes and it is no wonder, therefore, that Kullūka, or rather the scribes who copied his work, read and wrote *Nicchivi* in the place of Licchivi. Hence, we have no hesitation in rejecting Kullūka's reading *Nicchivi* and any attempt to connect the Licchivis with *Nisibis* in Persia[12] on such a flimsy foundation is not worthy of much consideration. Kullūka in his reading has made a mistake like the one found in Nandanācārya's commentary called *Nandinī* or *Manvarthạvyākhyāna* where we have the name in the form *Lichikhi,*[13] 'kh' being evidently a clerical error for 'v.' It should be observed, however, that here also the word begins with *l* and not *n.* Nowhere but in Kullūka and the editions dependent on him do we meet with, the form with an initial *N.*

That Nicchivi was only an accidental clerical error and had nothing to do with the name of the people we are dealing with, appears from the Sanskrit inscriptions of the early Gupta Emperors. In the Allahabad posthumous stone pillar inscription of Samudragupta that great monarch is described as the *Licchavi-dauhitra* or 'the son of the daughter of the Licchavis,'[14] so that we have here the very same form as in the Pāli Buddhist works. We have the same form in many other inscriptions of the monarchs of this family, for example, in the Mathurā stone inscription of Candragupta II,[15] the Bilsād stone pillar inscription of Kumāra Gupta Of the year 96,[16] the Bihar stone pillar inscription of Skanda gupta,[17] etc. On the other hand, the other variant, Licchivi, is found to occur in the Bhitarī stone pillar inscription of Skanda Gupta[18] and the Gayā copper plate inscription of Samudra Gupta,[19] which is considered to be spurious. Some of the coins of Candragupta I. have the name Licchavi on them. Moreover, in the inscriptions of the Nepal kings who claim to be descended from the family of the Licchavis, the expression used is always Licchavi-kula-ketu 'the banner or glory of the Licchavi family.'[20] In the Sanskrit inscriptions, therefore, the usual form of the name is Licchavi, and the form Licchivi is also met with occasionally. Coming now to the form of the name as used in countries outside India, we have seen that in the Chinese translations which are based on Sanskrit Buddhist texts, the form is Licchavi or Lecchavi; Fā Hien speaks of them as Licchavis[21] ; in Hiuen Tsiang's *Records of the Western World,* the form is Li-ch'e p'o which would correspond to the form Licchavi,[22] The Tibetans who began to have the Buddhist books translated into their own language from the eighth century A.D., have also the form *Licchavi*. In the Tibetan Dulva from which Rockhill quotes in his *Life of the Buddha* (p. 97 foll.) the form is Licchavi. Schiefner, in his German translation of Tārānātha's *History of Buddhism in India,* spells the word as *Litschtschhavi*[23] the consonantal group *tsch* representing, according to German orthography, the Indian च (c)

The Kṣartiya Origin of the Licchavis

The Licchavis were neither Tibetan nor Iranian in their origin: there is very clear evidence in the Buddhist literature to show that they belonged to the Aryan ruling caste—the Kṣatriya. In the Mahāparinibbāṇa Suttanta to which we have already referred, we read that after the decease of the Buddha, his body was preserved for a week by the Mallas of Kuśīnārā, while in the meantime, the news of the passing away of the Master reached the people of the countries far and near. Now, the Licchavis of Vaiśālī claimed a share of the remnants of his body. We read there, "And the Licchavis of Vesālī heard the news that the Exalted One had died at Kuśīnārā. And the Licchavis of Vesālī sent a messenger to the Mallas, sayings : 'The Exalted One was a Kṣatriya and so are we. We are worthy to receive a portion of the relics of the Exalted One. Over the remains of the Exalted One, will we put up a sacred cairn and in their honour, will we celebrate a feast.' "[24]

Here we see that the claim of the Licchavis was based on the fact that they were Kṣatriyas or people of the same caste as the Divine Master; hence, they were entitled to a portion of the relics. Similar claims based on the same argument were forwarded also by Ajātaśatru, the powerful king of Magadha, who also sent a messenger with the message, "The Lord is a Kṣatriya and so am I. Therefore, I deserve a share of the relics." (Bhāgavā pi Khattiyo, ahaṁ pi Khattiyo. Ahaṁ pi Bhāgavato sarīrānaṁ bhāgaṁ arahāmi"). The very same claim was preferred by the Bulis of Allakappa the Koliyas of Rāmagāma, the Mallas of Pāvā and the Monyas of Pipphalivana, all of whom advanced theif right on the ground, "The Lord is a Kṣatriya and so are we," while the Śākyas of Kapilavastu claimed him as their very kin.[25] A Licchavi named Mahāli says, "I am a Khattiya, so is the Buddha. If his knowledge increases and he becomes all-knowing, why should it not happen to me."[26] It is apparent, therefore, that the Licchavis were as good Kṣatriyas as Ajātaśatru of Magadha and the other Kṣatriya peoples in north-eastern India in the Buddha's time. In the introduction to the Sigāla Jātaka, we read of a Licchavī girl, "the daughter of a Kṣatriya and highborn."[27] Dr. Richard Fick in his well-known work, *The Social Organisation in North-east India in Buddha's time,* is rather sceptical as to whether the word Kṣatriya as used in the Pāli texts has exactly the same connotation as in the ancient Brāhmanical literature, while he has no such doubt with regard to the Brāhmaṇas, But, as Professor Oldenberg observes, there is no ground for this scepticism. "When it is admitted," says this distinguished savant, "that the families of Gautama, Bhāradvāja, etc., were all grouped together in the caste of Brāhmaṇas as being pervaded all of them by the mystic potency of the *Brahman,* I cannot see why just in the same way, and answering to exactly similar modes of expression in the texts, it should not be held that families like those of the Śākyas, Licchavis etc., all of whom felt in themselves the potency of the Kṣatra nobility, all of whom said, 'Māyaṁ pi khattiyā' are to be reckoned as belonging to a single caste of the Khattiyas (Kṣatriyas)—a single caste of which the members, when they said to each other 'I am a Khattiya,' 'I too am a Khattiya,' knew and acknowledged each other as persons of the same kind and nature."[28]

That the Licchavis were Kṣatriyas appears also from the Jaina sacred literature. Just as the Licchavis of Vaiśālī honoured the Buddha at his death by erecting a noble monument (*stūpa*) over their shares of the remnants of his body, so they had, before this, done honour to the memory of the great Mahāvīra, the founder of Jainism, at his death. The Jaina Kalpasūtra narrates: "In that night in which the venerable ascetic Mahāvīra died, went off, quitted the world, cut asunder the ties of birth, old age, and death; became a Siddha, a Buddha, a Mukta, a maker of the end (to all misery), finally liberated, freed from all pains, the eighteen confederate kings of Kāśī and Kośala, the nine Mallakiṣ and nine Licchavis, on the day lef new moon,, instituted an illumination on the Poshadha, which was a fasting day; for they said; 'since the light of intelligence is gone, let us make an illumination of material matter'. "[29] The Jaina works further tell us, as Professor Jacobi points out, that these nine Licchavis were tributary to Ceṭaka, King of Vaiśālī and maternal uncle of Mahāvīra[30] who was a Inātri Kṣatriya of the Kāśyapa Gotra, as we read in the Kalpasūtra. "The venerable ascetic Mahāvīra belonged to the Kāśyapa gotra.... The venerable ascetic Mahāvīra...., a Jñātṛ Kṣatriya, the son of a Jñātṛ Kṣatriya; the moon of the clan of the Jñātṛs, a Videha, the son of Videhadattā, a native of Videha, a prince of Videha,"[31] and there are reasons to believe that Mahāvīra was a native of a suburb of Vaiśālī.[32] Mahāvīra's mother, Triśalā, is always styled as Kṣatriyānī, and the Licchavis, therefore, must have been Kṣ -atriyas. That the Licchavis were looked upon as persons of very high pedigree appears from a passage in another work of the Jaina sacred literature, the Sūtrakṛtāṅga, where we read, "A Brāhmaṇa or Kṣatriya by birth, a scion of the Ugra race or a Licchavi, who enters the order eating alms given him by others, is not stuck up on account of his renowned Gotra." [33]

The Licchavis were Kṣatriyas of the Vāśiṣṭha gotra. In the account of the first meeting of the Buddha with the Licchavis as given in the Mahāvastu Avadāna, we read that the latter in order to avert a plague that was depopulating their town, brought the Master to Vaiśālī with great respect and honour, and the Buddha, when speaking to the Licchavis, always addressed them as Vāśiṣṭhas.[34] Again, according to the Tibetan Dulva, when King Ajātaśatru of Magadha was leading an army against the Licchavis, these latter also made preparations to meet him; and as they were starting out, they met Maudgalyāyana while he was entering Vaiśālī to get alms. They asked him whether they would be victorious. He answered them, "Men of Vaśiṣṭha's race, you will conquer,"[35] The Jaina sacred works lay down definitely that the Kṣatriyānī Trīśalā, the mother of Mahāvīra, was a sister of Ceṭaka, one of the kings of Vaiśālī, and belonged to the Vāśiṣṭha gotra (S.B.E., Vol. XXII, p. xii). We read in the Āyārāṅga Sūtra (11. 15. 15): "The venerable ascetic Mahāvīra's father belonged to the Kāśyapa gotra; he had three names, Siddhārtha, Sreyāṁsa, and Gasaṁsa. His mother belonged to the Vāśiṣṭha gotra, and had three names, Triśalā, Videhadattā and Priyakāriṇī." [36]

Thus, we observe that, both according to the Buddhist and Jaina Canonical works, the Licchavis belonged to the Vāśiṣ ṭha gotra. In the Nepāl Vaṁśāvalī, the Licchavis have been allotted tb the Sūryavaṁśa or solar race of the Kṣatriyas.[37] This ts quite in agreement with the fact elicited from the Buddhist records that they were Vāśiṣṭhas by gotra, for we know from the Aitareya Brāhmaṇa that the gotra or pravara of a Kṣatriya is the same as that of his purohita or family priest, who makes him perform the sacrifices.[38] Sir R.G. Bhāndārkar also points out that the gotra of a Brāhmaṇa "could be assumed for sacrificial purposes by a Kṣatriya, for according to Aśvalāyana (Sr. S. XII, 15.), the Gotra and the ancestors invoked of the Kṣ atriyas are those of their priests or chaplains, and the only Ṛṣi ancestors that all the Kṣatriyas have, are Mānava, Aila and Paurūravasa. The names of these do not distinguish one Kṣatriya family from another and, to. answer the purposes of such a distinction, the Gotra and ancestors of the priest are assumed."[39] The Vāśiṣṭha gotra was, therefore, the gotra of their family priest, and we know that the Vāśiṣṭhas were the family priests of the kings of the solar race, especially of the Ikṣvākus; there is thus an agreement between the Nepāl Vaṁśāvalī and the evidence from the Buddhist sources, and the Jaina records also corroborate the same. As Professor Jacobi observes, "According to the Jainas, the Licchavis and Mallakis were the chiefs of Kāśī and Kosala. They seem to have succeeded the Aikṣvākas who ruled there in the times of the Rāmāyaṇa."[40] The Sanskrit epic tells us that the city of Vaiśālī was founded by Viśāla, a son of Ikṣvāku and the heavenly nymph, Alamvuṣā,[41] while the Viṣṇu Purāṇa substitutes Tṛṇabindu, a later scion of the Ikṣvāku family, as the father of the eponymous hero, who founded the city. This shows at least that, at the time when these Brāhmanical Sanskrit books were composed, the ruling family of Vaiśālī was believed to have been descended from the Ikṣvākus.

Kinship the with the Mallas and the Śākyas

We may point out here that in the Mahāparinibbāṇa Suttanta, the Mallas of Kuśīnārā are addressed by the venerable Anuruddha and the venerable Ānanda as Vāseṭṭhas,[42] that is, Vāśiṣṭhas; thus corroborating the Jaina account of the close connection of these two Kṣatriya tribes, both having the same gotra. In the Sangīti Sutta of the Dīgha Nikāya, we find the Mallas of Pāvā also addressed as Vāṣeṭṭhas by the Buddha.[43] Their association with the Śākyas is also well-known. We read in the Karma-Śaṭaka (a French translation of the Tibetan version of which, has been given by M.L. Feer) that Prabodha (Rab-sad), king of the Vṛjis, gave away his two daughters, Māyā and Mahāmāyā, as brides to Śuddhodana, son of Simhahanu.[44] Besides, the Mahāvastu tells us of a contest at archery in which the Licchavi princes were asked to take part but they were incapable of doing so and at last the Bodhisatta succeeded.[45] Rockhill in his *Life of the Buddha* derived from Tibetan works, speaks of a tradition according to which, the Śākyas and the Licchavis are branches of the same people. He refers to Sanang Setsen, who "in his History of the Eastern Mongols, p. 21, says that the Śākya race (to which the Buddha belonged) was divided into three parts, whose most celebrated representatives were Śākya the Great (the Buddha), Śākya the Licchavi, and Śākya the Mountaineer. Gnya Khri bstan po, the first Tibetan king, belonged to the family of Śākya the Licchavi."[46] The above legend is of very little historical value but it shows at least that the Śākyas and the Licchavis were considered to be allied races.

Mythical account – Paramatthajotikā on the Dhuddakapāṭha and the Pūjāvaliya

We have seen above the affinity of the Licchavis with the Mallas and the Śākyas. Now we come to the account of the mythical origin of the Licchavis, which can be gathered from Buddhaghoṣa's Paramatthajotikā on the Khuddakapāṭha :–

"There was an embryo in the womb of the chief queen of Benares. Being aware of it, she informed the king who performed the rites and ceremonies for the protection of it. With the embryo thus perfectly protected, the queen entered the delivery chamber when it was fully mature. With ladies of great religious merit, the delivery took place at the dawn of day. A lump of flesh of the colour of lac and of bandhu and jīvaka flowers came out of her womb. Then the other queens thought that to tell the king that the chief queen was delivered of a mere lump of flesh while a son, resplendent like gold, was expected, would bring the displeasure of the king upon them all; therefore, they, out of fear of exciting displeasure of the king, put that lump of flesh into a casket, and after shutting it up, put the royal seal upon it, and placed it on the flowing waters of the Ganges. As soon as it was abandoned, a god wishing to provide for its safety, wrote with a piece of good cinnabar on a slip of gold the words, "The child of the chief queen of the King of Benares" and tied it to the casket. Then he placed it on the flowing current of the Ganges at a place where there was no danger from aquatic monsters. At that time an ascetic travelling along the shore of the Ganges close by a settlement of cow-herds. When he came down to the Ganges in the morning, and saw a vessel coming on, he caught hold of it thinking that it contained rags *(pamsukula),* but seeing the tablet with the words written thereon and also the seal and mark of the King of Benares, he opened it and saw that piece of flesh. Seeing it, he thus thought within himself :—"It may be an embryo, and there is nothing stinking or putrid in it," and taking it to his hermitage, he placed it in a pure place. Then after half a month had passed, the lump broke up into two pieces of flesh; the ascetic nursed them with still greater care. After the lapse of another half a month, each of the pieces of flesh developed fine pimples for the head and the two arms and legs. After half a month from that time, one of the pieces of flesh became a son resplendent like gold, and the other became a girl. The ascetic was filled with paternal affection for the babies and milk came out of his thumb. From that time forward, he obtained milk with rice; the rice he ate himself and gave the babies the milk to drink. Whatever got into the stomach of these two infants looked as if put into a vessel of precious transparent stone (maṇi), so that they seemed to have no skin (nicchavi) ; others said : "The two (the skin and the thing in the stomach) are attached to each other (līnā-chavi) as if they were sewn up together" ; so that these infants owing to their being *nicchavi, i.e.,* having no skin, or on account of their being *Līnāchavi, i.e.,* attached skin or same skin, came to be designated as *Licchavis.* The ascetic having to nurse these two children had to enter the village in the early morning for alms and to return when the day was far advanced. The cowherds coming to know this conduct of his, told him, "Revered sir, it is a great trouble for an ascetic to nurse and bring up children; kindly make over the children to us, we shall nurse them, do you please attend to your own business."The ascetic assented gladly to their proposal. On the next day, the cowherds levelled the road, scattered flowers, unfurled banners and came to the hermitage with music. The ascetic handed over the two children with these words: "The children are possessed of great virtue and goodness, bring them up with great care and when they are grown up, marry them to each other ; please the king and getting a piece of land, measure out a city, and instal the prince there." "All right, sir," promised they, and taking away the children, they brought them up. The children, when grown up, used to beat with fists and kicks, the children of the cowherds whenever there was a quarrel in their sports. They cried and when asked by their parents, "Why do you cry?" They said, "These nurselings of the hermit, without father and mother, beat us very hard." Then the parents of these other children would say, "These children harass the others and trouble them, they are not to be kept, they must be abandoned *(Vajjitabbā)*." Thenceforward that country measuring three hundred yojonas is called *Vajji*. Then the cowherds securing the good will and permission of the king, obtained that country, and measuring out a town there, they anointed the boy, king. After giving marriage of the boy, who was then sixteen years of age, with the girl, the king made it a rule : "No bride is to be brought in from the outside, nor is any girl from here to be given away to any one." The first time they had two children—a boy and a girl, and thus a couple of children was born to them for sixteen times. Then as these children were growing up, one couple after another, and there was no room in the city for their gardens, pleasure groves, residential houses and attendants, three walls were thrown, up round the city at a distance of a quarter of a yojana from each other; as the city was thus again and again made larger and still larger (Viśālikatā), it came to be called Vesālī. This is the history of Vesālī."[47]

Another Mythical account in the Pūjāvaliya

The Pūjāvaliya,[48] a Ceylonese Buddhist work, also gives the same account though with some slight variations. These stories, of course, are entirely mythical and must have grown up in very recent times, there being no evidence in the sacred canon itself to corroborate any part of the narrative. It shows at least that the Licchavis were regarded as Kṣatriyas.

Derivations of the term 'Licchavi'

The two derivations of the name, Licchavi, offered by Buddhaghoṣa in the above story, are no doubt entirely fanciful. Licchavi is the name of a race or tribe. The people must have acquired that name ages before they come to our notice in the pages of the Buddhist or Jaina literature, or in Kauṭilya's Arthaśāstra. Attempts at finding a derivation for the word are at best only ingenious and are very likely to be fanciful. Buddhaghoṣa's derivations must have been invented in a late age when the Licchavis had acquired great renown and power, and it was found necessary to find out some meaning for the word which is rather peculiar and defies, easy analysis by the ordinary rules of grammar. Hence, they were associated with some myths, and we have the fanciful explanation given above. But it must be observed that the two derivations suggested by the great commentator are almost exactly the same as those given in Chincsc Buddhist works. According to the Shan-hsien-lū (Chapter 8) the word "Licchavi" (or Lecchavi) is said to mean 'skin thin' or 'same skin,' the name, being treated as a derivative of cchavi (chchhavi) which means 'skin.'[49] These are the same as Buddhaghoṣa's *Nicchavi* or 'no skin,' that is, 'thin skin' and 'līnā chavi' or 'joined skin, that is, 'same skin.' This close agreement between the two sets of analysis and interpretation shows that both of them most probably drew materials from a common source.

The story recounted by Buddhaghoṣa has no historical value, yet it is significant that even according to this account, the Licchavis were of Kṣatriya origin. There can be no doubt of this fact, and it is clear that at the time the great Buddha and Mahāvīra lived and preached, the Licchavis were recognised as Kṣatriyas who held their heads very high on account of their high birth and with whom the highest born princes of eastern India considered it an honour to enter into matrimonial alliance. We have seen how the great and powerful king Ajātaśatru was always designated by the family name of his mother in the Pāli Buddhist Tripiṭaka. Even two centuries later than the above two great preachers, in the time of Candragupta, the Licchavis were of equal rank and position with the great Kṣatriya peoples of Northern India, *viz.* the *Madras* in the North-west, the *Kuru-Pañcālas* in the central region, and the *Mallas* and others in the east—the tribes who were organised as corporations of warriors and lived upon their position as *rājās,* that is, as owners of land deriving an income from their tenants.

Licchavis in Manu's code

Coming down to the time when the present code of Manu was composed, we find that the Licchavis were still looked upon as Kṣatriyas though of the Vrātya variety. Manu says, "from a Vrātya of the Kṣatriya the Licchavi, the Naṭa, the Karaṇa, the Khasa, and the Drāvida."[50] (Manu S. x. 22.) And immediately before this, Manu takes care to tell us what he exactly means by the term Vrātya; he says, "Those (sons) whom the twice-born beget on wives of equal caste, but who, not fulfilling their sacred duties, are excluded from the Sāvitrī, one must designate by the appellation Vrātyas."[51] (Manu S.x. 20,) The expression avratāh (not fulfilling their sacred duties) in the above verse, means, as Dr. Bühler points out,[52] 'not being initiated at the proper time,' on the authority of what Manu himself states in an earlier chapter, where he fixes the upper limits of the age before which the initiation of the twice-born castes must take place. We read, "The (time for the) Sāvitrī (initiation) of a Brāhmaṇa does not pass until the completion of the sixteenth year (after conception), of a Kṣatriya until the completion of the twenty-second and of a Vaiśya until the completion of the twenty-fourth. After those periods, men of these three castes who have not received the sacrament at the proper time, become Vrātyas (outcastes) excluded from the Sāvitrī (initiation) and despised by the Āryans."[53] Here, in the definition of the term Vrātya as well as the upper limit of the initiation, Manu is in agreement with the earlier lawgivers, Gautama, Āpastamba, Vaśiṣṭha and Baudhāyana.[54] Now from the passages of Manu quoted above, it will be seen that Manu states explicitly that the Vrātya is a person whom a twice-born begets on a wife of equal caste and not on a wife of an inferior or of a superior caste, as is the case with the *Anulomas* and the *Pratilomas,* but the Vrātya is looked upon with disfavour by the orthodox people on account of his failure to get himself initiated at the appointed time. In the case of the Licchavis, therefore, there is no question that they were pure Kṣatriyas by origin, but what is averred about them is that they were not very careful in obeying the regulations about initiation and perhaps similar other matters, like the people in the Madhyadeśa,[55] the central region, where the Brahmanic form of faith prospered and continued in its pristine vigour. An interesting chapter in the history of the social systems in India in early times has been opened by M.M. Haraprasād Śāstrī's interpretation of the word vrātya as used in the Atharvaveda. He says, "He (a Vrātya) is not as we commonly understand him sāvitrīpatitaḥ, a fallen Aryan, but he is an Aryan outside the Vedic circle, an Aryan outside the Antaradeśa, the tract inhabited by the Vedic Aryans. He is on all sides of the Vedic settlement. He has no Brahmanic culture, no trade, no commerce. He is a warrior and a keeper of flocks. He has no permanent settlement and lives in a temporary one called Vrātya. They roam about in hordes. They fight the Vedic Aryans." The learned scholar further says, "They are admitted to all the privileges of the Vedic Society—they can study the Vedas, perform the sacrifices, entertain Brāhmaṇas with food cooked by themselves, see mantras and even compile the Brāhmaṇas. They were in fact nomadic hordes of Aryans, but when they assumed a settled life, they were fully admitted into the Vedic society. "(J.A.S.B., Annual address, New Series, Vol. XVII, 1921, No. 2.) From what we know of the religious history of the Licchavis as a people, it is but natural to expect that they would fall off from the strict observance of the Brahmanic regulations. We have seen that Mahāvīra, the founder of Jainism, was of their very kin and most probably a fellow townsman and we also know that his followers were many among the residents of Vaiśālī, even among the highest officers as we see in the case of Sīha. Then, again, the fact that the Licchavis as a people had won, as we shall see in the chapters that follow, the good graces of the great Buddha as well as of the followers of the religion preached by the Enlightened One, appears to have been predominant in the Licchavi country during the centuries that intervened between the origin of Buddhism and the advent of Manu, the date of whose work, the Manusmṛti, according to Prof. Bühler, is about 200 B.C.—200 A.D.[56] During this long interval when the two great heretic faiths flourished in their country, it is but natural to expect that the Licchavis were not very particular about initiation and similar other ceremonies and practices that were required to be performed by the regulations of the orthodox Brahmins. Hence, we can very well understand how Manu, the great Brahmin law-giver, came to dub the Licchavis as Vrātyas and we have seen how the author of this code has taken care to avoid any chance of misunder-standing the exact connotation of the term Vrātya. He had already defined it in the second chapter of his book, yet he explains it again and says specifically that the term does not imply any of the castes,—that a Vrātya is begot by a twice-born person on a wife of the same caste and hence, the Licchavis were of pure Kṣatriya parentage on both sides. To claim the authority of this passage of Manu in support of a theory of non-Aryan origin of the Licchavis is quite unwarranted.

The above discussion, we hope, will also explain what the lexicographers and the author of the Vaijayantī declare about the origin of the Licchavis, *viz.*, that they were sons of a Kṣatriya Vrātya and a Kṣatriyā.[57] They have, all of them, followed Manu and a separate discussion of their statements is unnecessary.

At the same time, however, it must be admitted that the

Licchavis had not entirely fallen off from the Brahmanic society: in the fourth century A.D., just as Ajātaśatru had gloried in the title of *Vedehiputto,* the son of a daughter of Videha people, that is, of the Licchavis who occupied the Videha country, so also it was considered a glory to an orthodox Gupta Emperor to have been a *Licchavi-dauhitra* or the son of a daughter of the Licchavis.

Gupta-Licchavi Connection

Dr. Fleet who has edited the inscriptions in which the Gupta-Licchavi connection is mentioned, observes, "Proof of friendly relations between the early Guptas and the Licchavis, at an early time, is given by the marriage of Candragupta I. with Kumāra Devi, the daughter of Licchavi or of a Licchavi king. And that the Licchavis were then at least of equal rank and power with the early Guptas, is shewn by the pride in this alliance manifested by the latter; exhibited in the careful record of the names of Kumāra Devī, and of her father or her family, on some of the gold coins of Candragupta I, and by the uniform application of the epithet, 'daughters son of Licchavi or of a Licchavi,' to Samudra Gupta in the geneological inscriptions." [58] Fleet even goes so far as to declare "that in all probability the so-called Gupta era is a Licchavi era, dating either from a time when the republican or tribal constitution of the Licchavis was abolished in favour of a monarchy; or from the commencement of the reign of Jayadeva I, as the founder of a royal house in a branch of the tribe that had settled in Nepal."[59] The fact that this royal house that was planted by the Licchavis in Nepal about the period 330 to 355 A.D. by Jayadeva I[60] was all along Brahmanical, proves that the Licchavis had not entirely dissociated themselves from the Brahmanic faith. We thus observe that the power and glory of the Licchavis during the period of Brahmanic revival under the Guptas were as great as under the Śiśunākas and the Mauryas and that their position as one of the leading and honoured Kṣatriya families in Eastern India was fully recognised.

The late Dr.V.A. Smith's theory—the Tibetan origin

Before leaving this question of origin,, it remains for us to refer to the two theories about the Tibetan nd Persian affinities of the Licchavis started by and Satis Ch. Vidyabhūsaṇa respectively. Dr. Smith's conclusion about the Tibetan affinity rests on the agreement that is observed between the Tibetans and the Licchavis in the custom of exposure of the dead and in judicial procedure. We shall discuss these two points one by one. The prevalence among the Licchavis of the practice of exposing the dead to be devoured by wild animals is vouched for by a passage in *Beal's Romantic Legend of Śākya Buddha* [61] derived from Chinese sources. There we have the description of a visit paid by the Bodhisatta *(Gautama)* to a cemetery at Vaiśālī" where the Ṛṣis are stated to have answered his question thereanent. "In that place the corpses of men are exposed to be devoured by the birds; and there also they collect and pile up the white bones of dead persons, as you perceive; they burn corpses there also, and preserve the bones in heaps. They hang dead bodies also from the trees; there are others buried there, such as have been slain or put to death by their relatives, dreading lest they should come to life again ; whilst others are left there upon the ground that they may return, if possible, to their former homes." From this statement Dr. Smith argues, "whatever obscurity may exist in this passage it certainly proves a belief that the ancient inhabitants of Vaiśālī disposed of their dead sometimes by exposure, sometimes by cremation, and sometimes by burial. The tradition is supported by the discoveries made at prehistoric cemetries in other parts of India, which disclose very various methods of disposing of the dead"[62] He then concludes from the similarity which these customs of the disposal of the dead bear with those of Tibet that the Liccha vis had Tibetan affinities. But it may be observed that we need not go to Tibet for these customs, inasmuch as they were prevalent among the Vedic Aryans from whom the Licchavis were descended. We read in the well-known funeral hymn of the Atharva Veda (XVIII. 2.34). [63]

"They that are buried, and they that are scattered *(vap)* away, they that are burned and they that are set up *(uddhita)*—all those Fathers, O Agni, bring thou to eat the oblation."[64] 'Prof. Whitney, whose translation of the verse we have quoted here, observes on the expression *Uddhitāḥ,* "It evidently refers to exposure on something elevated, such as is practised by many peoples."[65] Prof. Whitney also refers to an analogous passage in Āpastamba (I. 87.) where the divisions are *(Ye garbhe mamruḥ), paroptāḥ, uddhitāḥ* and *nikhātāḥ,* so that there also we find a reference to the customs of burial and exposure on a raised platform *(Uddhitāḥ)*. Zimmer in his Altindisches Leben[66] thinks that in this passage there is "a parallel to the Iranian practice of casting out the dead to be devoured by beasts" though he takes the word *paroptāḥ* in this sense, and explains *uddhitāḥ* otherwise.[67] The Vedic literature shows that cremation was one of the methods of the disposal of the dead. Methods other than cremation were in vogue, it seems, in particular localities and among particular classes or peoples. It. is evident, therefore, that the custom of exposure of the dead was not a practice unknown to the Vedic Aryans but was apparently brought by them from their cradle into India inasmuch as we find the same to be the most approved method among the most closely allied branch of their family, *viz.,* the Iranians. To seek for the origin of this ancient Aryan custom in Tibet is absolutely unwarranted. The other argument of Dr. Smith that the ancient judicial procedure at Vaiśālī as given in the Aṭṭhakathā, is substantially identical with the modern procedure at Lhāsā as observed by the Bengali traveller in Tibet, the late Rai Bahadur Sarat Chunder Das, C.I.E., need not detain us very long. This procedure the Tibetans may have imbibed along with Buddhism from the province of Tirhut, which was nearest to their frontiers and which was inhabited by the descendants of the Licchavis of old.

The Late Dr. Vidyābhūṣaṇa's Theory—Persian Origin

Dr. Satis Chandra Vidyābhūsaṇa holds that they were of Persian origin. His strongest argument is the verbal coincidence between *Nisibis* in the Persian Empire and the word *Nicchivi* which occurs in Manu. We have already demonstrated that it was a misreading for which Kullūka was responsible, and as such it offers no basis for building up a theory of Persian affinity for the Licchavis. Dr. Vidyābhūsaṇa avers, "It appears to me very probable that while about 515 B.C., Darius, king of Persia, sent an expedition to India, or rather caused the Indus to be explored from the land of the Pakhtu (Afghans) to its mouth, some of his Persian subjects in Nisibis (off Herat) immigrated to India, and having found the Punjab over-populated by the orthodox Brāhmaṇas, came down as far as Magadha (Bihar) which was at that time largely inhabited by Vrātyas or out-caste people."[68] This is absurd on the face of it. The Licchavis were already a flourishing people, long established in the Videha country and had built up a splendid capital at Vaiśālī at the time of the Buddha's death; and whether we take the date of this event to be 487 B.C., as the late Dr. V.A. Smith thought, or what is more probable, to be 544 B.C., the traditional date maintained by the Ceylonese Buddhist monks, it is simply absurd to identify the Licchavis with the followers or subjects of Darius who were exploring the Indus about 515 B.C.

Beal's theory —Yuechi

It remains for us to refer to another theory about the foreign origin of the Licchavis, started by that they were 'Yuechi.[69] It hardly requires to be refuted as the Yue-chi came to India about the beginning of the Christian era and the Licchavis were a highly civilised and prosperous people in the fifth and sixth centuries B.C., when the Ephthalites or white Huns had not started from their original home in the east.

II. VAIŚĀLĪ, THE CAPITAL OF THE LICCHAVIS

Vaiśālī—Its Importance

Vaiśālī, 'the large city' par excellence is renowned in Indian history as the capital of the Licchavi rājās and the headquarters of the great and powerful Vajjian confederacy.[70] This great city is intimately associated with the early history of both Jainism and Buddhism, it carries with itself the sacred memories of the founders of these two great faiths that evolved in north-eastern India, five hundred years before the birth of Christ.

Vaiśālī and Mahāvīra

Vaiśālī claims the founder of Jainism as its own citizen. The Sūtrakṛtāṅga[71] one of the Jaina canonical works, says about Mahāvīra, the last *Tīrthaṅkara* of the Jainas as follows: "*Evaṁ se udāhu aṇuttaramaṇī aṇuttaradaṁsī aṇuttaraṇāṇadaṁsaṇadhare arahā Nāyaputte bhagavaṁ Vesālie Viyāhie (vyākhyātavān) iti bemi.*"[72] "Thus spoke the Arahat Jñātriputra, the reverend, famous native of Vaiśālī, who possessed the highest knowledge and the highest faith, who possessed (simultaneously) the highest knowledge and faith. This passage is also repeated in another Jaina work, the Uttarādhyayanasūtra with a slight variation.[73] Mahāvira is spoken of as Vesālie or Vaiśālika, *i.e.* a native of Vaiśālī.[74] Moreover Abhayadeva in his commentary on the Bhagavatī 2, I. 12, 2. explains Vaiśālika by Mahāvīra and speaks of Viśālā as Mahāvīrajananī or 'the mother of Mahāvīra.'[75] Besides, from a comparison of the Buddhist and Jaina scriptures, it appears that Kuṇḍagrāma, the birthplace of Mahāvīra, was a suburb of Vaiśālī.[76] Mahāvīra's mother Triśalā was a sister to Ceṭaka, one of the so-called rājās of that Lcchavi city.[77] The Jaina Kalpasūtra speaks of the connection of Mahāvīra with the Videha country and its capital, Vaiśālī in these words: "The venerable ascetic Mahāvīra—a Videha, the son of Videhadattā, a native of Videha, a prince of Videha—had lived thirty years in Videha when his parents went to the world of the gods *(i.e.* died) and he with the permission of his elder brother and the authorities of the kingdom fulfilled his promise" of going Out to "establish the religion of the law which benefits all living beings in the whole universe."[5] During his later ascetic life also Mahāvīra did not neglect the city of his birth and we are told by the Kalpa Sūtra that out of the forty-two rainy seasons of this period of his life, he passed no less than twelve at Vaiśālī.[80]

Vaiśālī and the Buddha

The connection of the Buddha with Vaiśālī is no less close and intimate. This city was hallowed by the dust of his feet early in his career and many of his immortal discourses were delivered here either at the mango-grove of Ambapālī, in the outskirts of the city or at Kūṭāgārasālā in Mahāvana, the great forest stretching out up to the Himālayas. The Exalted One was charmed with the conduct of the Vajjis or Licchavis residing within the town and looked upon them with kindness and approbation. The seven points of excellence with which he characterised the Licchavis in answer to the queries put to him by the Ministers sent by King Ajātaśatru of Magadha, are very well-known; we see there, how he spoke of the unimpeachable character of the people of Vaiśālī and tried to dissuade the Magadhan King from making fruitless attempts at robbing the people of that noble city of their independence. It is evident that the Enlightened One had a soft place in his heart for this mighty and noble people and their splendid and extensive capital. And when at last the days of his earthly existence were drawing to a close, he paid a last visit to the city that had received his blessing and affection, the city that was always ready to honour and worship him and as the Enlightened One felt within himself that the end was drawing nigh, that this was the very last view that he would ever have of this beautiful town, he cast a 'longing, lingering look behind.' In the words of the Mahāparinibbāṇa Suttanta, the Book of the Great Decease, "when the Exalted One had passed through Vesālī, and had eaten his meal and was returning from his alms-seeking, he gazed at Vesālī, with an elephant look,"[81] (that is, turning the whole body round as an elephant does, as Buddhaghoṣa explains), and then addressed the Venerable Ānanda, and said:—This will be the last time, Ānanda, that the Tathāgata will behold Vesālī.[82]

Vaiśālī and the Buddhist Church

Even after the Exalted One had entered into Nirvāṇa, Vaiśālī again drew to itself the care and attention of the whole

Buddhist Church, but this time it was not on account of the many good qualities of character and powers of organisation of its citizens, but of the objectionable tenets held by the Vaiśālī monks who twisted and turned the noble precepts of the Great Preacher to suit their own convenience and to lead a life of less austerity and greater enjoyment of the good things of the earth than the Master permitted; for example, they would have fresh meals even after the midday dinner and would accept gold and silver. The representatives of the entire congregation met at Vaiśālī itself and condemned in no equivocal terms the conduct of its pleasure-seeking bhikkhus. This was the second general council of the Buddhist Church.[83]

We have referred to a few only of the incidents connecting the great city of the Licchavis with the history of the growth and development of the Jain and Buddhist communities; there are innumerable references to the city and its people in their literature especially in the Buddhist Canon.

Foundation of Vaiśālī

To the fanciful stories told by Buddhaghoṣa of the origin of the town, we have already referred in the previous chapter. We may, however, glean from them two outstanding facts, namely : that the city was founded by the Licchavis and that the area covered by the town was very extensive; in fact, it owes its name Vaiśālī to its being Viśāla or very large and wide in area. Vālmīki in the Bālakāṇḍa[84] of the Rāmāyaṇa tells us a story (to which we have already referred) of the foundation of the city which is different from that of Buddhaghoṣa. He says that it was founded by a son of Ikṣvāku and the heavenly nymph (Apsarā), Alambuṣā ; after his name Viśāla, the cityit self came to be called Viśālā.

The Viṣṇupurāṇa Account

The Viṣṇupurāṇa says that it was Tṛṇabindu, who according to the geneological tree preserved in the Purāṇas, was descended from Ikṣvāku and had by Alambuṣā a son named Viśāla, who founded the city of Vaiśālī.[85]

The Rāmāyaṇa Account

The Rāmāyaṇa further tells us that when Rāma and his brother Lakṣmaṇa, guided by the sage Viśvāmitra, crossed the sacred river Ganges and reached its northern shore, on their way to Mithilā, the capital of the royal sage, Janaka, they had a view of the city of Vaiśāli. It does not tell us that it was exactly on the bank of the river, but it says that "while seated on the northern shore they saw the town."[86] It might be that the distant towers or the pinnacles of the temples met their gaze as they cast their glance northwards. Then the Rāmāyaṇa story continuing says that the eminent travellers went to the city of Viśālā which was an excellent town (Uttamā purī), "charming and heavenly, in fact a veritable svarga."[87] Viśwāmitra, the guide, narrates here a fairly long mythological account to show the importance of the locality where Indra himself had sojourned for about a thousand years. Then the Ṛṣi goes on to say that the Ikṣvāku prince ruling over the country at the time was Sumati by name, and adds that by favour of Iksvāku, the father of the eponymous founder of the city and the ruling dynasty, all the kings of Vaiśālī (*sarve vaiśālikā nṛpāḥ*) were long lived, high souled, possessed of strength and power and highly virtuous.[88] One may very well question whether the author of the Rāmāyaṇa has here an overt allusion to the Rājās of Vaiśālī in the phrase 'Vaiśālikā nṛpāh.'

Yuan Chwang's Account

From all the mythical stories above referred to, it is apparent that the name of the city had something to do with viśāla or extensive in area, and from what we read of the description of the ruins that Yuan Chwang saw in the seventh century after Christ, there can hardly be any doubt of its wide extent.The Chinese traveller relates, "The foundations of the old city Vaiśālī were sixty or seventy li in circuit and the 'palace city' (*i.e.* the walled part of the city) was four and five li in circuit."[89] This would mean an area of about twenty miles in circumference for the outer town; and the "Palace-city" of Yuan

Chwaug perhaps represents the earliest of the three cities which, according to Buddhaghoṣa, were built to accommodate the Licchavis as they were growing rather fast; but its area would not in that case agree with the statement that each of the three walls was at a distance of a gāvuta (gavyuti) or a quarter yojana, that is roughly a league from the other.

The Jātaka Account

The description of Buddhaghoṣa is also supported by the Jātakaṭṭhakathā to the Ekapaṇṇa Jātaka where we are told, "At the time of the Buddha, the city of Vesālī was encompassed by three walls at a distance of a gāvuta from one another and that at three places there were gates with watch-towers and buildings."[90] The three walls are adverted to in the Aṭṭhakathā to the Lomahaṁsa Jātaka also.[91]

The Dulva account

The Tibetan Dulva (iii. f.80) gives the following description. "There were three districts in Vaiśālī. In the first district were seven thousand houses with golden towers, in the middle district were fourteen thousand houses with silver towers, and in the last district were twenty-one thousand houses with copper towers; in these lived the upper, the middle and the lower classes according to their positions."[92]

Dr. Hoernle's Ṭheory—Vaiśālī and suburbs

Dr. Hoernle in his English translation of the Jaina work, Uvāsagadasāo, advances the suggestion that the three districts here referred to in the Dulva and in the Aṭṭhakathā, "may very well have been Vesāli proper, Kuṇḍapura and Vāṇiyagāma occupying respectively the south-eastern, north-eastern and western portions of the area of the total city. Beyond Kuṇḍapura, in a further north-easterly direction lay the suburb (or 'station,' sannivesa) of Kollāga which appears to have been principally inhabited by the Kṣatriyas of the Nāya (or Jñātri) clan, to which Mahāvīra himself belonged; for in it is described as the Nāya-kula."[93] He further observes that the phrases used in the Āyārāṅga Sūtra like "*Uttara-Khattiya-Kuṇḍapura-sannivesaor dahiṇa-māhaṇa-Kuṇḍapura-sannivesa*," "do not mean the northern Kṣatriya (resp. Southern Brahmanical) part of the place Kuṇḍapura, but the northern Kṣatriya, etc., suburb of Kuṇḍapura *i.e.* that suburb (sannivesa) of the city of Kuṇḍapura, which, lay towards the north and was inhabited by the (Nāya clan of) Kṣatriyas; it was distinguished from the southern suburb of the same city (Kuṇḍapura or Veśālī) which was inhabited by the Brahmins. This interpretation is confirmed by the parallel phrases in Kap (et passim), Khattiya-Kuṇḍagāme Nayare and Māhaṇa-Kuṇḍagāme Nayare, which are rightly translated by the Kṣatriya (resp. the Brahmanical) part of the town Kuṇḍagāma." He also points out that "the phrase uccanīya majjhimāirh kulāiṁ, 'upper, lower and middle classes,' applied to the town of Vāṇiyagāma (of the Uvāsagadasāp) curiously agrees with the description of Vesālī given in the Dulva."[95] The passage in the Uvāsagadasāo above referred to is the one in which Goyama, the senior disciple of Mahāvīra, addressed him thus: "I desire, Reverend Sir, with your permission, as the turn for the indulgence of my sixth meal has arrived, to go round the city of Vāṇiyagāma, to the upper, lower and middle classes, on a begging tour of house-to-house collection."[96]

Buddha's visit to the Licchavi capital

The great founder of the rival faith of Buddhism must have paid many visits to the Licchavi capital and the reports of at least two besides that already referred to, are preserved in Buddhist books. The earliest of his visits has been described at length in the Mahāvastu.[97] We are told there, how the people of Vaiśālī were troubled by a frightful pestilence which was laying their country waste and how they found all their efforts to stay the desolating plague entirely fruitless and in their dire distress sent for various holymen of great renown who failed to afford them any relief and as a last resort they sought the help of the Enlightened One who resided at the time at Rājagṛha, the Magadhan capital. The people of Vaiśālī sent a deputation headed by Tomara, a Licchavi chief of power and position, and at the same time of great learning, to Rājagṛha to bring the Exalted One to their city. Tomara went to Rājagṛha, fell down at his feet and sought his help with supplications, but was asked to apply to the King Śreṇika Bimbisāra who insisted on the condition that the Licchavis must welcome the Buddha at the border of their own dominions and that he himself would follow the great teacher to the boundaries of his own territory. To this the Licchavis readily assented and Bimbisāra secured the consent of the Buddha to save the Licchavis from the decimating disease.

To impress the Licchavis with an idea of his power and opulence, the Magadhan King had the road all the way from Rājagṛha to the Ganges, which formed the boundary between the two dominions, levelled, rendered clean like the palm of the hand, decorated with flags, garlands and richly embroidered cloth; besides, the whole road was watered, flowers were freely scattered upon it and the smoke of rich incense perfumed its whole length. He himself followed the Enlightened One with his whole court and numerous retinue. The Licchavis both the Abhyantara-Vaiśālakas, the Vaiśālī-cockneys proper, living within the walls of the city and the Bāhira-Vai ālakas, the people living in the outer town—the suburbs and surroundings—came in all their splendour and magnificence, in all the glory of their dazzling garments, blue, purple, green, yellow, brown and crimson; their appearance as they approached was so splendid and ravishing that even the Great Buddha was impressed with the sight and said addressing the monks, "Bhikkhus, you have never before beheld the Trayastriṁsa gods as they go out of their city Sudarśanā to the garden. Behold now the Licchavis of Vaiśālī who equal those gods in their prosperity and splendour. Look at the Licchavis with their elephants, with umbrellas of gold, their gold-covered litters, their chariots decorated with gold. See how they all come, both the young and the aged, as also those of middle age, all with ornaments on, with garments dyed crimson with lac and advancing with various beautiful movements. " The Licchavis of Vaiśālī decorated the road from the Ganges to Vaiśālī with a magnificence that left the preparations made by the Magadhan king far behind, they provided for the comfort of the Exalted One and the congregation of monks on a still more lavish scale. As soon as the Enlightened One crossed over to the northern side of the river and stepped on the Licchavi soil, all malign influences that had hung over the country and were making a havoc among the people, vanished, and the sick and the suffering were restored to health. The Licchavis received him with all honour and reverence and guided him to their city by asy stages with all the comfort and convenience that they were able to provide for him. Entering the city, the Enlightened One uttered the svastyayana-gāthā, the song of welfare, or according to the Pāli scriptures, the Ratana Sutta; they asked him whether he would live among the people of inner Vaiśālī or of outer Vaiśālī. The Exalted One would not live among either of them, but he accepted the invitation[98] of Bhagavatī Gośṛṅgi in the Mahāvana, the great forest extending from their city far away to the north.

Dedication of Kūṭāgārasālā

The Licchavis who wished that the Exalted One might be induced to live in their city, built the Kūṭāgārasālā, the peaked monastery, for him in the forest and paid their respects to him there. They offered it to him and the Buddhist congregation and the Blessed One permitted the bhikkhus to reside there. One day the Licchavis on coming to the Mahāvana learnt that Blessed One had repaired to the Cāpāla-Caitya for spending the day; they proceeded thither and presented it to him and the congregation of the śrāvakas or Buddhist monks.

Shrines dedicated to the Buddha and the Buddhist Church—Buddha 's discourse—Buddhist faith established.

Similarly finding the Enlightened One spending the day at the Saptāmra-Caitya, the Bahuputra-Caitya, the Gautama Caitya, the Kapinanya-Caitya and the Markaṭa-hrada-tira Caitya; the Licchavis made a gift of all these places of worship to the

Exalted One and the Buddhist Church. Next the courtesan, (gaṇikā) Āmrapālī made a gift of her ex- Itensive mango-grove to the congregation and similarly Bālikā made over Bālikāchavi [99] which is evidently the same as the Bālikārāma of the Pāli Buddhist books.[100] On this visit to their city, the Enlightened One delivered many discourses to the people of Vaiśālī and established the Buddhist faith on a strong foundation at the capital of the Licchavis as he had already done at Rājagṛha, the capital of their rivals, the Magadhas. A similar account differing in slight details is given by Buddhaghoṣa in the introduction to his commentary on the Ratana-Sutta. He says that Vaiśālī was suffering from three troubles — famine, pestilence and sprites. We read in the Buddhist books of many occasions when the Enlightened One paid visits to Vaiśālī in the course of his peregrinations.

Buddha and the Bhikkhus of Vaiśālī

The Mahāvagga tells us of an occasion when the Blessed One on his way from Rājagṛha to Vaiśālī noticed bhiksus with a superfluity of dress, 'almost smothered up in robes,' going along with their robes made up into a roll on their heads or on their backs or on their waists. The Blessed One stayed on that occasion at the Gotamaka Caitya; it was winter, the time between the Asṭakā festivals when the snow was falling and the Blessed One determined, by personal experience, the least quantity of robes that would suffice for keeping off the cold and preached accordingly to the Bhikkhus.[101] The Cullavagga[102] speaks of another occasion when the Blessed One lodged in the Kūṭāgāra Hall in the Mahāvana and the water being unfit for drinking, the use of strainers and filters was permitted for the Bhikṣus. This time, the Bhikṣus partaking freely of the abundant store of sweets offered by the laity, fell ill and were cured by the advice of Jīvaka Komārabhacca, the great physician. The sojourn of the Buddha on this occasion appears to have been rather long and the great teacher taught the Bhiksus many matters connected with the sort of houses they were to build and live in; and this time also the Blessed One ordered the saṁgha to turn down the bowl as regards Vaddha, the Licchavi, who had brought a false charge against one of the brotherhood but afterwards relented on Vaddha again making due reparations. The Cullavagga tells us of another visit when the Blessed One stayed in the Kūṭāgārasālā in the Mahāvana and spoke on the conduct of the Bhiksus with regard to the building of new houses for the use of the Order.

We read of the Buddha coming down to Vaiśālī from Kapilavastu and staying there at the Kūṭāgāra Hall in the Mahāvana. This was the great occasion when Mahāpajāpati Gotamī, the foster-mother of the Blessed One, came with a number of Śākya ladies from Kapilavastu and through the intercession of Ānanda, obtained permission for women 'to go forth from the household life and enter the homeless state under the doctrine and discipline proclaimed by the Tathāgata.'[103]

Valśālī—Rich and Prosperous

From the accounts that we get from the Buddhist books whether Pāli or Sanskrit, we observe that Vaiśālī is represented as a town that was rich and prosperous. The Mahāvagga, one of the oldest books of the Pāli Canon, tells us that at the time the Buddha lived, Vaiśālī "was an opulent, prosperous town, populous, crowded with people, abundant with food; there were seven thousand seven hundred and seven storeyed buildings, and seven thousand seven hundred and seven pinnacled buildings, and seven thousand seven hundred and seven pleasure grounds (ārāmas) and seven thousand seven hundred and seven lotus-ponds."[104]

A similar account of the prosperity of Vaiśālī is given in the Lalitavistara when the gods in the Tusita heaven were holding a discussion with regard to the family that would be the most suitable for the Bodhisattva to be born in. Some of the Tusita gods, the devaputras in advancing the claims of Vaiśālī for this great honour said, "This great city of Vaiśālī is prosperous and proud, happy and rich with abundant food, charming and delightful, crowded with many and various people, adorned with buildings of every description, with storeyed mansions, buildings with towers, and palaces, with noble gateways and charming with beds of flowers in her numerous gardens and groves. This resembling the city of the gods, is indeed fit for the birth of the Bodhisattva."[105] This recommendation was not accepted on other grounds, but the passage speaks of the splendour and prosperity of the capital of the Licchavis. It was a prosperous and gay city, full of music.[106]

Fā Hien's visit Mahāvana

We next come to the accounts of the city left by the Chinese travellers of whom Fa Hien visited it at the beginning of the fifth century A.D., that is, about a thousand years after the time the Buddha lived and delivered his discourses. Fā Hien says,[107] "North of the city so named is a large forest, having in it the double-galleried vihāra where Buddha dwelt and the tope over half the body of Ānanda."

Buddhaghoṣa on Mahāvana

The double-galleried vihāra is evidently the Kūṭāgārasālā in the Mahāvana which stretched right up to the Himālayas as Buddhaghoṣa explains in his Sumaṅgalavilāsinī to the Mahāli Sutta in the Dīgha-Nikāya. In commenting upon the word, "Mahāvana," he says, "outside the town lying in one stretch up to the Himālayas, there is a natural forest which on account of the large area covered by it, is called Mahāvana."[108] ("*Bahinagare Himavantena saddhiṁ ekābaddham hutvā ṭ hitaṁ sayañ-jāta-vanaṁ atthi, yaṁ mahantabhāvena Mahāvanaṁ ti vuccati.*") Legge remarks on the above quoted description given by Fā Hien of the Kūṭāgāra-Vihāra, "it is difficult to tell what was the peculiar form of this Vihāra from which it got its name; something about the construction of its door, or cupboards or galleries."[109] Here also Buddhaghoṣa offers a comment explaining the origin of the name. "In that forest was established a saṁghārāma or monastery. A pāsāda or a storeyed building was built on pillars and putting a pinnacle above, it was made into a kūṭāgārasālā resembling a chariot of gods (devavimāna). From it, the whole saṁghārāma or monastery is known as Kūṭāgārasālā."[110] This agrees with the description of the double-galleried vihāra, given by Fā-Hien. The upper storey was evidently built upon a large number of pillars instead of walls and on the top there was a peak or kūṭa, so that there were two galleries, one below and the other above, and from the upper storey rose a pinnacle as we see in the vimānas or rathas referred to by Buddhaghoṣa. Yuan Chwang who visited the city more than two hundred years after Fā-Hien, found this great vihāra in ruins. "To the east of the tope of the Jātaka narrative," the pilgrim continues, "was a wonder-working tope on the old foundations of the 'two-storey Preaching Hall' in which Ju-lai delivered the P'u-men-t'o-lo-ni and other sūtras."[111] The "two-storey Preaching Hall" is no doubt the Kūṭāgāra Hall of two storeys as described by Buddhaghoṣa and as spoken of by Fā-Hien. This is also evident from what Yuan Chwang says immediately after the above passage. "Close to the remains of the Preaching Hall," the pilgrim says, "was the tope which contained the half-body relics of Ānanda."[112] The story of the parinirvāṇa of Ānanda and the division of the remnants of the body has been told by Fā-Hien and the same account is also given in the Tibetan works. Fā-Hien narrates—"When Ānanda was going from Magadha to Vaiśālī, wishing his parinirvāṇa to take place (there), the devas informed King Ajātaśatru of it and the king pursued him, in his own grand carriage, with a body of soldiers and reached the river. (On the other hand), the Licchavis of Vaiśālī had heard that Ānanda was coming (to their city), and they on their part came to meet him. (In this way), they all arrived together at the river, and Ānanda considered that, if he went forward, King Ajātaśatru would be very angry, while if he went back, the Licchavis would resent his conduct. He thereupon in the very middle of the river burnt his body in a fiery ecstacy of samādhi, and his parinirvāṇa was attained. He divided his body (also) into two, (leaving) the half of it on each bank; so that each of the two kings got one half as a (sacred) relic, and took it back (to his own capital), and there raised a tope over it."[113]

Yuan Chwang's account

Yuan Chwang's account of the country of which Vaiśālī was the capital, agrees pretty well with the tradition of its prosperity preserved in the Buddhist books. We read, "The Vaiśālī country is described by the pilgrim as being above five thousand li in circuit, a very fertile region abounding in mangoes, plaintains and other fruits. The people were honest, fond of good works, esteemers of learning, and orthodox and heterodox in faith."

Tibetan Account

In the Tibetan works, a similar account is given of the prosperity and opulence of Vaiśālī which is invariably described in the Dulva as a kind of earthly paradise, with its handsome buildings, its parks and gardens, the singing birds and continual festivities among the Licchavis. "Nanda, Upānanda " exclaimed the Chabbaggiyā Bhikṣhus when they visited Vaiśālī, "the Blessed One never saw the like of this, even when he was among the Trayastrimcat devas." (Dulva X. f. 2,)[114] The Romantic Legend of Śākya Buddha[115] translated by Beal from Chinese sources, gives an account similar to that in the Lalita-Vistara.[116]

Chinese Account of Vaīśālī

Here we read of a god in the Tuṣita heaven who speaks thus, "This Vajora country has a city called Vaiśālī, rich in every kind of produce; the people in peace and contentment; the country enriched beautiful as a heavenly mansion; the king called 'Drumarāja'; his son without the least stain on his scutcheon; the king's treasuries full of gems, and gold and silver; perhaps you will be born there."

Identification of Vaīśālī

The identification of Vaiśālī, the capital of the Licchavis, had long been a point of discussion among scholars. General Cunningham with his immense knowledge of the country and of the Buddhist literature, identified the present village of Basārh in the Muzafferpur district in Tirhut as marking the spot where stood Vaiśālī in ancient days[117] and Mr. Vivien de Saint Martin agreed with him, but the evidence that led Cunningham to arrive at this conclusion was not put forward with such fulness and clearness as the question certainly deserved; so that scholars had doubts as regards the identity. Rhys Davids says that the site was quite uncer tain and that the site of Vaiśālī had still to be looked for somewhere in Tirhut.[118] Dr. W. Hoey sought to establish the identity, though on very insufficient evidence, of Vaiśālī with a place called Cherānd in the Chāprā or Sārān district. "Cherānd stands on the northern bank of the Ganges, in approximately N. lat. 25° 41' and E. long. 84°. 55' about seven miles south-east from Chāprā."[119] This identification has been proved to be entirely untenable by V.A. Smith in his paper on Vaiśālī[120] from which we have quoted above; and he has succeeded in establishing that the identification by Cunningham of the village of Basārh with Vaiśālī admits of no doubt. This identity has been proved still more decisively by the Archaeological explorations carried on in 1903-04 by Dr. T. Bloch on the site. Dr. Bloch excavated a mound called Rājā Viśāl kā garh and only eight trial pits were sunk. This was very insufficient considering the importance of the place. Three distinct strata have been found, the uppermost belonging to the period of Mahomedan occupation of the place, the second at a depth of about five feet from the surface, related to the epoch of the Imperial Guptas and the third at a still greater depth, belonging to an ancient period of which no definite date could be obtained, it being "represented only by a few scattered fragments, too scanty to offer any conclusive evidence as to their precise date or character."[121] The finds in the second stratum, however, are of very great value especially the find in one of the small chambers of "a hoard of seven hundred clay seals evidently used as attachment to letters or other literary documents. They belonged partly to officials, partly to private persons, generally merchants or bankers, but one specimen bearing the figure of a linga with a triśūla on either side and the legend 'Āmrātakeśvara' evidently belonged to a temple."[122]

The names of certain Gupta kings, queens and princes on some of these seals, coupled with palaeographic evidence, clearly demonstrate that they belonged to the fourth and fifth centuries after Christ when the Imperial Guptas were on the throne.[123] Some of the impressions show that the name Tīrabhukti (the original form of Tirhut) was applied to the province even in those early times and some show the name of the town itself, Vaiśālī. One of the clay seals of a circular area, shows a female standing in a flower group with two attendants and two horizontal lines below reading (i) [Vai]śātyam-araprakṛti-[Ku]-(2) tumbinā [m]—"(Seal) of the householders of.....at Vaiśālī." [124] Another seal also appears to have a similar legend. These things go to prove the identity of the site with Vaiśālī and there seems to be no ground to question this conclusion any longer. But it must be noted that the results so far obtained by excavations are very meagre, and it is a great pity that the Archaeological Department had to give up the explorations for shortness of funds. We know not what invaluable materials for the history of India might lie buried under the earth in the mounds of Basārh as at other ancient sites in India.

III. MANNERS AND CUSTOMS

Constltuent Elements of the Vajjian confederacy—The Līcchavīs and other Confederates

We have seen that the Licchavis were included in the great Vajjian confederacy that dominated over the Vajji or Vṛji country. But sometimes Vajji and Licchavi were used indiscriminately as syñonyms. At the time the Buddha lived, "the Vajjis were divided into several clans such as the Licchavis, the Vaidehis, the Tīra-bhuktis and so on and the exact number of those clans would appear to have been eight as criminals were arranged before the Aṭṭhakūlakā or eight clans which would appear to have been a jury composed of one member from each of the separate divisions of the tribe."[125]

Mutual sympathy amongst the Licchavis

All these Vajjis lived in great amity and concord which was a particular mark of their confederacy and this union coupled with their martial instincts and the efficiency of their martial institutions made them great and powerful amongst the nations of north-eastern India.[126] Their sympathy for one another was exemplary. If a Licchavi fell ill, other Licchavis, came to see him. The whole clan would join any auspicious ceremony performed in the house of a Licchavi if any foreigner of rank and power paid a visit to the Licchavi capital, they would all go out in a body to receive him and do him honour.[127]

Beauty in Appearance and Love for Cololurs

The young Licchavis were very handsome in appearance and very fond of brilliant colours in their dress and equipages.[128] The Buddha on his first meeting with the Licchavi nobles in their gay attire and rich and splendid equipages of various colours, was led to compare them to Tāvatiṁsa gods. A similar account we get from the Mahāparinibbāna Sutta, when the Licchavi nobles went out for the last time to meet the Blessed One as soon as they learnt that he had arrived at Vaiśālī and was staying at the mango-grove of Ambapālī in the outskirts of their city "Ordering a number of magnificent carriages to be made ready, they mounted one of them and proceeded with their train to Vesālī. Some of them were dark,[129] dark in colour and wearing dark clothes . and ornaments ; some of them were fair, fair in colour, and wearing light clothes and ornaments ; some of them were red ruddy in colour, and wearing red clothes and ornaments some of them were white, pale in colour, and wearing white clothes and ornaments."[130] Exactly the same description of the colours favoured by the Licchavis is given in the Aṅguttara Nikāya,[131] which shows that the Licchavis wore these colours not only on great festive occasions but in their ordinary daily life also. Once while the Enlightened One was staying at the Kūṭāgāraśālā in the Mahāvana, five hundred of the Licchavis were seated round him doing obeisance. Some of them were nīla or blue all over in clothes and ornaments and similarly others were yellow, red or white. We may compare these descriptions with the more detailed account in the Mahāvastu of the colours preferred by the Licchavis. Thus says the Sanskrit Buddhist work: "There are Licchavis. with blue horses, blue chariots, blue reins and whips, blue sticks, blue clothes, blue ornaments, blue turbans, blue umbrellas and with blue sword, blue jewels, blue footwear and blue everything befitting their youth"[132] and here the Mahāvastu quotes a verse, apparently from an older work or a traditional saying. In the very same terms the Mahāvastu speaks of the Licchavis decked all in yellow (pīta) and in light red, the colour of the Bengal madder (mañjiṣṭha), in red (lohita), in white (śveta), in green (harita), and some in variegated colours (vyāyukta).[133]

Classification of the Licchavis by colour

Perhaps the Licchavis were divided into separate septs as Senart suggested, distinguished by the colour worn by each ; otherwise it is difficult to explain why the same colour should be preferred for trappings of the horses, decorations of their carriages, as well as the articles of dress adorning their own persons.

Display of their Pomp and Grandeur

There was moreover a profusion of gold and jewels in everything in their equipage—carriages drawn by horses, gold-bedecked elephants, palanquins of gold set with all kinds of precious stones. Altogether there went out of the city of Vesālī twice eighty-four thousand conveyances decked in pearl and gold, with all the wealth and splendour of kings, (rājaṛddhiye and samṛddhiye).

Their Character as Depicted by the Buddha

All this speaks of a people who were greatly prosperous and in affluent circumstances and it may be expected that they would be given to luxury and indolence. But this was not their character at the time when Buddha lived and preached among them. The Saṁyutta Nikāya peserves a saying of the Exalted One: "Look ye Bhikkhus here, how these Licchavis live sleeping with logs of wood as pillows, strenuous and diligent, (appamattā) zealous and active (ātāpino) in archery. Ajātasattu, Vedehiputto, the Magadhan king, can find no defect in them, nor can he discover any cause of action (against them). Should the Licchavis, Oh Bhikkhus, in the time to come, be very delicate, tender and soft in their arms and legs, should they sleep in ease and comfort on cushions of the finest cotton up till the sun is up in the heavens, then the Magadhan king, Ajātasattu, Vedehiputto, will find defects and will discover cause of action."[134] This testimony of the Buddha goes to show that the Licchavis were hardy and active, ardent and strenuous in their military training, so that their enemies could have no chance of getting them at a disadvantage.

Not Vegetarians

The Licchavis used to kill animals on the 8th, 14th and 15th day of the lunar months and eat their flesh.[135]

Fond of manly pastimes

They were fond of manly pastimes such as elephant training and hunting. Among the Psalms of the Brethren (Theragāthā), we find one composed by Vajjiputtaka. the son of a Licchavirājā at Vaiśālī, who became known among the followers of the Buddha as the Vajjian's son and who, in his early life, was engaged in training elephants.[136]

Passion for hunding tempered by Buddha's influence

The Aṅguttara Nikaya narrates how a large number of Licchavi youths, armed with bows, ready with strings, set and surrounded by a pack of hounds, were roving about in the Mahāvana but finding the Buddha seated at the foot of a tree in the forest, threw away their bows and arrows and sending away the pack of hounds sat by the Great Teacher subdued by his presence, silent and without a word, in a reverent attitude with the palms joined. A Licchavi of apparently advanced years, Mahānāma by name, who came to pay his respects to the Buddha, expressed his great wonder at the sight of the Licchavi youths, full of life and vivacity, notorious for their insolent and wanton conduct in the city, thus sitting silent and demure, in an attitude of reverence before the great teacher; he pointed out the defects in their character, the defects that are found in youngmen of every country where the people are rich and powerful and of an imperious temper. "The Licchavi youths, Oh Lord!" goes on Mahānāma, "are rude and rough and whatever presents are sent to the families, sugarcane or plums, cakes, sweetmeats or preparations of sugar, these they plunder and eat up, throw dust at the ladies of respectable families and girls of good families; such youngmen are now all silent and demure, are doing obeisance with joined palms to yourself, O Lord."[137] Here we get an insight into the daily life of these young cockneys glorying within the walls of the city of Vaiśālī. It shows that the young Vaiśālians, though they indulged in the pranks and peccadillos of youth, were not so wild as to lose all sense of reverence or respect due to religious men.

Watters' view—Its Criticism

"In the Buddha's time, the young Licchavis of the city," says Watters, "were a free, wild, set, very handsome and full of life and Buddha compared them to the gods in Indra's Heaven. They dressed well, were good archers, and drove fast carriages, but they were wanton, insolent and utterly irreligious."[138] This is an exaggeration and is probably based on the Chinese translations of such passages as the following from the Lalitavistara, where some of the Tuṣita gods were pointing out the defects in the character of the Vaiśālians when their city was recommended by others among them as a suitable place of birth for the Bodhisatta. These Devaputras in the Tuṣita heaven averred, "Vaiśālī is unfit. What is the reason? Look here. They do not speak with propriety towards each other, there is no practice of religion among them, nor obedience to those in high or middle position, nor to the old and the elders. Each one of them thinks, 'I am a king, and I am a king.' They do not accept the discipleship of any one, nor the religion of any one. Therefore is Vaiśālī unfit."[139] Whatever might have been the opinions of these 'sons of heaven' before the birth of the

Bodhisattva, they must have changed their opinions about the people of Vaiśālī who showed such remarkable veneration towards the Enlightened One and received such marked favour from him. Do we not often read of five hundred Licchavis visiting him at the Kūṭāgāraśālā surrounding him and doing obeisance to him. The only conclusion we can draw from the above account in the Lalitavistara, is that the Licchavis were rather independent in character and would not easily accept a subordinate position to any one whether in politics or in religion or in ordinary daily life.

Moral Courage

Vaddha, a Licchavi, at the instigation of some dishonest Bhikkhus, had preferred a false charge of adultery against Dabba, a Mallian, but Vaddha afterwards made a clean breast of the whole ugly plot as soon as he saw the measure of his iniquity.[140]

Regard for Elders

Then again the statement that the Licchavis did not respect their elders or were irreligious, is in direct contradiction of what the Buddha said about them to Vassakāra, the Magadhan minister. "So long as they honour and esteem and revere and support the Vajjian elders, and hold it a point of duty to hearken to their words—so long as no women or girls belonging to their clans are detained among them by force or abduction—so long may the Vajjians be expected not to decline, but to prosper.[141]

Love of Education

The Licchavi youths went to distant countries for education. We read of a Licchavi named Mahāli who went to Taxila to learn śilpa or arts and returned home after completing his education. It is said that he in his turn trained as many as five hundred Licchavis who also, when educated, took up the same task and in this way education spread far and wide among the Licchavis[142] and some of them went so far as to write poems. For instance, we find in the Theragāthā[143] that a Vajjiputta, the son of a Licchavirājā at Vaiśālī, composed a psalm.

Artisans—Construction of Palaces and Shrines, etc.

Nor were the fine arts neglected by this gifted people. Artisans such as tailors, goldsmiths and jewellers must have been very much in requisition at the city of Vaiśālī to furnish the gay robes of seven thousand seven hundred and seven rājās or nobles, and we can very well imagine what a great strain the artisans were put to in order to devise suits of dress and ornaments to fit up the variously coloured Licchavis, the blues, the reds, the yellows, the greens and the whites. The art of architecture also was much developed in Vaiśālī; the magnificent palaces of the Licchavis are spoken of in the Lalitavistara.[144] They were equally enthusiastic in the building of temples, shrines, and monasteries for the Bhikkhus ; and we are told that the Bhikkhus themselves superintended the construction of these buildings for the order. The Cullavagga of the Vinaya Piṭaka tells us also how on one occasion when the Enlightened One was staying at the peak-roofed-hall in the Mahāvana, "the people were zealously engaged in putting up new buildings (for the use of the order), and as zealously provided with the requisite clothes, and food, and lodging, and medicine for the sick, all such Bhikkhus as superintended their work."[145] We are further told how a poor tailor of Vaiśālī intent on building himself a house for the Saṁgha, raised the walls of such a house, but, as the Cullavagga tells us, "by his want of experience the laying was out of line and the wall fell down." Then the poor tailor felt disturbed, grew angry and murmured thus:—"These Sākyaputtiya Samaṇas exhort and teach those men who provide them with the requisite clothes, food, lodging, and medicine, and superintend their buildings for them. But I am poor and no one exhorts or teaches me or helps me in my building."[146] This passage shows that some of the Bhikkhus themselves were master builders who supervised the erection of houses for the Buddhist order, just as in the medieval, times in Europe we find the monk excelling in many of the fine arts including painting, sculpture and architecture. The Licchavis of Vaiśālī had built many shrines or caityas inside and outside their great city and we have seen from the Mahāvastu passage quoted in the last chapter, with what great liberality and magnanimity they delivered over the best-among them to Buddha and the Buddhist Church. That these caityas were beautiful and fine buildings where one might prefer to dwell as long as one liked, even to the end of the kalpa, appears from a passage in the Dīgha Nikāya where Buddha while staying at the Cāpāla caitya said about each of the caityas that it was charming and then suggested to Ānanda that the Tathāgata might be inclined to live there for a kalpa[147] or the remaining part of a kalpa, meaning perhaps that in such beautiful surroundings, life would be pleasant and worth living.

Matrimonial rites—restrictions, Chastity

About the marriage rites ot the Licchavis, it is said in the Tibetan books that there were rules restricting the marriage of all girls born in Vaiśālī, to that city alone. They state, "The People of Vaiśālī had made a law that a daughter born in the first district could marry only in the first district, not in the second or third; that one born in the middle district could marry only in the first and second; but that one born in the last district could marry in any one of the three; moreover, that no marriage was to be contracted outside Vaiśālī."[148] A passage in the Bhikkhunī Vibhaṅga Saṅghādidesa[149] indicates that a Licchavi who wanted to marry could ask the corporation or the Licchavigaṇa to select a suitable bride for him. They appear to have a high idea of female chastity; violation of chastity was a serious offence amongst them. Buddha himself says that "no women or girls belonging to their clans are detained among them by force or abduction."[150] The Petavatthu Aṭṭhakaṭhā gives a story of a Licchavi rājā named Ambasakkhara who was enamoured of the beauty of a married woman, whose husband he engaged as an officer under him; he wanted to gain her love but was foiled in his attempts.[151]

Marriage Contract inviolable—its Exception

The punishment for a woman who broke her marriage

vow was very severe, the husband could with impunity even take away her life. But even an adulterous woman could save herself from the punishment by entering the congregation of nuns by getting the pabbajjā ordination, as can be seen from the Bhikkhunī Vibhaṅga Saṅghādidesa.[152]

An Example

A Licchavi wife committed adultery. The husband warned his wife many times but she heeded not. The Licchavi informed the Licchavigaṇa that his wife had committed adultery and he was resolved to kill her ; he then asked the gaṇa to select a suitable wife for him. When the lady heard that she would be killed, she took her valuables, went to Sāvatthi and asked for pabbajjā (ordination) from the titthiyas, by whom, however, she was refused : then she went to te bhikkhunis who in a body also refused; at last she went to a bhikkhunī who was persuaded to give ordination to her and thus she was successful. The Licchavi went to Sāvatthī and saw his wife ordained; complained to king Pasenadi of Kosala, who asked him to show his wife. The Licchavi informed the king that she had become a bhikkhuni. The king said that as she had become a bhikkhuni, no punishment could be inflicted on her. After the occurrence of this event, an agitation was set on foot among the Licchavis who reported the matter to the Buddha who told the bhikkhunis that they should not give ordination to such a woman.[153] Thus, we see that cases of adultery were tried by the Licchavigaṇa.

Disposal of the Dead

We have already referred in Chapter I, to the various methods prevalent among the Licchavis with regard to the disposal of thc dead. Besides cremation and burial, the custom of exposing the dead to be devoured by wild animals seems to have been in existence in Vaiśālī. When the Bodhisatta was at Vaiśālī, he is said to have observed a cemetery under a clump of trees and enquired about it from the Ṛṣis who explained that the corpses of men were exposed to be devoured by birds and there they used, to collect and pile up the white bones of dead persons. They burnt corpses there and the bones were preserved in heaps; the corpses were hung from the trees; there were others buried there such as had been killed by their relatives fearing lest they should be born again while others were left upon the ground that they might return if possible, to their former homes.[154] Dr.Vincent Smith finds in this story proof of the custom of the ancient inhabitants of Vaiśālī of disposing of their dead "sometimes by exposure, sometimes by cremation, and sometimes by burial."[155]

Festivals

The Licchavis had various festivals, of which the Sabbarattivāro or Sabbaratticāro was the most important. At the Sabbarattivaro or Sabbaratticāro festival, songs were sung, trumpets, drums and other musical instruments were used.[156] When a festival took place at Vaiśālī, all the people used to enjoy it and there were dancing, singing and recitation.[157]

Changes in Licchavi character

It was Sāriputta who said regarding the Vajjians that they were once good and afterwards took to evil ways. In other words, at first they were free from desires of senses, ill will, torpor, sloth, etc., but afterards they ere addicted to these evils. Then again they gave up all these vices and became good.[158]

IV. VIEWS AND PRACTICES

The Licchavis—a Religious People

All the information that we can get about the views and practices of the Licchavis is derived from Buddhist books and, to a smaller extent, from Jaina works. It is apparent from what we learn about them from these sources that the Licchavis, a vigorous, manly and heroic race, and highly prosperous too, were at the same time of a strongly religious and devotional bent of mind. Both Jainism and Buddhism found many followers among them. Even before the advent of the two new forms of religion, the licchavis, or to call them by their wider designation, the Vajjians, appear to have been imbued with a strong religious spirit and deep devotion. The Vajjis appear to have numerous shrines in their town as well as in the country and they worshipped the deities at these shrines with proper offerings and with the observance of due rites and ceremonies. Even after Jainism and Buddhism had obtained a strong hold on the Licchavis of Vaiśālī, the great body of the people of the Vajji country as well as of the capital remained staunch followers of their ancient faith, the principal feature of which was caitya worship, although they had due respect for the Jaina or Buddhist sages that wandered over their country preaching the message delivered by their respective teachers. The Mahāparinibbāṇa Suttanta tells us what the Buddha told Vassakāra, the prime minister (mahā-mātra) of Magadha, when the latter was sent by Ajātaśatru to learn from the Exalted One what he would predict with regard to the king's daring plan of exterminating the Vajjis. The Exalted One said : "So long as the Vajjians honour and esteem and revere and support the Vajjian shrines[159] in town, or country and allow not the proper offerings and rites, as formerly given and performed to fall into desuetude—so long as the rightful protection, defence and support shall be fully provided for the Arahants among them, so that the Arahants from a distance may enter the realm, and the Arahants therein may live at ease—so long may the Vajjians be expected not to decline but to prosper."[160] This was said by the Buddha on the eve of his last departure for Vaiśālī and shortly before he passed away from this world. Towards the end of his life, the Licchavis were devoted worshippers at the numerous shrines that were scattered about in their country. Buddhaghoṣa in his commentary, the Sumaṅgala-vilāsini, also informs us that the Licchavis observed their old religious rites.[161] We must here bear in mind the fact that Buddhism at the early stage, of which we are speaking, was a form of faith for ascetics only, not a religious creed for all people. The Buddhists at this period only formed one of the numerous ascetic sects of Northern India. Thus there was nothing unusual in the fact that many of the Licchavis who were householders and had not accepted the life of bhikkhus or Buddhist monks, should remain firm followers of their former faith. We must not also forget that there are strong reasons to suspect, as Kern observes, "that original Buddhism was not exactly that of the canonical books."[162] The Pāli Tripiṭaka represents the version acknowledged by a particular sect of the Buddhist, namely, the Vibhajjavādins of Ceylon and there can be no doubt that the sacred canon was moulded and modified by them when it was finally edited, and as it is said, was put down in writing in Ceylon. We cannot therefore, expect to find an impartial account of the religious tenets of the people of the country where the Enlightened One preached his new message. But as the Buddhist along with the Jaina books form the only source of our information about the religious beliefs of the Licchavis, we have to take them as the basis of our account of their ideas of religion. From the meagre mention of the caityas of the Licchavis in the Buddhist books, it is not easy to determine what the principal objects of their worship were. There is, however, nothing to show that the religious belief of the Licchavis was in any way different from the form of faith obtained in other parts of Northern India. The Vedic religion was still in full vigour in north-eastern India, as the references, though not very numerous, to Vedic sacrifices in the Buddhist books show. We should bear in mind that the country of the Vajjis was the sacred land of Videha where the great Samrāṭ Janaka had exercised his sway and where Yājñavalkya preached the white Yajurveda.

The Caitya worship—and Important Feature of the Licchavi Faith

We have already referred to the numerous caityas in Vaiśālī and its suburbs as mentioned in the Mahāvastu. These caityas are called the Cāpāla, the Saptāmraka, the Bahuputra, the Gautama, the Kapinahya and the Mārkaṭahradatīra. In the Mahāparinibbāṇa Suttanta, we also get the names of these shrines (caityas). The Exalted One on his last visit to Vaiśālī went one day to the Cāpāla caitya and said addressing the venerable Ānanda: "How delightful aspot, Ānanda, is Vaiśālī, and how charming the Udena Shrine, and the Gotamaka Shrine, and the Shrine of the Seven Mangoes (Sattambaka), and the Shrine of many sons, and the Sārandada Shrine, and the Cāpāla Shrine." The Pāṭika Suttanta which like the Mahāparinibbāṇa Suttanta, is included in the Dīgha-Nikāya, indicates the position of these caityas. Kandara-masuka, a naked ascetic of Vaiśālī, sought to please the Licchavis by professing a great attachment to their city; he says, "So long as I live, I will never go beyond the Udena Shrine on the east of Vaiśālī; the Gotamaka Shrine on the south; the Sattamba Shrine on the west and the Bahuputta Shrine on the north."[163] From this boasting of Kandara-masuka, it is evident that these shrines were situated in the outskirts of Vaiśālī marking its boundaries, as it were. A passage in the Divyāvadāna also gives a list of the caityas in almost the same words as the Mahāparinibbāṇa Suttanta: there also the Enlightened One speaks addressing Ānanda, of the beauties of the caityas called Cāpāla, Saptāmraka, Bahupatraka and Gautama-nyagrodha.[164] Bahupatraka is evidently the same as Bahuputraka of the other texts. Altogether we get the names of eight caityas or shrines in and about Vaiśālī. There can, therefore, be no doubt with regard to the existence of these caityas in the country of the Licchavis. Buddhaghoṣa in his commentary on the Mahāparinibbāṇa Suttanta explains cetiyāni in the text as Yakkhacetiyāni and about the Sārandada caitya where the Buddha preached, he says that "this was a Vihāra erected on the site of a former shrine of the Yakkha Sāran-dada."[165] So, that from Buddhaghoṣa's comments it is but reasonable to assume that the Yakkhas were worshipped in some of the caityas, but the materials at our command do not justify us to assume that the Yakkhas were the only deities worshipped at these shrines. The Buddhist books show that the Vedic gods, Indra and Prajāpati or Brahmā[166] were very popular deities in the regions where the Buddha preached. The Arthaśāstra of Kauṭilya [167] also speaks of many gods popularly worshipped besides the Vedic divinities. Some scholars are of opinion that the caityas were "Shrines of pre-Buddhistic worship" and that "they were probably trees and barrows."[168] Some of the caityas, as their names suggest, might have been named after the trees which marked the spots, but it would be going too far to imagine merely from the name that these shrines consisted of trees and nothing else, as some scholars would have us believe.

Jainism

Mahāvīra, the twenty-fourth Tīrthaṅkara of the Jains, as we have seen before, was a citizen of Vaiśālī. Even before his advent, the faith of which he was the last exponent, seems to have been prevalent in Vaiśālī and the country round, in some earlier form. It appears from the Jaina accounts that the religion as fixed and established by Pārśvanātha, who is revered as the twenty-third Tīrthaṅkara, was followed by some at least of the Kṣatriya people of north-eastern India, and especially amongst the residents of Vaiśālī. We read in the Āyārāṅga Sūtra, "The venerable Ascetic Mahāvīra's parents were worshippers of Pārśva and followers of the Śramaṇas. During many years, they were followers of the Śramaṇas, and for the sake of protecting the six classes of lives they obseived, blamed, repented, confessed, and did penance according to their sins. On a bed of Kuśa-grass they rejected all food, and their bodies dried up by the last mortification of the flesh, which is to end in death. Thus they died in the proper month, and leaving their bodies, were bora as gods in Adbhuta Kalpa."[169] Similar accounts are given in other Jaina works also of the prevalence in the country of a faith which was afterwards developed by Mahāvīra. The Śramaṇas or wandering ascetics had been in existence ever since the time of the earlier Upaniṣads and evidently the Śramaṇas that were followed so reverently by the parents of Mahāvīra, belonged to one of the numerous sects or classes amongst which the Indian ascetics appear to have been divided. After Mahāvīra developed his doctrines and preached his faith of unbounded charity to all living beings in the Vajji land and in Magadha, the number of his followers among the Licchavis appears to have been large and some men of the highest position in Vaiśālī appear to have been among them as is seen from the Buddhist books themselves. In the Mahāvagga of the Vinaya Piṭaka we read that Sīha, a general-in-chief of the Licchavis, was a disciple of Nigaṇṭha Nātaputta who has been shown by Profs. Bühler and Jacobi to be identical with Mahāvīra of the Jaina legends. We read here how general Sīha,[170] a follower of the Nigaṇṭhas, gradually felt attracted towards the Samaṇa Gotama by listening to the discussions among the Licchavis at the Santhāgāra or the Mote-Hall where they used to meet, discuss and settle all matters relating to politics or religion. One day "many distinguished Licchavis were sitting together assembled in the town hall and spoke in many ways in praise of the Buddha, of the Dhamma and of the Saṁgha. At that time, Sīha, the general-in-chief (of the Licchavis), a disciple of the Nigaṇṭha sect, was sitting in that assembly. And Sīha, the general, thought: Truly he, the Blessed One, must be the Arahat Buddha, since these many distinguished Licchavis who were sitting here together assembled in the town hall, speak in so many ways in praise of the Buddha, of the Dhamma and of the Saṁgha. What if I were to go and visit him, the Arahat Buddha." Sīha next asked permission to visit the Buddha from the Nigaṇṭha Nātaputta, who, however, tried to dissuade him from doing so, pointing out the defects in the doctrines preached by the former. "Why should you, Sīha, who believe in the result of actions (according to their moral merit) go to visit the Samaṇa Gotama who denies the result of actions? For the Samaṇa Gotama, Sīha, denies the result of actions; he teaches the doctrine of non-action; and in this doctrine he trains his disciples," Sīha's enthusiasm for the Buddha abated for the time but it was again roused by the discussions of the other Licchavis so that he at last did pay a visit to the Buddha who gave him a long discourse on the Buddhist doctrine. Sīha was at last converted to the Buddhist faith. That the number of the followers of Mahāvīra at Vaiśālī, however, was very large also appears from this story of Sīha. This general had invited Buddha and the Bhikkhus to take their meal at his house and procured meat from the market for feeding them. But the Jains spread a false report as we read in the Mahāvagga: "At that time a great number of Nigaṇṭhas (running) through Vesālī, from road to road and from cross-way to cross-way, with outstretched arms, cried : To-day Sīha, the general, has killed a great ox and has made a meal for the Samaṇa Gotama; the Samaṇa Gotama knowingly eats this meat of an animal killed for this very purpose and has thus) become virtually the author of that deed (of killing the animal)."[171] This false report circulated by them only made Sīha firmer in his zeal for the new faith, but the story shows that the number of the Nigaṇṭhas at Vaiśālī was sufficiently large to defy the influence of such a great man as Sīha, and the fact that the conversion of Sīha took place at the time that Buddha paid his last visit to the city, shows that though Buddhism had made many converts among the followers of the faith preached by Mahāvīra, yet they were still numerous and powerful at the capital of the Licchavis even after the numerous sermons preached by the Buddha. This is also confirmed by the story of Saccaka, a Nirgrantha, who had the hardihood to challenge the Buddha himself to a discussion on philosophical tenets before an assemblage of five hundred Licchavis.[172]

Buddhism

Accounts of the spread of Buddhism among the Licchavis, gleaned from the various works in the Buddhist sacred literature, are by no means meagre. The Enlightened One paid at least three visits, but probably many more, to the city and from the very first he appears to have met with great success among them. We have already seen from the Mahāvastu how great was the veneration with which he was received on his first visit to Vaiśālī. The Pāli works have recorded many occasions on which the Licchavis sought the aid of the Buddha for the solution of numerous problems about religion and dogma that presented any difficulty to them. These questions and answers put to and given by the Buddha though frequently of only a general character and such as would naturally arise in the mind of any Buddhist, may yet help us to get glimpses of the workings of the Licchavi mind with regard to matters of faith, and we think that the bringing together of all these Licchavi questions to the Master will well repay the trouble bestowed upon them.

Bhaddiya, a Licchavi and the Buddha

Once when the Buddha was staying in the Kūṭāgārāśālā at Mahāvana in Vaiśālī, a Licchavi named Bhaddiya paid a visit to the Buddha and told him, "I have heard that the Samaṇa Gotama is a magician who knows the magic spells by virtue of which he attracts the followers of the faiths. Do people speak rightly when they say thus ?" Thereupon, the Buddha explained to him kusala and akusala Dhamma. The Buddha accepted him as his disciple and said, "If I be successful in inducing all rich Kṣatriyas and Brahmins to give up all akusalas and perform kusalas, it will be for their welfare and happiness." Bhaddiya was much delighted with his expositions and declared himself a follower of the Buddha.[173]

Two Licchavis and the Buddha

On another occasion we find that when the Buddha was at Vaiśālī, a Licchavi named Sālho and another Licchavi named Abhaya approached the Buddha. Sālho, the Licchavi, said to the Buddha, "There are some Samanas and Brāhmaṇas who preach the crossing of flood in two ways, namely, (1) on account of purity of conduct (śīla), (2) on account of practice of self-mortification (tapa). What does the Exalted One say about it" The Buddha replied, "It is impossible for the Samaṇas and the Brāhmaṇas who are devoted to the practice of self-mortification as well as those who are not pure in deed, whether in body or in mind or in speech to cross the flood."[174]

Licchavi minister, Nandaka and the Buddha

A Licchavi minister (mahāmātra) Nandaka approached the place where the Blessed One was. saluted him and sat at a little distance. The Buddha explained to him the four Dhammas, namely unshakable faith in the Buddha, Dhamma and Saṁgha and possession of śīlas which are beloved of the Ariyas, by which a noble disciple can obtain emancipation. Nandaka was told that it was the time to take his bath. Nandaka replied, "No use having an external bath, my faith in the Blessed One will be my internal bath."[175]

Veneration of the Licchavi youths for the Buddha

We have already recounted how when the Blessed On was at Mahāvana, many young Licchavis who having taken well arranged bows, surrounded by dogs, used to wander about in the Mahāvana, now sat silent and demure by the Buddha, who was seated at the foot of a tree and how Mahānāma, a Licchavi of rather advanced age, expressed his surprise that these arrogant youths who were rather rowdy in their daily life, had become so mild and gentle before the Exalted one.[176]

Five hundred Licchavis and the Buddha

On another occasion when the Buddha was at Vaiśālī, there were five hundred Licchavis assembled at the Sārandada cetiya. There was a talk about the five kinds of rare gems, Hatthiratana, Assaratana. Maṇiratana, Itthiratana and Gahapatiratana. The Licchavis placed a man on the road with instruction to inform them when he would see the Buddha coming. He informed the Licchavis about his advent. They approached him and requested him to go to the Sārandada cetiya. The Licchavis informed the Buddha that a discussion had arisen among them about the five kinds of rare gems. Buddha said, "The Licchavis who indulge in kāma or desire speak of such a topic." The Buddha solved the problem by speaking of five kinds of precious gems. It is difficult to get such persons as strictly follow the Tathāgata's Dhamma. It is also difficult to find a person who is grateful and who is an exponent of gratefulness. The appearance of the Tathāgata on earth is rare. So also is the preacher of Tathāgata's Dhamma.[177]

Jubilations of the Licchavis to see the Buddha

The Aṅguttara Nikāya[178] speaks of a large number of distinguished Licchavis, who, when going to see the Buddha who was at Vaiśālī, resounded the Mahāvana with a great tumult of joy to see the Buddha, as they were greatly devoted to him and had a strong faith in him. This noise so greatly troubled the Bhikkhus that they were unable to proceed with their meditation, and the Buddha remarked, "Noise is the hindrance of meditation." The Aṅguttara Nikāya[179] narrates how on another occasion, when the Blessed One was at Vaiśālī, he was worshipped by five hundred Licchavis arrayed in various coloured garments, ornaments, and trappings. The Licchavis gave Piṅgiyāni five hundred upper garments, after listening to a gāthā in praise of the Buddha sung by him. Piṅgiyāni offered the Buddha all those garments. Then the Buddha spoke of the five rare gems before the Licchavis.

Añjana-Vaniya

Añjana-Vaniya was born at Vaiśālī in the family of a rājā of the Vajjians. During his adolescence, the three-fold panic of drought, sickness and non-human foes affected the Vajjian territory. Afterwards the Exalted One put a stop to the panic and addressed a great concourse. Hearing his discourse, the prince won faith and left the world. After passing through the preliminary training, he settled in the Añjana wood at Sāketa. When the rains drew near, he got a castaway couch and placing it on four stones and covering it with grass, he made a shelter for the rainy season. There he engaged himself in a strenuous study for one month. Then he won Arhatship.[180]

Vajjiputta

Vajjiputta or the son of the Vajjis was the son of a Licchavi rājā at Vaiśālī. He went to the vihāra to attain salvation when the Master was preaching. Hearing him he entered the order and in due course acquired six-fold Abhiññā.[181]

Sīha

Sīhā, a daughter of the sister of the Licchavi general Sīha was born at Vaiśālī at the time of Gotama Buddha. She was called Sīhā, after her maternal uncle, Sīha. When she attained years of discretion, one day she heard the Master teaching the Norm. She became a believer and obtained the consent of her parents to enter the order. When she was attempting to gain insight, she was unable to prevent her mind from running on objects of external charm. Thus harassed for seven years, she at last made up her mind to put an end to her life. Taking a noose, she hung it round the bough of a tree and having it tied round her neck, she made her mind bend upon insight. At last she won Arhatship with a thorough grasp of "the Norm in form and in meaning."[182]

Jentī or Jentā

Jentī or Jentā was born in a princely family of the Licchavis at Vaiśālī. She won Arhatship after hearing the Dhamma preached by the Buddha. She developed the seven sambojjhaṅgas.[183]

Vāsiṭṭhi

Vāsiṭṭhi was reborn in a clansman's family at Vaiśālī. Her parents gave her in marriage to a clansman's son of equal position. She had a son. When the child was able to run about, he died. She being worn and overwhelmed with grief, came to Mithilā. There she saw the Exalted One, self-controlled and self-contained. At the sight of the Buddha she got back her normal mind from the frenzy that had caught hold of her. The Master taught her the outlines or the Norm. Performing all proper duties, she acquired insight and struggling with the help of full knowledge, she soon attained Arhatship together with a thorough grasp of the Norm in form and in spirit.[184]

Ambapālī

Ambapālī was born at Vaiśālī in the king's gardens at the foot of a mango tree. She was brought by the gardener to the city. She was known as the mango-guardian's girl. She was so very beautiful that many young princes wanted to have her. She was made a courtezan. Later on, out of reverence for the Master, she built a vihāra in her own gardens and gave it over to him and the Order. When she heard her own son preaching the 'Norm,' she tried to acquire insight.[185] The evanescence of her own body was noticed by her and she saw transitoriness in every phenomenon of the universe. At last she attained Arhatship.[186]

Philosophical Speculations of the Licchavis

From what has been given above about the religious beliefs of the Licchavis, it must have become sufficiently clear that many of them were of a religious turn of mind. The people of Vaiśālī were philosophical speculators and very often dealt with questions relating to the means of attaining Nirvāṇa,[187] dosa, lobha, moha, alobha, adosa, amoha,[188] samādhi, saññā, vedanā, saṁkhāra and the influence of the purity of sīla, tapa, etc.[189]

The independent spirit of the Licchavis or Vajjians was manifested notably in the great schism brought about by the bhikkhus of their clan in the life of the Buddhist Order. Their national spirit was also displayed in bringing about a momentous change within the Buddhist doctrine. A school of Buddhist thought known as the Vajjiputtakas is said to have formulated a theory of personality (Puggalavāda) which was unacceptable to the orthodox interpreters of Buddhism.

Saccaka, a Nigaṇṭha, and the Licchavis

That the Licchavis used to take interest in philosophical and metaphysical discussions is evident from the following incident recorded in the Majjhima Nikāya. The Nigaṇṭhaputta Saccaka approached the place where the Licchavis were and said to them, "Let the Licchavis come out today; I shall hold a conversation with Samaṇa Gotama. If the Samaṇa Gotama places me in the same position in which I am placed by the monk Assajī who is a Sāvaka, I shall defeat Samaṇa Gotama by my argument like a strong man catching hold of a goat by its long hair and moving it in any way he likes." Saccaka mentioned various ways in which he was going to treat Samaṇa Gotama, if Samaṇa Gotama would be defeated. Some Licchavis enquired how Gotama would meet the argument of Saccaka, the Nigaṇṭhaputta, and *vice versa,* while others enquired how Nigaṇṭhaputta Saccaka would meet the arguments of Samaṇa Gotama and *vice versa.* Saccaka induced five hundred Licchavis to go with him to the Mahāvana to listen to his discussion with Gotama. He approached the place where the Bhikkhus were walking up and down and asked them, "We are anxious to see Gotama, the Blessed One." The Buddha was seated to spend the day in meditation at the foot of a tree in the Mahāvana forest. Nigaṇṭ haputta Saccaka with a large number of Licchavis went to the Blessed One and having exchanged friendly greetings with him, sat at a little distance. Some Licchavis saluting him took their seats; others exchanged friendly greetings with him and then took their seats; some saluting with folded hands, sat at a little distance, some prominent Licchavis giving out their names and family names, took their seats at a little distance. Some remained silent and sat at a little distance with great devotion to the Blessed One. Then arguments relating to the saṁghas and gaṇas, some knotty points of Buddhist psychology and metaphysics *e.g.*, the nature of rūpa (form), vedanā (sens' ātion), saññā (perception), saṁkhāra (confections) and viññāna (con-sciousness), were started between Nigaṇṭhaputta Saccaka and the Blessed One. Saccaka being defeated, invited the Blessed One who accepted the invitation. The Licchavis were informed of this and asked to bring whatever they liked at the dinner which would be held on the following day. At the break of day, the Licchavis brought five hundred dishes for the Buddha.[190] The Nigaṇṭhaputta and the Licchavis became greatly devoted to the Blessed One.

Mahālī, a Licchavi and the Buddha

In the Saṁyutta Nikāya,[191] we read of Mahāli, a Licchavi, who went to the Buddha and told him that Pūraṇa Kassapa was of opinion that there was no cause of the sin of beings and without cause they suffered and there was no cause of the purity of beings and without cause thev were purified. Buddha refuted this theory of Pūraṇa Kassapa by raising the subtle philosophical discussion about the five khaṇḍhas and afterwards the Buddha succeeded in making the Licchavi understand that what Pūraṇa Kassapa had taught him, did not hold good ; it fell to the ground.

Buddha on sin and merit

The Aṅguttara Nikāya[192] also speaks of a Licchavi named Mahāli who said to the Buddha, "What is the cause of sinful act" ? Blessed One answered," The causes of sinful act are avarice, hatred, delusion, absence of reasoning and cherishing wrong views in mind." Mahāli further asked the Buddha, "What is the cause of virtuous act " ? The Buddha answered, "Absence of avarice, hatred, delusion, reasoning and not cherishing wrong views in mind — these are the causes of a virtuous act."

Abhaya, a Licchavi

When Ānanda was at Vaiśālī, Abhaya, a Licchavi and another Licchavi named Paṇditakumāra went to Ānanda. Abhaya said to Ānanda. "Nigantha Nāthaputta is all-knowing, all-seeing, and knows the light of knowledge, *(i.e.* has insight into knowledge) he teaches the destruction of previous actions by austerities and says that by non-action the cause of fresh kamma is destroyed. From the destruction of action there is the cessation of suffering ; from the cessation of suffering, we have the destruction of sensation and from the destruction of sensation suffering will be no longer on earth. There is an overcoming of suffering by purity in the present existence." Thereupon Ānanda said that the three kinds of purity which were not subject to decay had beet: expounded by the Buddha. These three kinds of purity were the means of going beyond grief and lamentation, of disappearance of sorrow, of the attainment of knowledge and of the realisation of Nirvāṇa.[193]

Sāmaṇḍaka and Sāriputts

The Samyutta Kikāya[194] relates that when Sériputta dwelt at Ukkācelā among the Vajjians, a monk named Sāmandaka went to the place where Sāriputta was and asked him, "What is Nirvāṇa?" "It means rāgakkhaya, dosakkhaya and mohakkhaya ;

there is a path for the realisation of Nirvāṇa." "What is that path ? " "It is the sublime eightfold path *e.g.* right speech, right action, etc. "

The Samyutta Nikāya further relates that when the Blessed One was at Ukkācelā in the Vajji country with a large congregation of monks, he was told that owing to the passing away of Sāriputta and Moggallāna, the congregation seemed to be empty. Buddha said, "You depend on yourself and not on others. Meditate on four satipaṭṭhānas. Tathāgata has no grief or lamentation for the passing away of such great disciples because what is born for some cause is subject to decay."[195]

A Wicked Licchavi Prince

The influence that the teachings of the Exalted One exercised even upon the fierce Licchavis, is unique. Of the many stories showing how noble and inspiring were the Blessed One's teachings, we give below one indicating how they cured a wicked prince of the ferocity of his spirit and temper. It has been said of a wicked Licchavi prince[196] that he was so very fierce, cruel, passionate and vindictive that none could dare utter more than two or three words in his presence, even his parents, relations and friends, could not make him better. So at last his parents resolved to bring him to the All-wise Buddha for his rectification. Accordingly he was brought before the Buddha who addressed and said to him thus, "Prince! a man should not be cruel, passionate and ferocious because such a man is harsh and unkind to his father, mother, brother, sister, children, friends, relatives and to all and thus he is looked upon with terror and hatred by all. He will be reborn in hell of other place of punishment after this life; and however adorned he may be in this life, he looks ugly; although his face is beautiful like the orb of the full moon, yet it is loathsome like a scorched lotus or disc of gold overworn with filth. The violence of his rage impels him to commit suicide and thus meeting his death by reason of his own rage he is reborn into torment. So also those persons who injure others are not only hated in this life but will after their death, pass to hell and punishment, and when they are again born as men they are destined to be beset with disease and sickness of eye and ear. So let all men show kindness and also do good to others and thereby they will avoid hell and punishment." The magic power of this wholesome and edifying lecture had the beneficial effect of removing the arrogance and selfishness of the prince from the core of his heart, which became afterwards full of love and kindness.

Now, the influence of the Buddha's teachings which changed the mood of the wicked prince was observed by the brethren who talked together as to how a single lecture could tame the fierce spirit of the prince while the ceaseless exhortations of his parents were of no avail. They also remarked thus, "as an elephant-tamer or a horse-tamer makes the animal go to the right or left so the Blessed One—the All-wise Buddha, guides the man whithersoever he wills, along any of the eight directions and makes his pupil discern shapes external to himself. The Blessed One is hailed as chief of the trainers of men, supreme in bowing men to the yoke of truth. There is no trainer of men like unto the supreme Buddha." The people of Vaiśālī were so devoted to the Buddha that they made a cairn at Vaiśālī over the remains of the Buddha and celebrated a feast.[197]

Beal's opinion regarding the inhabitants of Vaiśālī

Mr. Beal in his Romantic Legend of Śākya Buddha[198] says that the people of Vaiśālī owing to their imperfect knowledge of the laws of self-discipline and mortification, could not use true discernment in their religious life and search after deliverance. There was an old king named Druma, for example, in the city of Vaiśālī, who retired into solitude, but afterwards forsaking his hermit-cell, came back to his kingdom. But we cannot agree with Mr. Beal. It is evident from the Psalms of the Brethren and Sisters that many people of Vaiśālī, both male and female, though they had fallen off from virtue at first, were, later on, greatly influenced by the preaching of the Norm and became self-controlled and self-disciplined. They advanced so far as to attain Arhatship which they could not have gained if they had failed to use true discernment in their religious life and search after deliverance.

Ten indulgences and Vajjiputtaka bhikkhus

A hundred years after the passing away of the Buddha, certain Vajjiputtaka bhikkhus, the residents of Vaiśālī, began to indulge in practices prejudicial to the interests of Buddhism. They proclaimed ten indulgences as permissible, namely:

(1) storing of salt;[199]
(2) the taking of the midday meal when the sun's shadow shows two finger-breadths after noon;
(3) the going to some village (or to another village) and there eating fresh food;
(4) residing (in the same parish and yet holding the Uposatha separately);
(5) sanction (of a solemn act in an incomplete chapter):
(6) the (unconditional) following of a precedent;
(7) the partaking of unchurned milk;
(8) of unfermented toddy;
(9) the use of a mat without fringes (not conform with the model prescribed);
(10) to accept gold and silver."[200]

The Vajjiputtaka Bhikkhus of Vaiśālī on the Uposatha day in question, filling a golden basin with water, and placing it in the midst of the assembled priests, thus appealed to the devotees of Vaiśālī, who attended there: "Beloved ones! bestow on the priesthood either a kahāpaṇa or half, or a quarter of one, or even the value of a māsa to the priesthood, it will afford the means of providing themselves with sacerdotal requisites."

Judgment of suppression finally pronounced

In order to suppress the heresies among them, the Buddhist Elders convened a council at Vaiśālī known as the 'Sattasatika' or the convocation of the Seven Hundred. At this meeting bhikkhus assembled, brought together by the exertions of the venerable Yaso. In the course of discussions. the interrogation of the venerable Revata, and the exposition of the Vinaya by the Thera Sabbakāmi, the ten indulgences being thoroughly inquired into, a judgment of suppression was finally pronounced.[201]

V. GOVERNMENT AND ADMINISTRATION OF JUSTICE

Republic—No Hereditary Ruler

The Licchavis formed a great and powerful republic in the sense that there was no hereditary monarch, the power of the state being vested in the assembly of citizens. It does not appear to have been a full-fledged democratic republic but an oligarchy in the sense that citizenship was confined to the members of the confederate clans. This form of government as described in the Buddhist books was not rare in ancient India; there is ample evidence to show that in ancient times, this form was much more in vogue than we are led to imagine from later literature. It is certainly a very remarkable phenomenon that while to the south of the Ganges, in Magadha, an empire was being built up first under the Śiśunāgas, next under the Nandas and later still under the Mauryas, to the north of the same river, the Licchavis formed a powerful corporation resisting for long the aggressive attempts of the Magadhan kings.

The Licchavi Saṁgha or Gaṇa

The Licchavis formed what is called in ancient Indian literature, a Saṁgha, or Gaṇa, that is, an organised corporation. One of the Buddhist canonical books, the Majjhima Nikāya,[202] speaks of the Vajjis and the Mallas as forming saṁghas and gaṇas, that is, clans governed by an organised corporation and not by an individual sovereign, the power of the state being vested in the corporation. The Mahāvastu[203] says that when plague raged in their city, one of them, Tomara, was elected by the Gaṇa to represent their difficulties before the Buddha and bring him over to their city.

Kauṭilya on the Licchavi Saṁgha

Kauṭilya, the great minister of the first Maurya Emperor,

has also indicated in his Arthaśāstra, the real nature of the Licchavi form of government. He speaks of the Licchavis in the chapter on the conduct of corporations.[204] He says that the saṁghas or corporations of the peoples like the Licchavis, the Vṛjis, the Mallas, the Madras, the Kukuras, the Kurus, the Pañcālas and others were rājaśabdopajivinah.[205] This apparently means that among these peoples, each citizen had the right to call himself a rājā *i.e.,* dignitary who did not owe allegiance or pay revenue to any one else; but each of whom held up his head high and, not merely looked upon himself as a rājā , but considered that the word rājā was his usual designation recognised not only by his fellow clansmen but also by the other peoples of India. This is corroborated by the description given of the Licchavis in the Lalita Vistara, which, though a late work, preserves the right tradition when it says that at Vaiśālī, there was no respect for age, nor for position, whether high or middle or low, each one there thought that he was a rājā.[206] Kauṭilya's account shows that this designation of each individual clansman was not confined to the Licchavis alone but was shared by them along with many other warrior peoples of northern India from the land of the Madras on the north-western frontier up to the Vṛji land in the east; we happen to possess independent corroboration of this statement of Kauṭilya's in the Buddhist literature with regard to the Licchavis. The same state of things must have been in existence among the other tribes mentioned by Kauṭilya. Savaraswāmī in his commentary on the Pūrvamīmāṁsā Sūtra, Book II,. says that the word 'rājā' is a synonym for Kṣatriya, and he supports his statement by the fact that even in his time, the word was Used by the Āndhras to designate a Kṣatriya. From the authority of Savaraswāmī it can be said that the word 'rājā' in early times designated a Kṣ atriya and subsequently came to mean a king.

In practice the rank of 'rājā' must have been restricted to a comparatively small section of the community because we learn from the Ekapaṇṇa Jātaka that besides the rājās, there were the uparājās, senāpatis, etc. What the real number of the de facto rājās was, we do not know. Tradition gives various numbers of a widely divergent character. The Mahāvastu[207] speaks of the twice eighty-four thousand Licchavi rājās residing within the city of Vaiśālī. The Pāli commentaries, as for example, the preambles to the Cullakāliṅga Jātaka[208] and the Ekapaṇṇa Jātaka[209] speak of seven thousand seven hundred and seven rājās of Vaiśālī. The Kalpa Sūtra speaks of only nine. (Jaina Sūtras, pt. I, S.B.E,, Vol. XXII, p. 266.)

Unity of the Licchavis

Kauṭilya[210] observes that all these saṁghas by virtue of their being united in such corporations, were unconquerable by others. He further observes that for a king, the winning over to his side of such a corporate body was the acquisition of a best friend, that of all his allies, a corporation was the best and most helpful because of the power derived from their union which made them invincible.[211] Buddhist books inform us that the Licchavis were so strong as to defy the aggression of their country by any foreign power on account of their unity and concord and their practice of constantly meeting in their popular assemblies, and that this made them almost invincible. When Ajātaśatru sent his prime minister (*mahāmātra*) to ascertain the views of the Buddha with regard to his proposed extermination of the Vrjis, the Blessed One said addressing Ānanda, "Have you heard, Ānanda, that the Vajjians hold full and frequent public assemblies ?" "Lord, so I have heard," replied he, "so long, Ānanda," rejoined the Blessed One, "as the Vajjians hold these full and frequent public assemblies; so long may they be expected not to decline but to prosper'."[212] And in like manner questioning Ānanda and receiving reply, the Exalted One declared the other conditions which would ensure the welfare of the Vajjian confederacy:—"So long, Ānanda, as the Vajjians meet together in concord and rise in concord and carry out their undertakings in concord—so long as they enact nothing not already established, abrogate nothing that has been already enacted, and act in accordance with the ancient institutions of the Vajjians as established in former days—so long as they honour and esteem and revere and support the Vajjian elders and hold it a point of duty to hearken to their words—so long may the Vajjians be expected not to decline but to prosper."[213]

Santhāgāra – public hall—procedure of the Assembly

From the above statements about the Vajjians of whom the Licchavis were the most important clan, we come to learn that they were governed by an assembly where the people of their clan met for discussion about all matters and we see further that these meetings were held often and frequently. The public hall where they used to hold these meetings was called the Santhāgāra and there they discussed both religion andpolitics. We have seen in the story of the conversion of Sīha that the Licchavis met at the Santhāgāra to discuss the teaching of the Buddha. The procedure that was followed in these assemblies in arriving at a decision on any particular matter brought before the council of the Licchavi saṁgha, may be gathered, as Professor D.R. Bhandarkar[214] has pointed out, from an account of the procedure followed at a ceremony of ordination at the saṁgha of the Buddhist Bhikkhus. There can be no doubt, that in organising the Buddhist saṁgha, the Buddha had, as his model, the political saṁghas of north-eastern India, especially that of the Licchavis whose corporation, as we have seen above, from the discourse of the Buddha with Vassakāra, the Magadhan minister—he esteemed very highly. And we further observe from the Mahāparinibbāna Suttanta[215] that just after speaking of the great merits of the Licchavi institutions, the Exa-lted One called together in the Service-Hall at Rājagṛha all the members of the Buddhist congregation in the neighbourhood of that city and impressed on them the virtues that he had extolled in the Licchavis, as being indispensable for the welfare of every organised community. Fortunately for us, the rules of procedure followed in the Buddhist community or saṁgha have been preserved in the description of the upasaṁpadā or ordination ceremony in the Pātimokkha section of the Vinaya Piṭaka, and from it, we can form an idea of the procedure followed in the political saṁgha of the Licchavis. First of all, it appears, was elected an officer called the *Āsana paññāpaka* or regulator of seats whose function seems to have been to seat the members of the congregation in the order of their seniority.[216] As in the Buddhist congregation, so among the Licchavis, the elders of the clans were highly respected as we see from the Mabā-parinibbāṇa Suttanta of the Dīgha Nikāya.[217]

We next come to the form of moving a resolution in the council thus assembled and seated by the *Āsana-paññāpaka.* "The mover first announces to the assembled Bhikkhus what resolution he is going to propose : this announcement is called *Ñatti.* After the *Ñatti,* follows the question put to the Bhikkhus present if they approve the resolution. This question is put either once or three times; in the first case, we have a *Ñattidutiya Kamma*; in the second case, a *Ñatti-catuttha Kamma.* "[218] This last process in which the question is put three times after the *Ñatti* or *Jñāpti* is illustrated by the process prescribed by the Buddha for the upasarhpadā ordination given in the Mahā-vagga. "I prescribe; O Bhikkhus, that you confer the upasaṁpadā ordination by a formal act of the Order in which the announcement (ñatti) is followed by three questions."

'And you ought, O Bhikkhus, to confer the upasaṁpadā ordination in this way. Let a learned, competent Bhikkhu proclaim the following ñatti before the Saṁgha :

'Let the Saṁgha, reverend sirs, hear me. This person N.N., desires to receive the upasaṁpadā ordination from the venerable N.N.,(*i.e.* with the venerable N.N., as his Upajjhāya or Upādhyāya). If the Saṁgha is ready, let the Saṁgha confer on N. N., the upasaṁpadā ordination with N. N., as Upajjhāya. This is the *ñatti.*

'Let the Saṁgha, reverend sirs, hear me. This person N. N., desires to receive the upasaṁpadā ordination from the venerable

N.N., The Sarhgha confers on N.N., the upasaṁpadā ordination with N. N. as Upajjhāya. Let any one of the venerable brethren who is in favour of the upasaṁpadā ordination ot N.N., with N.N., as Upajjhāya, be silent, and any one who is not in favour of it, speak.

'And for the second time I thus speak to you : Let the Saṁgha (etc., as before).

'And for the third time, I thus speak to you : Let the Saṁgha.....etc.

'N.N., has received the upasaṁpadā ordination from the saṁgha with N.N., as Upajjhāya. The Saṁgha is in favour of it, therefore, it is silent. Thus I understand.' "[219]

Disputes settled by votes

As might be expected in such an assembly, there were often violent disputes and quarrels with regard to controversial topics. In such cases, the disputes were settled by the votes of the majority and this voting was by ballot; voting tickets or salākas were served out to the voters and an officer of approved honesty and impartiality was elected to collect these tickets or voting papers. This is evidenced by the Cullavagga which recounts it thus: "Now at that time the Bhikkhus in chapter (Saṁgha) assembled, since they became violent, quarrelsome and disputatious, and kept on wounding one another with sharp words, were unable to settle the disputed question (that was brought before them). They told this matter to the Blessed One."

"I allow you, O Bhikkhus, to settle such a dispute by the vote of the majority. A Bhikkhu who shall be possessed of five qualifications, shall be appointed as taker of voting ticket—one who does not walk in partiality, one who does not walk in malice, one who does not walk in folly, one who does not walk in fear, one who knows what (votes) have been taken and what have not been taken."[220] The appointment of this officer who was called the Salākā-gāhāpaka was also made by the whole assembly.

Absentee's vote counted

There was also a provision for taking votes of the members who could not for any reason be present at a meeting of the assembly. The Mahāvagga mentions an example. On an occasion when the Buddha asked all the Bhikkhus to assemble in the saṁgha, "a certain Bhikkhu said to the Blessed One: 'There is a sick Bhikkhu, Lord, who is not present.' I prescribe, O Bhikkhus, that a sick Bhikkhu is to declare (lit, to give) his consent (to the act to be performed) etc."[221] This declaration of consent of an absent member to an official act was called Chanda.

Quorum

A quorum was required and difficulty was often experienced in getting the right number, so that the Buddha exhorted the Bhikkhus to help to complete the quorum.[222] There are other detailed rules in the Vinaya Piṭaka for the regulation of the assembly. This elaboration and perfection of the procedure as well as the use of so many technical names to designate each particular detail shows that the organisation of these popular assemblies had already been developed and elaborated among the political saṁghas like that of the Licchavis and that the Buddha only adopted them for the regulation of his religious saṃgha or congregation.[223]

Nāyaka—Chief magistrate

The Tibetan works mention a Nāyaka who was the chief magistrate of the Licchavis and "was ruling clans of Licchavis."[224] We do not know exactly what his functions were; perhaps he was an executive officer for carrying out the decisions of the assembly.

Rājās

There does not appear to have been any outstanding figure of the position of Śuddhodana among the Śākyas. The preamble to the Ekapaṇṇa Jātaka[225] relates that, of the *rājās* who lived in Vaiśālī permanently exercising the rights of sovereignty, there were seven thousand, seven hundred and seven and there were quite as many *Uparajās* or subordinate officials, quite as many *Senāpatis* or generals and quite as many *Bhaṇḍāgārikas* or treasurers. A passage in the preamble to the Cullakāliṅga Jātaka[226] also says, "of the Licchavi Rājās, seven thousand, seven hundred and seven Licchavis had their abodes at Vaiśālī. All of them were given to arguments and disputations." The number, seven thousand, seven hundred and seven cannot be the number of all the Licchavis living in the town of Vaiśāli; it would be too small a number for a great people that commanded respect for many centuries for their prowess and power and also it is too small a number for a people that filled almost the whole of such a large city as Vaiśālī; in fact, we are told by the Mahāvastu that the Licchavis who went out of their capital, Vaiśālī, to meet the Buddha on his first visit to their city, numbered so many as twice eighty-four thousand which was not an incredible number for such an extensive city as Vaiśālī. We, however, do not insist upon seven thousand, seven hundred and seven representing the exact number of members of the ruling assembly; it is evidently an artificiall concocted number seven being used from the idea that it has some magic potency; seven thousand, seven hundred and seven means simply a large number. It is significant that none of the canonical texts themselves give this number, which occurs only in a later commentary, the Nidānakathā of the Jātakas.

Uparājā, Senāpati and Bhāṇḍāgārika

Professor Bhāndārkar says that an Uparājā or viceroy, a Senāpati or general and a Bhāṇḍāgārika or treasurer formed the private staff of every Licchavi rājā. If stress is laid upon the fact that all these officers were equal in number with the rājās, it would mean that each of them had a personal staff of these three officers who helped him in dischargeing his duties to the state. Professor Bhāndārkar adds that each rājā had a personal property of his own which was managed by himself with the help of the three officers mentioned above. This seems to be likely because the existence of a Bhāṇḍāgārika attached to each rājā necessarily implies that each rājā had his own separate Bhāṇḍāgāra or treasury. There must have been officers who recorded the decisions of the council. A passage in the Mahā Govinda Suttanta of the Dīgha Nikāya seems to justify this conclusion. In describing a meeting of the thirty-three gods in the Tāvatiṁsa heaven, it is said that after the deliberations were over, four great kings recorded the conclusions arrived at. We read in the Suttanta, " Then the three-and-thirty gods having thus deliberated and taken counsel together concerning the matter for which they were assembled and seated in the Hall of Good Counsel, with respect to that matter the Four Kings were receivers of the spoken word, the Four Great Kings were receivers of the admonition given, remaining the while in their places not retiring."[227] On this passage the translators observe, "This sounds very much as if the Four Great Kings were looked upon as Recorders (in their memory, of course) of what had been said. They kept the minutes of the meeting. If so (the gods being made in the image of men) there must have been such Recorders at the meetings in the Mote-Halls of the clans."[228] This remark is quite justified and without such officers to record the proceedings of such a vast assembly as that of the Licchavis, any practical work would have been impossible.

Coronation Ceremony

A passage in the preamble to the Bhaddasāla Jātaka mentions a tank, the water of which was used at the ceremony of abhiṣeka or coronation of the kulas or families of the gaṇa rājās of Vaiśālī.[229] This coronation may refer to the ceremony performed when a Licchavi rājā was elected to a seat in the assembly of the state, or it may denote that the ceremony of coronation was performed when a young Licchavi kumāra or prince as he was called, succeeded to the title and position of his father.

Administration of Criminal Justice

The Aṭṭhakathā or commentary of Buddhaghoṣa on the Mahāparinibbāṇa Suttanta, gives an account of the judicial procedure. When a person was presented before the Vajjian rājās as having committed an offence, they without taking him to be a malefactor, surrendered him to the *Viniccaya-Mahāmāttas* or *Viniścaya-Mahāmātras,* that is, officers whose business it was to make enquiries and examine the accused with a view to ascertain whether he was guilty or innocent. If they found that the man was not a culprit, they released him but if, on the other hand, they considered him guilty, then instead of proceeding to inflict punishment upon him, they made him over to the *Vohārikas* or *Vyavahārikas,* that is, persons learned in law and custom. They could discharge him if they found him innocent; if they held him guilty, then they transferred him to certain officers called *Suttadharas,* that is, officials who kept up the sūtra or the thread of law and custom existing from the ancient times. They in their turn made further investigation and if satisfied that the accused was innocent, they discharged him. If, however, he was considered guilty by them, then he was made over to the *Aṭṭhakūlakū*[230] (lit. "the eight castes or tribes") which was evidently a judicial institution composed of judges representing eight kūlas or tribes.

The *Aṭṭakūlakā,* if satisfied of the guilt of the offender, made him over to the *Senāpati* or commander of the army who made him over to the *Uparājā* or sub-king, and the latter in his turn, handed him over to the *Rājā.* The *Rājā* released the accused if he was innocent; if he was found guilty, the *Rājā* referred to the *Paveṇipotthaka,* that is, the pustaka or book recording the law and precedents. This book prescribed the punishment for each particular offence. The *Rājā*[231] having measured the culprit's offence by means of that standard, used to inflict a proper sentence.[232]

VI. POLITICAL HISTORY

No mention of the Licchavis to the Vedic and Epic literature

It is from the Buddhist literature that we first realise the importance of the Licchavis as a great and powerful Kṣatriya race in north-eastern India. In the Brāhmaṇa literature, though there is repeated mention of Videha, which, in the Buddha's time, joined with the Licchavis and formed a confederation, there is no mention of the Licchavis. It is likewise remarkable that while the Mallas, their immediate neighbours, are mentioned in the great Epic, the Mahābhārata, the Licchavis are not found among the races or peoples that were met by the Pāṇḍava brothers either in their peregrinations on pilgrimage, or on their mission of conquest at the time of the Rājasūya or the Aśvamedha. In the sixth century B.C. they come to our notice in the Jaina and Buddhist books but we meet them there as a powerful people in the enjoyment of great prosperity and of a high social status among the ruling races of eastern India, and as we have seen in the previous chapter, they had already evolved a system of government and polity bearing not a little resemblance to some of the democracies[233] of the western world, embodying all the latest methods of voting. It must have taken a long time to develop such an institution which can only have grown in the course of many centuries. But we must not imagine that the system was a creation of the Licchavis ; on the other hand, it seems that the saṁgha form of government was the normal form in ancient India even among the peoples that had a king at the head. The earliest Indian tradition of a king is that of a person elected by the people and ruling for the good of the people. This is clearly proved by the story of Beṇa and Pṛthu in the Mahābhārata.[234] The procedure of conducting the deliberations of an assembly must have been developing from the earliest Vedic times as the samiti and the pariṣad were well known institutions in the Ṛgveda. The Licchavis must have modelled their procedure on that which was already in vogue among the Indian Aryans and adapted it to their own use. We may allow a century for the evolution of the particular form of government of the Licchavis from the already existing system. Their emergence from obscurity may fairly be placed at the beginning of the seventh century B.C. It is true that we do not find the Licchavis among the Vedic peoples but in the fourth century B.C. to which Kauṭilya's Arthaśāstra may be supposed to belong, they have been mentioned along with the Kurupāñcālas and the Madras, *i.e.* with some of the powerful races of the Brāhmanic period.

Bimbisāra's marriage with a Licchavi girl

We know nothing of the history of the Licchavis during the period they grew up and developed into the noble and powerful people as we find them in the Buddhist works. The earliest political fact of any importance that we know of, is that they had given one of their daughters in marriage to Seṇiya or Śreṇika Bimbisāra, king of the gradually extending monarchy of Magadha. The Licchavi lady, according to the Nirayāvalī Sūtra, one of the early works of the Jainas, was Cellanā, the daughter of Ceṭaka,[235] one of the rājās of Vaiśālī, whose sister Ksatriyānī Triśalā was the mother of Mahāvīra, the founder of Jainism. In a Tibetan life of the Buddha, her name is Śrībhadrā[236] and in some places, she is named Maddā.[237] This lady, however, is usually called Vaidehī in the Buddhist books, and from her, Ajātaśatru is frequently designated as Vedehiputto[238] or the son of the Videha princess. In the commentary on the Saṁyutta Nikāya, III, 2. sections 4-5, Buddhaghoṣa gives an alternative meaning of the word Vedeha in Vedehiputta by resolving it "into vedaiha, vedena-ihati or intellectual effort." He says that here the other meaning deriving the expression from Videha, the country, is not admissible. Some of the commentaries, those, for example, on Thusa and Taccha-sukara Jātakas,[239] state that Ajātaśatru's mother was a sister of the king of Kośala. Here the commentators have evidently made a confusion between the two queens of Bimbisara. Buddhaghoṣa himself in other passages[240] has taken the more natural sense of the word but sometimes, as here, he has been misled into a fanciful interpretation.

The Divyāvadāna speaks of Ajātaśatru as Vaidehīputra in one of the Avadānas[241] and in another place,[242] it states, "At Rājagṛha, reigns the King Bimbisāra. Vaidehī is his Mahādevī (or chief queen) and Ajātaśatru, his son and prince." There can, therefore, be no doubt that the Videha princess was the mother of Ajātaśatru. The Tibetan Dulva gives the name of Vāsavī to Ajātaśatru's mother and narrates a story which cannot be traced in the Pāli Buddhist books. We give here the story for what it is worth :—"Sakala, a minister of king Virudhaka of Videha, had been obliged to flee from his country on account of the jealousy of the other ministers of the king; so he went to Vaiśālī together with his two sons, Gopāla and Sinha. Sakala soon became a prominent citizen in Vaiśātī, and after a while he was elected Nāyaka. His two sons married at Vaiśālī, and Sinha had a daughter whom they called Vāsavī; it was foretold that she would bear a son who would take his father's life, set the diadem on his own head, and seize the sovereignty for himself. Sinha's wife bore him, moreover, another daughter, whom they called Upavāsavī, and the seers declared that she would bear a son endowed with excellent qualities."

"Gopāla was fierce and of great strength, so he ravaged the parks of the Licchavis. To restrain him, the popular assembly gave him and his brother a park ; and thus it is said by the sthaviras in the sūtras, 'The Blessed One went out from Vesālī to the sāla forest of Gopāla and Sinha.' "

"When Sakala died, the people appointed Sinha, his son Nāyaka; and Gopāla slighted at this, departed from Vaiśālī and took up his residence at Rājagṛha in Magadha where he became the first minister of Bimbisāra."

"A little later on, king Bimbisāra married Vāsavī, Gopāla's niece, and as she was of a family from Videha, she became known as Vaidehī. After a while she bore a son, who on account of the prediction made to his mother, received the name of Ajātaśatru, or the enemy (while) not (yet) born."[243]

Professor D.R. Bhāndārkar holds that "this matrimonial alliance was a result of the peace concluded after the war between Bimbisāra and the Licchavis"[244] and that "Bimbisāra thus appears to have seized Magadha after expelling the Vajjīs beyond the Ganges."[245] The only evidence, however, that he has put forward in support of these theories is that Vaiśālī is spoken of, in an early Buddhist work, the Sutta-Nipāta,[246] as Māgadhaṁ puraṁ.

Birth of Abhaya, son of Bimbisāra by a Licchavi Woman

Dr. D.R. Bhāndārkar's theory is based on Rhys Davids' supposition that the expression, Vesāliṁ Māgadhaṁ puraṁ in verse 1013 of the Sutta-Nipāta (P.T.S.) refers to one and the same city, taking Māgadharii purarh in apposition to Vesālī. But the commentator has taken Māgadhaṁ puraṁ to be a synonym of Rājagaha.[247] Mention of the Pāsāṇa cetiya in the same verse also goes to show that Māgadham puram was not Vaiśālī. In several places we find mention of the caityas or cetiyas round about Vaiśālī but nowhere do we come across a Pāsāṇa cetiya. From verse 1014 of the Sutta-Nipāta, it appears that this cetiya (caitya) was situated on a mountain peak. It is quite possible that the cetiya referred to was one of the cetiyas round about Rājagaha and most probably it was the Gijjhakūṭa monastery. There seems to have been some basis, however, to conclude that there was a war between Bimbiśāra and the Lcchavis. as such a war is referred to incidentally in the Tibetan Dulva. We shall quote the whole passage from Rockhill's Life of the Buddha inasmuch as the story traces the birth of Abhaya, another son of Bimbisāra, also by a Licchavi woman. The Dulva says, "There lived at Vaiśālī, a Licchavi named Mahānāman. From a kadali tree in an āmra grove in his park was born a girl, lovely to look upon, perfect in all parts of her body, and he called her name Āmrapāli. When she was grown up, as there was a law of Vaiśālī by which a perfect woman was not allowed to marry, but was reserved for the pleasures of the people, she became a courtesan. Bimbisāra, king of Magadha, heard of her through Gopāla; he visited her at Vaiśālī, though he was at war with the Licchavis, and remained with her seven days. Āmrapālī became with child by him, and bore him a son whom she sent to his father. The boy approached the king fearlessly and climbed up to his breast which caused the king to remark 'This boy seems not to know fear'; so he was called Abhaya or fearless."[248] This story which makes Abhaya or Abhayakumāra, as the Jaina books have it, a son of Ambapāli (Āmrapāli), the courtezan of Vaiśālī. is not vouchsafed by the Pāli books where her son through Bimbisāra, is called Vimala-Kondañña who became a Bhikkhu and whose preachings are said to have given her a deep spiritual insight.[249]

The Licchavis and King Prasenajit of Kośala

The Licchavis appear to have been on friendly terms with King Prasenajit of Kośala. Who speaks of them as his friends in a passage of the Majjhima Nikāya. Prasenajit proceeded to arrest Aṅgulimāla, the murderer, and on his way met the Buddha who enquired whether he was going to fight with Bimbisāra of Magadha or the Licchavis of Vaiśālī or some other rival kings; thereupon Prasenajit replied that all of them were his friends.[250]

The Relation of the Licchavis with the Mallas

The relation of the Licchavis with their neighbours, the Mallas, also seems to have been, in general, friendly as is evidenced by the Mallas standing by the Licchavis against their common foe, Ajātaśatru. The Jaina books also speak of nine Malla chiefs and nine Licchavi chiefs showing reverence to Mahāvīra at the time of his passing away from the world. There were, however, occasional hostilities, as is shown by the story of Bandhula, a Mallian prince.

In the Bhaddasāla Jātaka,[251] we find that the Licchavis hearing the sound of the chariot of Bandhula, put a strong guard by the side of the tank. Bandhula came down from his chariot and put the guards to flight and in the tank he bathed his wife and gave her water to drink and put her in his chariot and then left the town. The Licchavi chiefs were informed and they were angry. Five hundred Licchavis mounting as many chariots, followed the general. They were asked not to follow but they heeded not and followed on and on till they were half dead. Bandhula said, "I cannot fight with the dead." They after wards died. Bandhula, the Mallian general, at last became victorious.

The Relation of the Licchavis with Ajātaśatru

We next come to the relation of the Licchavis with Ajātaśatru, the son and successor of Bimbisāra. It cannot be expected that the man whose greed for power and position did override even the natural instinct of regard for his father's life, would show any tender feeling towards his mother's relations. On the other hand, he must have felt from the very beginning that the Licchavis formed the greatest bar to the realisation of his idea of Magadhan expansion and we find him taking the dreadful resolve, "I will root out these Vajjians, mighty and powerful though they be, I will destroy these Vajjians, I will bring these Vajjians to utter ruin."[252]

Downfall of the Licchavis

The city of Vaiśālī reached the zenith of prosperity but her prosperity could not be sustained by the Vajjians, who, it seems, attacked Ajātaśatru, king of Magadha, many times. This enraged him very much and in order to baffle their attempts, two of his ministers, Sunīdha and Vassakāra built a fort at Pāṭaligāma[253] and at last Ajātaśatru annihilated the Vajjians. We agree with Prof. Rhys Davids[254] in holding that it was distinctly a political motive which led him to do so. We call it political on the ground that although the existing records of the Buddhists or of the Jainas may lead one to think that the motive was no more than personal grudge, it will be found that in the case of Ajātaśatru, ambitious for domination over the neighbouring powers, the personal motive cannot be distinguished from the political.

Estrangement between Ajātaśatru and the Licchavis—Abhaya. Quarrel over the treasure. Intrigues of Vsssakāra. The sowing of dissensions among the Licchavis

Ajātaśatru was not on friendly terms with the Licchavis. He was under the impression that his foster brother, Abhaya, (son of Bimbisāra by Ambapāh, a courtezan of Vaiśali) had Licchavi blood in him and he liked the Licchavis very much. At this time, the Licchavis were gaining strength day by day, and Ajātaśatru thought that if Abhaya sided with them, it would be very difficult for him to cope with the Licchavis. So he made up his mind to do away with them. In the Sumaṅgalavilāsinī,[255] we find that there was a port near the Ganges extending over a yojana, half of which elonged to Ajātaśatru and half to the Licchavis and their orders were obeyed in their respective yojanas. There was a mountain not far from it, and at the foot of the mountain, there was a mine of precious substance (mahogghabhaṇḍa). Ajātaśatru was late in coming there and the avaricious Licchavis took away all the precious Substance. When Ajātaśatru came and learnt that all the precious substance had been taken away by the Licchavis, he grew angry and left the place. This happened also in the succeeding year. Having sustained a heavy loss he thought that there must be a fight between him and the Licchavis. He realised, however, that the Licchavis being numerically stronger, he would fail to carry out his purpose. So, he conceived the design of destroying the independence of the Licchavis by sowing seeds of dissension. Formerly, the Licchavis were not luxurious but very strenuous and exerting, so Ajātaśatru could not get an opportunity of subduing them. He sent Vassakāra, one of his ministers, to the Buddha, who predicted that in future the Licchavis would be delicate, having soft hands and feet, would use very luxurious and soft beds with soft pillows made of cotton, would sleep till sunrise[256] and further declared: "By no other means will the Vajjians be overcome but by propitiating them with tributes or dissolving the subsisting union." Vassakāra returned from the Buddha and stated to the king what the latter said about the Licchavis. The rājā did not agree to propitiate the Vajjians with tributes as that would diminish the number of elephants and horses. So, he decided to break up their union and Vassakāra advised him to convene a meeting of the councillors to bring up some discussions regarding the Vajjians when in the midst of the sitting, he (Vassakāra) would quit the council after offering a remonstrance saying, "Mahārāja, what do you want with them ? Let them occupy themselves with the agricultural and commercial affairs of their own (realm)." Then he said to Ajātaśatru, "Mahārāja, completely cut off all my hair, bringing a charge against me for interdicting your discussion without either binding or flogging me. As I am the person by whom ramparts and ditches of your capital were formed and as I know the strong and the weak, high and low parts (of your fortification), I will tell the Vajjians that I am able to remove any obstacle you can raise." The rājā acted up to the advice of his minister, Vassakāra. The Vajjians heard of the departure of Vassakāra and some of them decided not to allow him to cross the river while others observed, "He (Ajātaśatru) has so treated him because he advocated our cause"; that being the case, they said (to the guards who went to stop him) "fellows, let him come." Accordingly, the guards permitted him to come in. Now Vassakāra being questioned by the Vajjians, told them why he was so severely punished for so slight an offence, and that he was there a Judicial Prime Minister. Then the Vajjians offered him the same post which he accepted and very soon he acquired reputation for his able administration of justice and the youths of the (Vajji) rulers went to him to have their training at his hands. Vassakāra, on a certain day taking aside one of the chavi rulers (mysteriously) asked, "Do people plough a field?" "Yes, they do; by coupling a pair of bullocks together." On another occasion, taking another Licchavi aside he significantly asked, "With what curry did you eat (your rice) ?" and said no more. But hearing the answer, he communicated it to another person. Then upon a subsequent occasion, taking another Licchavi aside, he asked him in a whisper, "Art thou a mere beggar ? " He enquired, "Who said so ? " and the Brahmin, Vassakāra, replied: "That Licchavi." Again upon another occasion, taking another aside, he enquired, "Art thou a cowherd ? " and on being asked who said so, he mentioned the name of some other Licchavi. Thus by speaking something to one person which had not been said by any other person, he succeeded in bringing about a disunion among the rulers in course of three years, so completely that none of them would tread the same road together. When matters stood thus, he caused the tocsin to be sounded as usual. Some of the Licchavi rulers disregarded their call saying "Let the rich and the valiant assemble. We are beggars and cowherds." The Brahmin sent a mission to the rājā saying, "this is the proper time, let him come quickly." The rājā on hearing this announcement, assembled his forces by beat of drum and started. The Vajjians on receiving intimation there of, sounded the tocsin declaring, "Let us not allow the Rājā to cross the river." On hearing this also, they refused to meet together saying, "Let the valiant rulers go." Again the tocsin was sounded and it was thus declared : "Let us defend ourselves with closed gates." No one responded to the call. Ajātaśatru entered by the wide open gates, and came back after putting them to great calamities.[257] Thus, the Magadhan kingdom was very much extended during the reign of Ajātaśatru.

The Licchavis and Candragupta Maurya—The Licchavis and Aśoka

Of the subsequent history of the Licchavis we know very little. But this much is certain that they were not exterminated by Ajātaśatru. What Ajātaśatru seems to nave succeeded in doing, was that the Licchavis had to accept his suzerainty and pay him revenue, but they must have been independent in the matter of internal management and maintained in tact the ancient democratic institution of personal liberty. Kauṭilya speaks of them two centuries after Ajātaśatru as living under a saṁgha form of government, and the same learned author advises king Candragupta Maurya seek the help of these saṁghas which on account of their unity and concon were almost unconquerable. This shows that the Licchavis though they might have been forced to acknowledge suzerainty of Magadha, enjoyed a great deal of independen under Candragupta. There can be no doubt that under his grandson Aśoka, the Licchavis accepted his suzerainty. The Licchavis in Manu's Code.

We next meet the Licchivis (Licchavis) in Manu's Code,[258] the recension of which, was made according to Dr. Bühler,[259] sometime during the period 200 B.C.— 200 A.D.; in our opinion the date is likely to fall within the period of a Brāhmanic revival under Puṣyamitra Sunga, so that about a century after the time of Aśoka, we find the Licchavis still living in Northern India as a Kṣatriya people. We do not hear of them again until the fourth century A.D. when their name appears on the records of the Imperial Guptas.

The Licchavis and the Imperial Guptas

At the beginning of the fourth century A.D., Candragupta I a son-in-law of the Licchavi family and son of Ghaṭotkaca Gupta, established a new kingdom.[260] A gold coin was introduced under the name of Candragupta I. by his great son, Emperor Samudragupta who, by his many conquests, established his suzerain right over a great part India. On the obverse were incised the figures of Candragupta and his Queen Kumāradevī and the former with his right hand offers an object which on some coins is clearly a ring to Kumāradevī who stands wearing a loose robe, ear-rings, necklace and armlets, and tight-fitting headdress; the words "Candragupta" and "Kumāradevī," "Śrī Kumāradevī" or "Kumāradevī Śrīḥ," are inscribed in the Brāhmī character of the fourth century A.D., and on the reverse were engraved the figure of Lakṣmī, the goddess of Fortune, seated on a lion couchant with the legend "Licchavayah,' the Licchavis.[261] With this is to be combined the significant fact that the great Samudragupta in his Allahabad inscription takes pride in describing himself as "Licchavidauhitra,' 'the son of a daughter of the Licchavis.' These things combined together, justify the conclusion that about the fourth century A.D., when the Guptas rose to power, the Licchavis must have possessed considerable political power in north-eastern India. It is quite probable that Candragupta's dominions received considerable expansion by the country which he obtained through his Licchavi wife, perhaps by succession ; and very, likely it was the accession of the Licchavi districts to his kingdom that enabled him to adopt the title of Mahārājādhirāja. His son and successor wants apparently to emphasise this fact by issuing a gold coin delineating the Licchavi connection, and it is very likely that the goddess Lakṣmī mounted on a lion couchant is the Licchavi symbol adopted by the Guptas, otherwise, the legend "Licchavayaḥ" by its side becomes unmeaning. We cannot agree with Dr. Allan when he avers, "Too much emphasis should not be laid on the pride of the Guptas in their Licchavi blood, but it was probably due rather to the ancient lineage of the Licchavis than to any material advantages gained by this alliance." (p. xix.) The probabilities are, however, quite the reverse for reasons which we have already expatiated upon. It is significant that the epithet "Licchavidauhitra" is not only asserted by Samudragupta about himself, but it continues to be a permanent appellation of this sovereign in the inscriptions of his successors. Mr. Allan presumes that it was to keep up the memory of his father, Candragupta, and mother, Kumāradevī, that the coin bearing their names and that of the Licchavis was issued by Samudragupta. It is not improbable that the inscription 'Licchavayah' which occurs in Candragupta's gold coins together with the name of his queen Kumāradevī may signify that she belonged to a royal family of the Licchavis previously reigning at Pāṭaliputra[262] (modern Patna) which seems to have been the original capital of the Gupta Empire. A similar opinion is also held by Dr. V.A. Smith who says that Candragupta, a local rājā at or near Pāṭaliputra, married Kumāradevī, a princess belonging to the Licchavi clan, famous in the early annals of Buddhism in or about the year 308.[263] In ancient times, the Licchavis of Vaiśālī had been the rivals of the kings of Pāṭaliputra. Chandragupta's position was elevated through his Licchavi connections from the rank of a local chief.[264] His son and successor often felt pride in describing himself as the son of the daughter of the Licchavis.[265] Before his death, his son by the Licchavi princess, Samudra Gupta, was selected by him as his successor.[266]

The Nepal inscriptions point out that there were two distinct houses, one of which, known as the Thākuri family, is mentioned in the Vaṁśāvalī but is not recorded in the inscriptions; and the other was the Licchavi or the Sūryavaṁś family which issued its charters from the house or palace called Mānagriha and uniformly used an era with the Gupta epoch.[267] Thus we find that the Licchavis were not inferior to the Imperial Guptas so far as rank and power were concerned.[268] Their friendly relations with the Guptas were established by the marriage of Candra Gupta I with Kumāradevī, a daughter of the Licchavis.

REFERENCES

1. *Divyāvadāna* edited by E.B., Cowell and R.A., Neil, pp. 55-56, 136.
2. *Mahāvastu* edited by E., Senart, Vol. I, p. 254, etc.
3. T., Walters—*On Yuan Chwang,* Vol. II, p. 77.
4. Dr. M. Winternitz, *Geschichte der Indischen Litteratur* II Band, p. 295.
5. *Kalpasūtra, section* 128. *Sīrkalpasūtram,* Bhavnagar edition, p. 192; See also Jaina *Sūtras by* H. Jacobi, S.B.B., vol. xxii, p. 266 f. n. I., Vol. xiv, part, II, p. 321, f.n. 3.
6. *Jaina Sūtras,* by H., Jacobi, S.B.E., Vol, xxii, part I, p. 266, f. n. 1.
7. Kauṭilya's Arthaśāstra translated by R. Shamśastry. B.A., p. 455. The Sanskrit text has:—"Licchivika-Vṛjika-Mallaka-Madraka-Kukura-Kura-Pāñcālādayo Rājaśabdopajivinaḥ." The 'Ka' at the end of the words does not change the meaning at all. It will be seen that Kauṭilya distinguishes the Licchivikas from the Vṛjikas.' Regarding this H. Panday ("Notes on the Vajji country and the Mallas of Pāvā." J.B. and O.R.S., Vol. VI, pt. II, June 1920, p. 259 foll.) says that it appears from the Pāli Suttas that the names Vajji and Licchavi are interchangeable to some extent. In Kauṭilya's Arthaśāstra (2nd. Ed., p. 378), we find that both the Licchavis and Vṛjis (Vajjis) are mentioned together in the list of republics. It at once starts an enquiry whether the Licchavis and Vṛjis (Vajjis) were two separate republics. The Pāli literature will answer it in the negative but the accounts of the Chinese pilgrims lead to a different conclusion. Pa Hien calls the country of which Vaiśālī was the capital, "the Kingdom of Vaiśālī" and the people of the country, "Licchavis." Fa Hien does not mention Vṛiji. Hiuen Tsang describe Vaisālī and Vṛji as two distinct countries and Watters is inclined to

disbelive the accuracy of Hiuen Tsang's description of the Vṛji country. Dr. Rai Chaudhury reconciles the evidence of the Pāli literature with that of Kauṭilya and Hiuen Tsang, saying that "Vajji was not only the name of the confederacy but also of one of the constituent clans. But the Vajjis like the Licchavis are sometimes associated with the city of Veśālī which was not only the capital of the Licchavi clan, but also the metropolis of the entire confederacy." (Political History of India, p.60.)

8. For the various readings see *Mānava Dharmaśāstra* edited by J. Jolly, Ph.D., p. 325. 'See also *The Laws of Manu* by G. Bühler, S.B.E., Vol. XXV., p. 406. notes.
9. R.D., Banerji, The Origin of the Bengali Script, Cal. Univ. 1919, p. 82.
10. Ibid., p. 108.
11. Ibid., p. 109,
12. Mahāmahopādhyāya Dr. Satish Ch. Vidyābhūṣaṇa, Indian Antiquary, Vol. XXXVII, pp. 78-80
13. Jolly *Mānavadharmaśāstra*, p. 325
14. Inscriptions at the Early Gupta Kings, edited by J.F. Fleet—*Corpus triscriptionum Indicarum,* Vol. III, P. S.
15. J.F. Fleet, op. cit. p. 27.
16. Ibid., p. 43.
17. Ibid., p. 50.
18. Ibid., p. 53.
19. J.F. Fleet, *Inscriptions of the Early Gupta Kings, Corpus Inscriptionum Indicarum,* Vol.III, p. 256.
20. J.F. Fleet, *Inscriptions of the Early Gupta Kings,* pp. 177 f.n., *Indian Antiquary,* Vol. IX, pp. 168 ff.
21. Legge, Fā-Hien, pp. 71, 76.
22. *Buddhist Records of the Western World,* by S. Beal, Vol., II, p. 73.
23. *Tārānātha's Geschichte des Buddhismus Indien*—translated into German by Anton Schiefner, pp. 9. 41, 146.
24. *Mahāparinibbāṇa Suttanta*—Translated by T.W. & C.A.P. Rhys Davids in *Dialogues of tht Buadha,* Vol. Ill, p. 187.

    Note. The original Pāli text here is also interesting and we quote it in full. ("Bhagavā pi khattiyo, mayaṁ pi khattiyā. Māyāṁ pi arahāma Bhagavato sarīrānaṁ bhāgaṁ, mayam pi Bhagavato sarīrānaṁ thūpañca mahañ ca karissāmāti." Dīgha Nikāya, P.T.S., Vol. II, pp. 164-165.)
25. *Mahāparinibbāṇa Suttanta in.* the Dīgha Nikāya, P.T.S. Vol. II., pp. 104 (foll ."Bhagavā amhakamñāṭī-seṭṭho."
26. *Sumaṅgala—Vilāsinī,* Pt. I. P.T.S., p. 312.

    "Ahaṁ Khattiyo, ayaṁ pi Khattiyo va, sac' assa naṇena vaḍḍhissati ayaṁ pe sabbaññū bhavissatīti, usuyāya mayhaṁ na katheti."

27. Licchavi kumārikā khattiyadhītā jātisampannā'—Jātaka edited by V. Fausboll, Vol. II, p. 5.
28. Prof. H., Oldenberg, *On the History of the Indian Caste System* translated into English from the Z.D.M.G., Vol. LI, by Prof. H.C., Chāklādār, Ind. Ant. Vol. XLIX., Decem. 1920, p. 227.
29. *Kalpa Sūtra See.* 128 translated by Prof. H. Jacobi, S.B.E., Vol. XXII, p. 266.
30. Jacobi, op. cit., note 1, p. 266.
31. Jacobi, op. cit., See. 108-110. pp, 255-56.
32. Ibid., pp. x-xii.
33. Jacobi, *Jaina Sūtras,* part II, S.B.E., Vol. XLV, p. 321.
34. "Licchavikā āhansu. Anyadapi Bhagavan. Bhagavānāha, anyadāpi Vāsiṭṭhā. Bhūtapurvaṁ Vāsiṭṭhā atītamadhvāne Pāñcāle janapade Kaṁpillanagare Rājā Brahmadatto nāma rājyam kāresi."

    La Mahāvastu, edited by E. Senart, Vol. I, p. 283. The Licchavis are addressed as Vāśiṣṭhas many times in this account, Vol. I, pp. 286, 289, 290, 300 etc.
35. Rockhill, *Life of the Buddha,* pp. 97 ff.
36. Jacobi, *Jaina Sūtras*, S.B.E., Vol. XXII, p. 193.
37. *Indian Antiquary,* Vol. XXXVII, p. 79.
39. Aitareya Brāhmaṇa, Ch. 34, Kāṇḍa 7, verse 25.
39. Sir R. G. Bhāndārkar, *Vaiṣṇavism, Śaivism, and minor Religious Systems,* p. 12.
40. Jacobi, *Jaina Sūtras,* Part II, p. 121, note 3.
41. *Rāmāyaṇa,* Bombay edition, Bālakāṇḍa, Ch., 47, verses 11-12.

    "Ikṣvākostu naravyāghra putraḥ paramadhārmika. Alamvuṣāyām utpauuo viśāla itivisutaḥ" (11) "teuacāsidiha sthāne Viśāleti purīkritā" (12).
42. *Buddhist Suttas,* S.B.E., Vol. XI., pp. 121-122.
43. *Dialogues of the Buddha,* Part III, p. 202.
44. *Karma-saṭaka,* 20. II. 7, Translated from Tibetan by M. L. Feer, Reprint, p. 40.
45. Senart, *Mahāvastu Avadāna,* Vol. II, p. 76.
46. Rockhill, *The Life of the Buddha* (popular edition), p. 203, note.
47. *Paramatthajotikā on the Khuddakapāṭha* edited by H. Smith, P.T.S., pp. 158-160.
48. Spence Hardy, *Manual of Buddhism,* 2nd edition, 1880, pp. 242-243.
49. T. Watters, *On Yuan Chwang,* Vol. II, p. 77.
50. Bühler, *Laws of Manu,* p. 406.
51. Ibid., pp. 405-406.
52. Ibid., pp. 405-406, note 20.

53. Bühler, *Laws of Manu*, pp. 36-37.
54. Gautama, XXI, 11, Āpa. 1, I etc. Vaś. XI, 74-79, Baudh. I. 16, 16.
55. See *Manusaṁhitā*, II. 21.
56. Bühler, *Manu*, Introduction, p. CXVII.
57. See Monier Williams, Sanskrit English Dictionary, 1899, p. 902.
    The Vaijayantī, edited by Gustav Oppert, p. 76. "Licchivim kṣatriyā Vrātyāt."
58. J. Fl:et, *Gupta Inscriptions—Corpus Ins. Ind.*, Vol. III, Introduction, p. 135.
59. *Corpus Ins. Ind.*, Vol. III, p. 136.
60. Ibid., p. 135.
61. S. Beal, Ramantic Legend Śākya Buddha pp.159-160.
62. *Indian Antiquary*, Vol. XXXII, 1903, p. 234.
63. "Ye nikhātā ye paroptā ye dagdhā ye coddhitāḥ sarvāṁstāngna a vaha pitṛn havișe attave." *Atharvaveda Saṁhitā* edited by R. Roth and W. D. Whitney, p. 339.
64. *Atharva Saṁhitā* translated by W.D. Whitney and revised and edited by C. R. Lanman, Harvard. Or. Series, Vol. VIII, p. 840.
65. Ibid., p. 841.
66. Ibid., p. 402.
67. Macdonell and Keith, *Vedic Index*, Vol. I, p. 8.
68. *Indian Antiquary*, Vol. XXXVII, 1908, p. 79.
69. *The Life of Hiuen-Tsiang* by Beal, Intro., p. xxii
70. Rhys Davids, *Buddhist India*, p. 40.
71. Sūtrakṛtāṅga, 1. 2. 3. 22.
72. Jacobi, *Jaina Sūtras*, S. B. E., pt. II. p. 261.
73. Ibid., pt. II, Lecture VI, 17, p. 27.
74. Ibid., pt. I, Introduction, XI.
75. Weber, Indische studien, Band XVI, p. 263.
    Auch Abhayadeva zu Bhag. 2, 1. 12, 2. erklärt Vaicalika dutch Mahāvīra, und zwai als Metronymicum (!) ; Viśālā Mahāvīrajananī."
76. Jacobi, Jaina Sūtras, S.B.E., Vol. XXII, pp. X-XI.
77. Ibid., p. XII.
78. Jacobi, *Jaina Sūtras*, Vol. I, p. 256, *Kalpa Sūtra*, See. 110.
    "Samaṇebhagavaiṁ Mahāvīre dakkhe dakkhapaīnne padiruve allīne bhaddae viṇie nāe nāyaputtenāyakulacande videhe videhadinne videhajacu, videhasamāle tīsaṁvāsāiṁ. Videhaṁsikaṭṭu ammāpi īhiṁ devattagaehiṁ gurumahattaraehiṁ abbhanunnāte samattapainne punaraviloyanti ehiṁ Jīyakappiehiṁ........evaṁ vayāsī." (*Kalpa Sūtra*, Dhanpat Singha's edition, pp. 64-65.)
79. Jacobi, *Jaina Sūtras*, Vol. I, *Kalpa Sūtra*. See 111.

80. Jacobi, *Jaina Sūtras,* Kalpa Sūtra, See. 122.
81. Nāgāpalokitaṁ Vesāliyam apaloketvā (Dialogues of the Buddha, pt., II, pp 131. f.).
82. Dialogues of the Buddha, pt. II, p. 131.
83. Kern, Manual of Indian Buddhism, pp. 103-109.
84. Rāmāuaṇa Bālakāṇḍa, Chap. 47, Verses 11. and 12.
85. The Viṣṇupurāṇa by H. H. Wilson, Vol. III, p. 246.
86. Rāmāyaṇa (Bombay Edition), chap. 45, verse 9. "Uttaramtīrarhāsādya sampūjyarsigaṇaṁ tataḥ Gaṅgākūle nivisṭāste Viśilāta dadrisuh puriṁ."
87. Rāmāyaṇa (Bombay Edition), chap. 45, verses 10 and 11.—" Viśālāṁ nagariṁ ramyāṁ divyāṁ svargopamām tadā " (10).
88. Rāmāyaṇa (Bombay Edition), chap. 47, verse 18.
89. Watters, on Yuan Chwasg, vol. II, p. 63.
90. Jātaka (Fausboll) Vol. I, p. 504.
"Vesālinagararṁ gāvutigavutantare tīhi pākārehi parikkhittaṁ tīsu ṭhānesu gopuraṭṭālokayuttaṁ."
91. Ibid., vol. I, p. 389.
92. Rockhill, Life of the Buddha, p. 62.
93. Hoernle, Uvāsagadasāo, vol. II, Translation, p. 4. Note. 8.
94. Hoernle, Uvāsagadasāo, vol. II, p. 5.
95. Hoernle, Uvāsagadasāo, vol. II, Translation, p. 6.
96. Ibid., p. 52.
"Icchāmi naṁ, bhante, tubbhehiṁ abbhaṇunāe chaṭṭakkhamaṇassa pāraṇagaṁsi vāniyagāme nayare uccanīya majjhmāiṁ kulāiṁ gharasamuddābhikkh ā ariyāe adittae" (upāsakadasāo-sūtram, vol. I, p. 36, para 77, Hoernle's edition).
97. Le Mahāvastu, Ed., by E. Senart, vol. I, pp. 253. ff.
98. Ibid., Vol. I, pp. 295-299.
99. Ibid., Vol. I, p. 300.
100. Vinaya Texts, S.B.E., pt. III. p. 408.
101. Vinaya Texts. pt. II, S.B.E., pp. 210-211.
102. Ibid., pt. III, S.B.E., p. 101.
103. Vinaya Texts, pt. Ill, p. 322.
104. Vinaya Texts, pt. II, S.B.B., p. 171.
105. Lalitavistara, E.d. by Lefmann. Chap. III, p. 21. "Iyaṁ Vaiśālī mahānagarī ṛddhāca sphītāca khemāca subhikkhāca ramanīyā cākīrnabahujanamanussā ca vitardi-niryuhatoraṇagavākṣa-harmyakūṭāgāraprāsādatalasamalackritā ca puṣ-pavāṭikā-vanarājisaiukusumitā ca. Amarabhavanapuraprākāśyā sāpratirūpāsya Bodhisattvassa garbhapratisaṁsthānayeti."
106. Fausboll, Dhammapada, old Ed., p. 391.

107. Legge, Fā-Hien, p. 72.
108. Sumaṅgalavilāsinī, pt. I, (P.T.S.) p. 309.
109. Legge, Fā-Hien, p. 72. Note. I.
110. Sum. V. pt. I, P.T.S., p. 309. "Tasmin vanasaṇde saṅghārāmaṁ patiṭṭhāpesuṁ. Tattha kaṇṇikaṁ yojetvā thaṁbhānaṁ upari Kūṭāgārasālā-saṁkhepena deva-vimāna sadisaṁ pāsādaṁ akaṁsu. Taṁ upādāya sakalo pi saṁghārāmo Kūṭāgātasālā ti paññāyittha."
111. Watters, On Yuan Chwang, Vol. II, p. 71.
112. Ibid., Vol. II, p. 71.
113. Legge. Fā-Hien, pp. 75-77.
114. Rockhill, Life of the Buddha, p. 63.
115. S. Beal, The Ramantic Legend of Śākye Buddha, *p.* 28.
116 Ed. by Dr. S. Lefmann, Text, p. 21.
117. Arch. S., Report, Vol. I, pp. 55, 56 and Vol. XVI, p. 6.
118. Rhys Davids, Buddhist India, p. 41.
119. J.A.S.B., 1900, Vol. LX1X., pt. i, pp. 78, 79, 80, 83.
120. V.A. Smith, J.R.A S.1902. p. 267, n. 3.
121. Sir John H. Marshall , Arch. Surv. of India, Annual Report, 1903-04, p.74.
122. Ibid.,
123. Ibid., p. 110.
124. Ibid.,
125. Cunningham, Ancient Geography of India, p. 447.
126. Buddhist Suttas, S.B.E., Vol. XI, p. 3; vide also Turnour, Pāli Buddhistic. Annals, No. 5,J.A.S.B., Dec. 1838, p.992.
127. Sumaṅgala, vilāsinī (Burmese edition), pp. 103-105.
128. Watters, On Yuan Chwang, Vol. II, p. 79.
129. Nīla (Dīgha Nikāya, Vol. II, p. 96) has been translated as 'dark' by Rhys Davids; though for the complexion this may be a fair rendering, it is not so for the attire and the equipage.
130. Buddhist Suttas, S.B.E., Vol. XI, p. 31. "Atha kho te Licchavi bhaddāni bhaddāni yānāni yojāpetvā bhaddaṁ yānaṁ bhirūhitvā bhaddehi bhaddehi yānehi Vesāliyā niyyiṁsu. Tatrekacce Licchavī nīlā honti, nīlavaṇṇā, nīlavatthā, nīla laṅkārā, ekacce Licchavi pītā honti... ekacce Licchavi lohitakā... ekacce Licchavi odātā honti. (Mahāparinibbāṇa suttanta.)
131. Aṅguttara Nikāya, P.T.S., pt. Ill, p 239.
132. Mahāvastu, Vol. I. p. 259, for the text. The author is responsible for the English translation.
133. We have here followed the interpretation, suggested by Senart, of Vyāyukta (*vide* Mahāvastu, note, p. 574); this meaning, however, is very doubtful.
134. Saṁyutta Nikāya, (P.T.S.) pt. II, pp. 567-268.
135. Divyāvadāna (Cowell and Neil), p. 136.
136. Psalms of the Brethren, By Mrs. Rhys Davids, p. 106.

137. Aṅguttara Nikāya, P.T.S., pt. III, p. 76.
138 T.Watters, On Yuan Chwang, Vol. II, p. 79.
139. Lalitavistara, ed. by S. Lefmann, Vol. I, p. 21. "Apara āhuḥ sāpyaprati' rūpā... tena sāpyapratirūpā."
140. Vinaya Texts, S.B.E., pt. III, pp. 118-125.
141. Dialogues of the Buddha, part II, p. 80.
142. Fausboll, Dhammapada, (old Ed.) p. 211.
143. Psalms of the Brethren, By Mrs. Rhys Davids, p. 106.
144. Lalitavistara, Chap. 3, p. 23. (Bibliotheca Indica Series.)
145. Cullavagga, VI, translated by Drs. Rhys Davids and Oldenberg, S.B.E., Vol. XX, pp. 189-190.
146. Cullavagga VI, translated by Drs., Rhys Davids and Oldenberg, S.B.E., Vol. XX, p. 190.
147. Buddhist Suttas, S.B.E., Vol. XI, p. 58.
148. Rockhill, Life of the Buddha, p. 62.
149. Bhikkhunī Vibhaṅga Saṅghādidesa II Vinaya Piṭākam Ed. by H. Oldenberg, Vol. IV, p. 225.
150. Buddhist Suttas, S.B.E., Vol. XI, pp. 3-4.
151. Petavatthu-Aṭṭhakathā, Sinhalese edition, Simon Hewavitaraṇa's Beques Series, No. 1, pp. 154-156; See my "The Buddhist conception of spirits," pp. 49-51
152. Vinaya Piṭaka by H. Oldenberg, Vol. IV, pp. 225-226.
153. Bhikkhunī-Vibhaṅga Saṅghādidesa, Vol. II, p. 225.
154. Beal's *Romantic Legend of Śākya Buddha*, pp. 159-160.
155. Indian Antiquary, Vol. XXXII, p. 234.
156. Saṁyutta Nikāya, Vol. I, pp. 201. 202.
157. Psalms of the Brethren, p. 63.
158. Psalms of the Brethren, p. 348.
159. The word in the text is 'Cetiyāni. T.W. Rhys Davids' translation seems to be too exclusive for, as Kern points out, the name Cetiya was applied not only to shrines but also to sacred trees, memorial stones, holy spots, images, religious inscriptions (Manual of Indian Buddhism, p. 91).
160. T.W., and C.A.F., Rhys Davids-Dialogues of the Buddha, Pt. II, p. 80.
161. Sumaṅgala-vilāsinī (Burmese edition), pp. 103-105.
162. Kern, Manual of Indian Buddhism, p. 50.
163. Dialogues of the Buddha, part III, p. 14. "Puratthimena Vesāliyaṁ Udenaṁ nāma cetiyaṁ taṁ nātikkameyyaṁ: dakkhiṇena Vesāliyam Gotamakaṁ nāma ceiāyaṁ taṁ nātikkameyyaṁ: pacchimena Vesālīyaṁ sattaṁbaṁ nāma cetiyaṁ tath nātikkameyyaṁ: uttarena Vesālīyaṁ Bahuputtaṁ nāma cetiyaṁ taṁ nātik kameyyanti." (Pāṭika Suttanta.)
164. Divyāvadāna, p. 201.
165. Dialogues of the Buddha, part II, p. 80, notes 2 and 3.

166. For Brahmā see S.N., 122. seq; Samy VI. i, 1-3, 10, etc. M.P.S., VI. 15, etc., etc.
167. Arthaśāstra of Kauṭilya, ed. by R. Shāma Śāstrī, and edition, p. 244.
168. Prof, and Mrs. Rhys Davids, Dialogues of the Buddha, pt. II, p. 110, footnote 2. See also Mr. R.P. Chanda's Medieval Sculpture in Eastern India, Cal. Unit, I, Journal (Arts), Vol. III.
169. Jaina Sūtras, pt. i, Ākārāṅga Sūtra translated by H. Jacobi, S.B.B., Vol. xxii, p. 194.
170. Vinaya Texts translated by T.W. Rhys Davids and H. Oldenberg, S.B.E., Vol. XVII, pp. 108f.
171. Vinaya Texts, S.B.E., Vol. xvii, p. 116.
172. The story of Saccaka is given in detail in this chapter, a few pages below.
173. Aṅguttara Nikāya, P.T.S., Vol. II, pp. 190-194.
174. Aṅguttara Nikāya, P.T.S., Vol. II, pp. 200-202.
175. Saṁyutta Nikāya, P.T.S., Vol. V, pp. 389-390.
176. Aṅguttara Nikāya, P.T.S., Vol. III, pp. 75-78.
177. Aṅguttara Nikāya, Vol. III, pp. 167-168.
178. P.T.S., Vol. V, p. 133.
179. P.T.S., Vol. III, p. 239.
180. Psalms of the Brethren, p. 56.
181. Psalms of the Brethren, p. 106.
182. Psalms of the Sisters by Mrs. Rhys Davids, pp. 53-54.
183. Psalms of the Sisters, pp. 23-24.
184. Psalms of the Sisters, pp. 79-80.
185. Ibid., pp. 120-121.
186. Ibid., p. 125
187. Aṅguttara Nikāya, pt. I, pp. 220-222.
188. Ibid., pt. II, pp. 190-194.
189. Ibid., pt. II, pp. 200-202.
190. Cūḷasaccaka Suttaṁ, Majjhima Nikāya, Vol. I, pp. 227-237.
191. Saṁyutta Nikāya pt. III, pp. 68-70.
192. Aṅguttara Nikāya Vol. V. pp. 86-87.
193. Aṅguttara Nikāya, Vol. I, (P.T.S.), pp. 220-221.
194. Saṁyutta Nikāya, Vol. IV, (P.T.S.) pp. 261-262.
195. Ibid., Vol. V, pp. 163-165.
196. Ekapaṇṇa Jātaka (Cowell's edition), Vol. I, p. 16.
197. Mahāparinibbāna Suttanta, Buddhist Suttas (S.B.E.), Vol XI, p. 134.
198. S. Beal Romantic Legend of Śākya Buddha, 167-168.
199. *Note*—Priests can keep salt only for seven days. But if kept in horn, they would be able to retain it for any length of time—J.A.S.B., Vol. VI, pt. II, p. 728 (1837).

200. Kern's Manual of Buddhism, p. 103.
201. Examination of the Pāli Buddhistical Annals, Vol. VI, pt. II, p. 729, J.A.S.B., 1837. (September).
202. P.T.S., Vol. I, p. 231.
203. Vol. I, p. 254.
204. Arthaśāstra translated by R. Shāmaśāstry, p. 455.
205. Dr. Shāmaśastrī's rendering "lived by the title of arājā" is rather too literal to convey the real meaning.
206. 'Ekaika eva manyate ahaṁ rājā, ahaṁ rājeti.' Ed. by Lefmann, Vol. I, p. 21; Lalita Vistara (Bibliotheca Indica series), Chap. III. 23.
207. Vol. i. p. 271.
208. Faüsboll, Jātaka, Vol. III, p. 1.
209. Ibid., Vol. I, p. 504.
210. Saṁghābhisaṁhatatvāt dhṛṣyān pareṣām—Arthaśāstra (2nd. Ed.), p. 378.
211. Saṁgha lābho daṇḍa mitralābhānāmuttamaḥ—Ibid., p. 378.
212. Buddhist Suttas, S.B.E., Vol. XI, p. 3.
213. Buddhist Suttas, S.B.E., Vol. XI, pp. 3-4.
214. Carmichael Lectures, 1918, p. 181.
215. Buddhist Suttas, pp. 5-11. (S.B.E., Vol. XI.)
216. Vinaya Texts, S.B.E., Vol. XX p. 408, f. n.
217. Buddhist Suttas, S.B.E., Vol. XI, p. 3.
218. Rhys Davids and Oldenberg—Vinaya Texts, pt. I, p. 169, Note 2.
219. Rhys Davids and Oldenberg—Vinaya Texts, pt. I, pp. 169-170. See also Dr. R.C. Majumdar, Corporate life in Ancient India, pp. 202-295.
220. Cullavagga, S.B.E., Vol. XX, Vinaya texts, pt. III, p. 25.
221. Mahāvagga, S.B.E., Vol. XIII, p. 277.
222. Ibid., pp. 307-309.
223. For the democratic organisation of the Licchavis, see Prof. D. R. Bhandarkar's Carmichael Lectures, 1918, pp. 179-184.
224. Rockhill, Life of the Buddha, p. 62.
225. Fausboll, Jātaka, Vol. I, p. 504—"Niccakālam rajjaṁ kāretvā vasantānaṁ yeva rājūnaṁ sattasahassāni satta ca rājāno honti, tattakā yeva uparājāno, tattākā senāpatino, tattakā bhāṇḍāgārikā."
226. Ibid., Vol. III, p. 1. "Licchavirājūnaṁ sattasahassāni sattasatāni satta ca Licchavi vasiṁsu. Te sabbe pi paṭipucchāvitakkā ahesuṁ."
227. Dialogues of the Buddha, pt. II, p. 263.
228. Ibid., p. 263, f.n. 1.
229. "Vesālinagare gaṇarājakulānaṁ abhisekamaṅgalapokkharaṇiṁ, etc. "—Faüsboll, Jātaka, Vol. IV, p. 148.

See also Prof. D. R. Bhandarkar's Carmichael Lectures, 1918, pp. 150-151.

230. Hon'ble G. Turnour says that no satisfactory explanation can be obtained as to the nature of tlie office held by these functionaries. It is inferred to be a judicial institution composed of judges from all the eight castes. (An examination of the Pāli Buddhistical Annals by G. Tumour, p. 993, f. n., J.A.S.B., Dec. 1838.)

231. It seems that 'Rājā' who was the highest authority in the administration of criminal justice was different from ordinary rājās who constituted the popular assembly. He was perhaps the seniormost amongst the rājās or was one elected from time to time to administer criminal justice.

232. G. Turnour, An examination of the Pāli Buddhistical Annals, J.A.S.B., December 1838, pp. 993-94, f. n.

233. It may, no doubt, be argued that the Licchavi constitution was not a democracy because citizenship was confined only to the Licchavi clan, but in reply it may be pointed out that even in the great democracy of Athens, every resident was not a citizen. The Metics and the Slaves, for instance, were excluded from citizenship.

234. Mahābhārata, Śāntiparva, Vaṅgavāsī Ed. Ch. 60, verse 94.

235. Jacobi, Jaina Sūtras, S.B.E., Vol. XXII, Intro., p. XIII.

236. Ibid., p. XIII, note 3.

237. Mrs. Rhys Davids and S. Sumaṅgala Thera, The Book of the Kindred Sayings, pt. I, p. 38, n. I.

238. Saṁyutta Nikāya, pt. II, p. 268.

239. Faüsboll, Jātaka III, 121. and IV, 342.

240. Commentary on Dīgha, I. 47, on Majjhima Nikāya, I. 125, on Saṁyutta Nikāya, II. 215, quoted by Mrs. Rhys Davids in "The Book of the Kindred Sayings, part I, p. 109, f. n.

241. Divyāvadāna, (Cowell & Neil), p. 55.

242. Ibid., p. 545. "Rājagṛhe Rājā Bimbisāro rājyaṁ kārayati.. tasya Vaidehī Mahādevī Ajātasatruḥ putraḥ kumāro."

243. Rockhill, Life of the Buddha, pp. 63-64.

244. Carmichael Lectures, 1918, p. 74.

245. Ibid., p. 73.

246. Sutta-Nipāta (New edition) P.T.S., p. 194.

247. See Sutta-Nipāta commentary, p. 584. "Māgadhaṁ puranti Māgadhapuraṁ Rājagahanti adhippāyo."

248. Rockhill, Life of the Buddha, p. 64.

249. Psalms of the Sisters, pp. 120-21, Psalms of the Brethren, p. 65. 3. Majjhima Nikāya P.T.S. Vol. II, pp. 100-101, Aṅgulimāla Suttam.

250. Jātaka (Cowell's edition), Vol. IV, p. 94.

251. Buddhist Suttas, S.B.E., Vol. XI, pp. I & 2. "Ahañhī me vajjī evaṁ-mahiddhike evaṁ-mahānubhāve ucchejjāmi vajjī vīnāsessāmī vajjī anaya-vyasanaṁ āpādessāmi vajjīti." (Mahāparinibbāṇa Suttanta.)
252. Buddhist Suttas (S.B.E.) Vol. XI, p. 18.
253. Buddhist India, p. 12.
254. "Gaṅgāyatṁ kira ekam paṭṭanagāmaṁ nissāya aḍḍha Ajātasattuno āṇā aḍḍha yojanaṁ Licchavinaṁ. Ettha pana āṇāpavattiṭṭhānaṁ hotiti attho. Tatrāpi ca pabbatapādato mahogghabhaṇḍaṁ otarati. Tam sutvā ajjayāmi sveyāṁiti. Ajātasattuno samvidahantasseva Licchavi-rājāno samaggā sammodamānā puretaraṁ gantvā sabbaṁ gaṇhanti. Ajātasattu pacca āgantvā taṁ pavattiṁ ñātvā kujjhitvā gacchati. Te puna samvacchare pi tath' eva karonti. Attha so balavā ghāṭajāto tadā evaṁ akāsi. Tato cintesi, "gaṇena saddhim yuddham nāma bhāriyatṁ. Ekopi moghappahāro nama n'atthi." (Suttanta Piṭaka, Mahāvagga Aṭṭhakathā, edited by U. Pe, p. 96.)
255. Saṁyutta Nikaya, (P.T.S.), pt. II, p. 268.
256. G. Turnour, An Examination of the Pāli Buddhistical Annals, No. V., Dec. 1838. pp. 994, f. n.—996, f. n.
257. Manusaṁhitā, X. 22.
258. Bühler, Laws of Manu, S.B.E. Intro., p. cxvii.
259. R.D., Banerjce, Prācīn Mudrā, p. 12.
260. Allan, Gupta Coins, pṭ. 8-11.
261. Rapson, Indian Coins, pp. 24, 25.
262. V.A. Smith, Early History of India, 3rd Ed., p. 279.
263. 3. V. A. Smith, Early History of India, 3rd. Ed., p. 280.
264. Ibid., p. 280.
265. Ibid., p. 281.
266. Fleet, Corpus Inscriptionum Indicarum, Vol. III, p. 135.
267. Ibid., p. 135.

CHAPTER 2

THE JÑĀTRIKAS

Importance of the Jñātrikas in Indian Religious History

The Jñātrikas formed the clan which gave India one of its greatest religious reformers. This was Mahāvīra, the last Tīrthaṅkara of the jains. The name of the clan is also given as the Nāya or Nātha clan.[1]

Their location

The Jñātrikas or the Khattiyas of the Nāya (or Jñātri clan) as Dr. Hoernle says,[2] used to dwell in Vaiśālī (Basārh), Kuṇḍagrāma and Vāṇiyagāma. Dr. Hoernle holds, "Beyond Kuṇḍapura in a further north-easterly direction lay the suburb (or station, sannivesa) of Kollāga which appears to have been principally inhabited by the Kṣattriyas of the Nāya (or Jñātri) clan, to which Mahāvīra belonged."[3] It is stated in the Cambridge History of India[4] that just outside Vaiśālī, there was the suburb of Kuṇḍagrāma, probably surviving in the modern village of Basukuṇḍa. Mrs. Sinclair Stevenson says that some two thousand years ago, in Basārh, the same divisions existed as would be found to-day, and there, in fact, the priestly (Brāhmaṇa), the warrior (Kṣatriya) and the commercial (Vaṇiyā) communities lived so separately that their quarters were sometimes spoken of as though they had been distinct villages, as Vaiśāli, Kuṇḍagrāma and Vāṇijyagrāma. Strangely enough it was not in their own but in the Kṣatriya ward that Mahāvīra was to be the great hero of the Vaṇiyā.[5] Vaiśālī was undoubtedly a Kṣatriya settlement and commercial people might have lived in it but we do not find any refrerence in the ancient literature and in coins and inscriptions to Vaiśālī being exclusively a Brahmin setttlement. Mrs. Stevenson has not cited any authority in support of the above statement. We are not prepared to acept it. Leaving aside the question of Vaiśālī being inhabited by the Brahmins, the other statements of Mrs. Stevenson seem to be appropriate.

Characteristics of the clan Religion

The Jain writers give an idealised picture of the Jñātrikas and tell us that they avoided what was sinful and were afraid of sin. They abstained from wicked deeds, did not do any mischief to any being and therefore they did not partake of meat.[6] Dr. Hoernle says, "outside their settlement at Kollāga, the Jñātrikas (Nāyaclan) possessed a religious establishment (or Cheyia) which bore the name Duipalasa. Like most Cheiyas, it consisted of a park enclosing a shrine, hence in the Vipāka Sūtra, it is called the Duipalāsa Park (Ujjāna) and that it was owned by the Nāya clan is shown by its description in Kap 115 and Āy, 11, 15 22, where it is called Nāya-Saṇḍavaṇe Ujjāne or Nāya-Saṇḍe Ujjane, i.e., the park of the Saṇḍavaṇa (or Cheiya) of the Nāya clan."[7] Thus, we see that the Jñātrikas used to honour the Cheiyas or Caityas or shrines. The Nāya clan seems also to have supported a body of monks who followed Pārśvanātha, an ascetic, who lived some 250 years before Mahāvīra.[8] It is stated in the Uvāsagadasāo that Mahāvīra's parents (and with them probably the whole clan of Nāya Kṣattriyas) are said to have been followers of the tenets of Pārśvanātha.[9] Lastly, when Mahāvīra appeared, the members of his clan became his devoted followers. The Sūtrakritāṅga tells us that those who followed the law proclaimed by Mahāvīra were virtuous and righteous and they were established in law.[10]

Government

Dr. Hoernle says that Vaiśālī, one of the settlements of the Jñātrikas, was an oligarchic republic, the government of which was "vested in a senate composed of the heads of the resident Kṣatriya clans and presided over by an officer who had the title of king and was assisted by a viceroy and a commander-in-chief."[11] 'Mrs. S. Stevenson says that the government of Vaiśālī seems to have resembled that of a Greek state."[12]

Siddhārtha, the chief of the clan

The chief of the Kṣatriya Nāta Clan was Siddhārtha who married Triśalā who was the sister of Ceṭaka, the most eminent amongst the Licchavi princes. Siddhārtha and Triśalā were the parents of Mahāvīra, the last and the most famous of the Jaina Tīrthaṅkaras. The Śvetāmbaras hold that the embryo of the Tīrthaṅkara, which first entered the womb of the Brāhmin lady Devanandā, was then transferred to the womb of Triśalā. This story is believed to be untrue by the Digambaras. Siddhārtha and his wife were worshippers of Pārśva and gave their son the name of Vardhamāna (Mahāvīra). Dr. Hoernle speaks of Siddhattha thus, "Though as may be expected, the Sacred Books of the Jains speak of him in exaggerated terms, they do not, I believe, ever designate him as 'the king of Kuṇḍapura or Kuṇḍagāma'; on the contrary, he is, as a rule, only called the khattiya Siddhattha (Siddhatthe khattiye) and only exceptionally he is referred to simply as King Siddhattha. This is perfectly consistent with his position as the chief of the Kṣatriyas of Kollāga. Accordingly Mahāvīra himself was born in Kollāga and naturally when he assumed the monk's vocation, he retired to the Cheīya of his own clan, called Duīpalāsa and situated in the neighbourhood of his native place, Kollāga. Mahāvīra's parents are said to have been followers of the tenets of Pārśvanātha"[13] as we have already said. Mahāvīra on renouncing the world would probably first join Pārśva's sect, in which, however, he soon became a reformer and chief himself.[14]

Māhavīra

Mahāvīrā, the son of Siddhārtha and Triśalā, is undoubtedly the most notable scion of the Jñātrika clan. A side-light on the tremendous influence exercised by this remarkable man on his fellowmen is thrown by a passage occurring in the canonical literature of his bitter antagonists, the Buddhists. This passage may be translated thus, "He is the head of an order, of a following, the teacher of a school, well-known and of repute as a sophist, revered by the people, a man of experience, who has long been a recluse, old and well-stricken in years"[15] (Dialogues of the Buddha, II, p. 66). A detailed sketch of the life and work of Mahāvīra will fill a volume and is beyond the scope of the present treatise. We may, however, mention the fact that it was he who brought the Jñātrikas into intimate touch with the neighbouring com munities of eastern India and developed a religion which is still professed by millions of Indians. Another celebrity of the Jñātrika clan was Ānanda, a staunch follower of Mahāvīra. The Jaina work, Uvāsagadasāo, mentions that he had with him a treasure of four kror measures of gold deposited in a safe place. Again he is represented as a person whom many kings, princes and other dignitaries down to merchants found it necessary to consult on many matters requiring advice. He had a devoted wife named Śīvanandā.[16]

REFERENCES

1. Uvāsagadasāo, vol. II, p. 4, f. n.
2. Ibid., vol. II, p. 4, f.n.
3. Ibid., Vol. II, p. 4, f .n.
4. Cambridge History of India, Ancient India, edited by Rapson, vol. I, p. 157.
5. Mrs. Sinclair Stevenson, Heart of Jainism, pp. 21-22.
6. Jains Sūtras. pt. II. S.B.E., Vol. XLV, p. 416.
7. Uvāsagadasāo, vol. II, pp. 4 & 5 f. n.
8. Mrs. Sinclair Stevenson,, Heart of Jainism, p. 31.
9. Hoernle's ed. vol. II, p. 6.
10. Jaina, Sūtras, pt. II, pp. 256-257.
11. J. A.S.B., 1898, p. 40.
12. Heart of Jainism, p. 22.
13. Uvāsagadasāo, vol. II, pp. 5-6.
14. Ibid., p. 6.
15. "Saṅghī ceva gaṇī ca gaṇācariyo ca ñāto yasassī titthakaro sādhusammato bahujanassa rattaññu ciropabbajito addhagato vayo anupatto."
16. Uvāsagadasāo, II., Tr. pp. 7-9.

CHAPTER 3

THE VIDEHAS

Vedic Evidence

The Videhas are mentioned as a people in a very advanced state of civilisation in the Brāhmaṇa portion of the Vedas. That part of the country where they lived, appears to have been known by the name of Videha even in the still more ancient times of the Saṁhitās. The Saṁhitās of the Yajurveda menton the cows of Videha which appear to have been specially famous in ancient India in the Vedic times.[1]

Kośala-Videha Confederacy

According to Julius Eggeling, there lived to the east of the Madhyadeśa at the time of the redaction of the Brāhmaṇas, a confederacy of kindred peoples known as the Kośalavidehas occupying a position of no less importance than that of the Kurupāñcālas. He further states that the legendary account is that these people claimed Videgha Māthava to be their common ancestor and they are said to have been separated from each other by the river Sadānīrā (corresponding to either the Rāpti or the Gaṇḍak). In his opinion the Videhan country was in those days the extreme east of the land of the Aryans.[2] Dr. Weber points out that the Aryans apparently pushed further up the river Sarasvatī led by Videgha Māthava and his priest as far east as the river Sadānīrā which formed the western boundary of the Videhas or more probably the Gaṇḍaka which was the boundary between the Kośalas and the Videhas.'[3]

Origin of the Name

The country is said to have derived its name from this kin

Videgha Māthava or Videha Mādhava who introduced the sacrificial fire; and according to some, this introduction of the sacrificial fire is symbolical of the inauguration of the Brahrnanical faith in the region. As the legend is of importance in connection with the question of Aryan settlement in the Videha country, we quote it here in full from the Śatapatha Brāhmaṇa:—

"Māthava, the (king of) Videgha, carried Agni Vaiśvānara in his mouth. The Ṛṣi Gotama Rāhūgaṇa was his family priest. When addressed (by the latter), he made no answer to him, fearing lest Agni might fall from his mouth.

He (the priest) began to invoke the latter with verses of the Ṛgveda, 'We kindle thee at the sacrifice, O wise Agni, thee the radiant, the mighty caller to thc sacrificial feast (Ṛgveda, V., 26, 3)!—O Videgha!'

He (the king) did not answer. (The priest went on), 'Upwards, O Agni, dart thy brilliant, shining rays, thy flames, thy beams, (Ṛgveda VIII. 44, 16)—O Videgha— a—a!

Still he did not answer. (The priest continued), 'Thee, O butter-sprinkled one! we invoke. (Ṛgveda, V. 26, 2); so much he uttered, when at the very mentioning of butter, Agni Vaiśvānara flashed forth from the (king's) mouth: he was unable to hold him back; he issued from his mouth, and fell down on this earth.

Māthava, the Videgha, was at that time on the (river) Sarasvatī. He (Agni) thence went burning along this earth towards the east; and Gotama Rāhūgaṇa and the Videgha Māthava followed after him as he was burning along. He burnt over (dried up) all these rivers. Now that (river), which is called 'Sadānīrā,' flows from the northern (Himālaya) mountain : that one he did not burn over. That one the Brāhmans did not cross in former times, thinking, 'it has not been burnt over by Agni Vaiśvānara.'

Now-a-days, however, there are many Brāhmans to the

east of it. At that time it (the land east of the Sadānīrā) was very uncultivated, very marshy, because it had not been tasted by Agni Vaiśvānara.

Now-a-days, however, it is very cultivated, for the Brāhmans have caused (Agni) to taste it through sacrifices. Even in late summer that (river), as it were, rages along: so cold is it, not having been burnt over by Agni Vaiśvānara.

Māthava, the Videgha, then said (to Agni), 'Where am I to abide ?' 'To the east of this (river) be thy abode,' said he. Even now this (river) forms the boundary of the Kośalas and the Videhas; for these are the Māthavas (or descendants of Māthava)."[4]

Very great importance has rightly been attached to this passage which, since the days of Professor Weber, has been taken by scholars to indicate the progress of Vedic Aryan civilisation from north-western India towards the east. Though we cannot be sure about this point, yet it shows at least that in times that the Śatapatha Brāhmaṇa considers as ancient, the Videha country had received Vedic civilisation and the cult of offering sacrifices in fire had developed there in those early days. According to tradition, the Śatapatha Brāhmaṇa was compiled in the Videha country by Yājñavalkya who flourished in the court of Samrāt Janaka, though parts of it bear testimony to having originated in the country lying farther to the west like the other great Brāhmaṇas.

Magadha and Videha's contact with Vedic culture

In the later mantra period, Videha must have been organised so far as to take a leading part in Vedic culture, and the Śatapatha Brāhmaṇa clearly indicates that the great spiritual and intellectual lead offered by Samrāt Janaka and Ṛṣi Yājñavalkya had to be accepted by the whole of Northern India. Ṛṣis from the Kurupāñcāla regions flocked to the court of Janaka and took part in the discussions held about the supreme Brahman and had to admit the superior knowledge of Yājñavalkya. In our opinion, however, the Videha country must have received Vedic culture long before the time of the compilation of this Brāhmaṇa, as we find in the Bṛhadāraṇyaka Upaniṣad which forms a part of it, that Samrāt Janaka of Videha was a great patron of Vedic culture and that to his court repaired Ṛṣis from the whole of Northern India. Thus, we read there : "Janaka Vaideha (the King of the Videhas) performed a sacrifice at which many presents were offered to the priests of (the Aśvamedha). Brāhmaṇas of the Kurus and the Pāñcālas had come thither, and Janaka Vaideha wished to know, which of those Brāhmaṇas was the best read. So, he enclosed a thousand cows, and ten pādas (of gold) were fastened to each pair of horns. And Janaka spoke to them : 'Ye venerable Brāhmaṇas, he who among you is the wisest, let him drive away these cows.'

Then those Brāhmaṇas durst not, but Yājñavalkya said to his pupil: 'Drive them away, my dear.'

He replied: 'O glory of the Sāman,' and drove them away.

The Brāhmaṇas became angry and said: 'How could he call himself the wisest among us ?'

Now, there was Aśvala, the Hotṛ priest of Janaka Vaideha. He asked him: 'Are you indeed the wisest among us, O Yājñavalkya?' He replied: 'I bow before the wisest (the best knower of Brāhman), but I wish indeed to have these cows.'

Then Aśvala, the Hotṛ priest, undertook to question him." Yājñavalkya gave full and satisfactory answers to all the questions put by Aśvala, so that at last 'Aśvala held his peace,' as we are told in the naive language of the Upaniṣad.

Then Jāratkārava Ārtabhāga took up the questionnaire, and he also was forced to hold his peace like his predecessor, Aśvala. Then followed in succession Bhujyu Lāhyāyani, Uṣasta Cākrāyana, Kahola Kauṣītakeya, Gārgī Vācaknavi, Uddālaka Āruṇi. and all of them had ultimately to hold their peace. Then again Gārgī Vācaknavī came to their rescue, and the way she put the question is interesting, showing that the Videhas put two arrows to their bow-string at the same time. We read here:—

"Then Vācaknavī said: 'Venerable Brāhmaṇas, I shall ask him two questions. If he will answer them, none of you, I think, will defeat him in any argument concerning Brahmān.' "

"Yājñavalkya said, 'Ask,O Gārgi.'"

"She said: 'O Yājñavalkya, as the son of a warrior from the Kāśīs or the Videhas might string his loosened bow, take two pointed foe-piercing arrows in his hand and rise to do battle, I have risen to fight thee with two questions. Answer me these questions." 'But these questions fared no better than those had been asked before, and Gārgī at last exhorted the Ṛṣis thus, "Venerable Brāhmans, you may consider it a great thing, if you get off by bowing before him. No one, I believe, will defeat him in any argument concerning Brahmān." Then she held her peace.

Then rose Vidagdha Śākalya, evidently from the Kuru-Pāñcāla country, the Brāhmaṇas of which held up their heads very high in the early Brāhmaṇa period. He in the course of the discussion that followed, said: 'Yājñavalkya, because thou hast decried the Brāhmaṇas of the Kuru-Pāñcālas, what Brahmān dost thou know ?'

Yājñavalkya non-plussed him, as he had done the rest, and at last threw out a challenge: "Reverend Brāhmaṇas, whosoever among you desires to do so, may now question me, or question me, all of you. Or whosoever among you desires it, or I shall question all of you." "But," the Upaniṣad adds, "those Brāhmaṇas durst not (say anything)." (Bṛhadāraṇyaka Upaniṣad, III. 1-9).

We have quoted this episode from the Upaniṣad to show that at the time of the Śatapatha Brāhmaṇa, the Videha Brāhmaṇas were superior to the Kuru-Pāñcālas as regards the Upaniṣadic phase of the development of Vedic culture.

In other works of the Brāhmaṇa period as well as of the Sūtra period that followed, other celebrated kings of Videha are mentioned *(vide* Vedic Index, II, 298), so that there can be no question that the Videhans maintained a high position in Vedic society at least in the Brāhmaṇa period, and from the superior intellectual position that they had attained in this period it is legitimate to assume that Vedic Aryan culture had taken its root in Videha long before the Brāhmaṇa age, and most probably in the early Saṁhitā age of the Ṛgveda.

Sacrifices in Videha

Besides the great Vahudakṣiṇā sacrifice performed by Janaka,[5] and attended by the Brahmins of Kuru and Pāñcāla to which we have already referred, the Jātaka stories, too, refer to sacrifices performed by the Videhan kings. Goats were sacrificed in the name of religion .[6] We are told in the Purāṇas that Nimi, Ikṣvāku's son, a king of Videha, performed a sacrifice for a thousand years with the help of Vaśiṣṭha who had previously officiated as high-priest at a certain Yajña lasting for a long time performed by Indra. the completion of that ceremony Vaśiṣṭha went to Mithilā to commence the sacrifice of King Nimi.[7]

The evidence of the Adhyātma Rāmāyaṇa also testifies to the Yājñika activities of the Videhan royal family. Viśvāmitra is represented as saying to Rāma who was with Lakṣmaṇa, "Dear, we are going to Mithilā, of which Janaka is the ruler. After attending the great Yajña of Janaka, we shall make for Ayodhyā." (Adhyātma Rāmāyaṇa, Bālakāṇḍa, Chap. VII, p. 68, Kālī Śaṅkara Vidyāratna's edition).

Videha in the Epics

Coming to the Epic age we find Rāmacandra, the hero of the Rāmāyaṇa, marrying Vaidehī, the adopted daughter of Janaka, King of Mithilā.[8] This Janaka is probably not the same person as the patron of Yājñavalkya; it appears that several sovereigns of the dynasty bore that title which had been rendered glorious by the intellectual and political powers of the Vedic King. The Rāmāyaṇa gives a splendid picture of the Videha capital and the wide and richly equipped sacrificial place of King Janaka.

Mithilā, the capital

The distance between Mithilā and Ayodhyā may also be gathered from the fact that during the reign of Janaka, king of Videha, when Viśwāmitra came to Mithilā with Rāma and Lakṣmaṇa, it took them four days to reach Mithilā from Ayodhyā. They took rest for one night only at Viśālā on their way.[9]

The messengers sent by Janaka reached Daśaratha's capital in three days of very fast travelling and Daśaratha on his journey to the Videhan capital in his chariots took four days. Mithilā, the capital, is identified by tradition with modern Janakapura in the hills in the present Nepalese territories; a large number of pilgrims visits it every year.

In the Mahābhārata, Videha, its capital Mithilā, and its king Janaka are mentioned many times. After Yudhiṣṭhira's accession to the throne of Indraprastha, before the Rājasūya sacrifice, Bhīma defeated in the course of his *digvijaya,* the king of the Videha people (Vaidehakañ can Rājānaṁ) [Sabhā, Ch. 30]; Karṇa also conquered Mithilā the Videha capital in his *digvijaya* (Vana, 254); the celebrated sacrifice of Janaka is referred to in several places (Vana, Chs. 132, 134, etc.), a conversa-tion between Janaka and Yājñavalkya is related in the Śāntiparva (Ch. 311). There are many references to Janaka's spiritual enlightenment, his talks with Pañcaśikha, with Sulabhā and others and the teaching imparted by him to the young Śuka (Śānti-parva, Chap. 327, etc.). Kṛṣṇa with Bhīmasena and Arjuna visited Mithilā, the capital of the Videhas, on his way from Indraprastha to Rājagṛha (Sabhā 20). The Videhas are mentioned twice in the list of peoples in the Bhīṣmaparval once as *Videhas* along with the Magadhas and again as *Vai-dehas* along with the Tāmraliptakas.

Videha in the Purāṇas—its kings

The Viṣṇu Purāṇa also mentions the Videha country, furnishes a list of its rulers from ancient times and gives an account of the origin of the name of Videha and also that of Mithilā, the capital. It relates that Vaśiṣṭha having performed the sacrifice of Indra proceeded to Mithilā to commence the sacrifice of King Nimi. On reaching there he found that the king had engaged Gautama to perform the sacrificial rites. Seeing the king asleep he cursed him thus : "King Nimi will be bodiless (Videha, vi—vigata, deha) inasmuch as he having rejected me has engaged Gautama." The king being awake cursed Vaśiṣṭha saying that Vaśiṣṭha too would perish as he had cursed a sleeping king. Ṛṣis churned the dead body of Nimi. As a result of the churning, a child was born, afterwards known as Mithi, his birth being due to churning. The most important Videhan king was, no doubt, Janaka but we have reference to other kings in our ancient literature, namely, Sāgaradeva, Bharata, Aṅgirasa, Ruci, Suruci, Patāpa, Mahāpatāpa, Sudassana, Neru, Mahāsammata, Mucala, Mahā mucala, two Kalyāṇas,[10] Śatadhanu of ill-fame,[11] Makhādeva, Sādhina, Suruci, Nimi and others. Mithilā was founded by King Mithi better known as Janaka. According to the Bhaviṣya Purāṇa, Nimi's son, Mithi founded a beautiful city near Tirhoot which was named Mithilā after him. From the fact of his having founded the city, he came to be known as Janaka.[12] The Mahāgovinda Suttanta of the Dīgha Nikāya gives another account of its origin and states that Mithilā of the Videhas was built by Govinda.[13]

Matrimonial relations with dthe neighbouring powers—marriage of a Videhan princess with a prince of Kośala, Udayana, the Vaidehīputra

Kings of Videha usually maintained friendly relations with neighbouring powers. We have already referred to the marriage of Sītā daughter of Janaka king of Videha, with Rāmacandra, the son of Daśaratha, king of Kośala mentioned in the Rāmāyaṇa. Instances of matrimonial alliances concluded by the kings of Videha with the neighbouring royal families occur also in later literature. Dr.D.R. Bhāndārkar points out that in the play of Bhāṣa, Udayana is called Vaidehīputra. This clearly indicates that his mother was a princess of Videha.[14]

Ajātaśatru, the Vaidehiputra

In the Buddhist literature, we have a reference to another Videhan princess who was the mother of Ajātaśatru and was no doubt a queen of Bimbisāra. Her name was Vāsavī.[15]

Vardhamāna Mahāvira and Mithilā

Vardhamāna Mahāvīra, the great founder of Jainism, "a Videha, son of Videhadattā, a native of Videha, a prince of Videha, had lived thirty years in Videha when his parents died." [16] Mithilā was his favourite resort. Here six monsoons were spent by him.[17]

Videha—its area

At the time when the Buddha preached his religion, we find the ancient Videha country cut up into parts, the Licchavis occupying the foremost position among the tribes that occupied it in former times. Eight peoples are named as making up the Vajjian confederacy, the Licchavis and the Videhas named as such, occupying a prominent position. The confederacy, according to Kauṭilya, was a Rājaśabdopajivin Saṅgha.[18] Videha was 24 yojanas in length from the river Kauśikī to the river Gaṇḍak and sixteen yojanas in breadth from the Ganges to the Himālayas (Brihat Viṣṇupurāṇa, "Kauśikiṁ tu samārabhya... .Mithilā nāma nagarī tatrāste loka viśrutā"). The capital of Videha was Mithilā situated about thirty-five miles northwest from Vesālī. [19]

It is stated in the Jātakas that the city of Mithilā, the capital of the Videhans, was seven leagues and the kingdom of Videha three hundred leagues in extent.[20] It was the capital of the kings Janaka and Makhādeva in the district now called Tirhut.[21] The city of Mithilā in Jambudvlpa had plenty of elephants, horses, chariots, oxen, sheep and all kinds of wealth of this nature together with gold, silver, gems, pearls and other precious things.[22] From a Jātaka description, we learn that the kingdom of Videha had 16,000 villages, storehouses filled, and 16,000 dancing girls.[23] Magnificent royal carriages were drawn by four horses. The Videhan king was seen seated in a carriage drawn in state around his capital.[24]

In the Si-Yu-Ki (Buddhist Records of the Western World) we find that the Chinese traveller, Hiuen Tsiang, describing the kingdom of Fo-li-shi (Vrijji) says that the capital of the country is Chen-shu-na. At the foot of page 77 we find a note by the translator who calls our attention to the fact that the country of the Vrijis was that of the confederated eight tribes of the people called the Vrijis. He quotes V. de St. Martin who connects the name Chen-shu-na with Janaka and Janakapur, the capital of Mithilā.[25]

Videha, a Resort of Merchants

From a very early time, Videha figured as a place frequented by merchants. At the time of Buddha Gautama we find people coming from Sāvatthī to Videha to sell their wares. When the Buddha was at Sāvatthī, a disciple of his, who was an inhabitant of Sāvatthī, took cart-loads of articles and went to Videha for trade. There he sold his articles and filled the carts with articles got in exchange and then proceeded towards Sāvatthi. When he was proceeding through a forest, one wheel of a cart broke down. Then another man who had gone out of his own village with an axe to cut down trees, reached the very spot while wandering in the forest. He saw the disciple dejected on account of the breaking of the wheel. Taking pity on the traveller, he cut down a tree, made a strong wheel out of it, and fixed it to the cart and thus got him out of the trouble. The latter then succeeded in reaching Sāvatthī.[26]

The People charitable

The Videhans were a charitable people. Many institutions of charity were in existence. Daily six hundred thousand pieces were spent in alms-giving.[27] We find it stated in the Makhādeva Jātaka how a Videhan king, when he renounced the wordly life, gave a village to his brother which fetched him much.

Long-lived

The Jātaka stories occasionally make extravagant demands upon popular credence as when they relate how the average length of human life at the time of the Buddha Gautama was thirty thousand years. More fortunate than the average mortal, King Makhādeva of Mithilā had a lease of life for eighty-four thousand years,[28] in the earlier portion of which he amused himself as a royal prince and later on was appointed a viceroy, and last of all he became a king. We, however, come to a more sober estimate when we find it related that there lived in Mithilā, a Brahmin named Brahmāyu, aged one hundred and twenty years, who was well versed in the Vedas, Itihāsas, Vyākaraṇa, Lokāyata and was endowed with all the marks of a great man.[29]

Polygamous

Polygamy appears to have been in vogue among the kings of Videha. Brahmādatta. king of Benares, had a daughter named Sumedhā whom he declined to give in marriage to a Videhan prince who had a large number of wives, fearing that her cowives would make her life very miserable. So, he thought that he would marry his daughter to a prince who would wed her alone and take no other wife.[30]

Many writers bear testimony to the devotion and faithfulness of Videhan princesses. The story of Sītā is too well-known to be repeated. It is stated in the Amitāyurdhyāna Sūtra that when Ajātaśatru arrested his father Biṁbisāra at the instigation of Devadatta and confined him in a room with seven walls, declaring that none should approach him, Vaidehi, the queen-mother, who was very faithful to her husband, having purified herself by bathing and washing, having anointed her body with honey and ghee mixed with corn-flour and having concealed the juice of grapes in the various garlands she wore, saved his life. Ajātaśatru enquired about his father and he was informed by the warder of the gate about what Vaidehī had done. This enraged him much and he wanted to kill his mother. At this the ministers remonstrated with him and he had to give up this idea. Vaidehi was kept in seclusion. She showed great respect to the Buddha who appeared before her and gave her a long discourse on peace and contentment.[31]

Public Opinion in Videha

We read in one of the Jātakas that in Videha the people reproached the king for his childlessness and suggested to the king various devices which could be accepted or rejected by the king who might ask for the advice of the people as to what to do.[32]

Videhan Kings's Love of Learning

The kings of Mithilā were men of high culture. We have already referred to Janaka, the great Rājarṣi of the Brahmanic period, who had received Brahmāvidyā or Ātmavidyā from the great sage Yājñavalkya, the reputed author of the Yājñavalkyasaṁhitā.[33] In the Buddhist age, we find Sumitra, king of Mithilā, devoted to the Practice and study of the true law. [34] King Videha of Mithilā had four sages to instruct him in law. [35]

Royal Princes Educated at Texila

In the past when King Videha was reigning at Mithilā, his queen bore him a son who grew up and was educated at Taxila. [36] Taxila was the seat of learning where the Videhan princes, like the princes of the other States,[37] used to receive education.

Story of Nimi, King of Videha

Stories regarding the religious proclivities of the royal family of Videha are frequently met with in our ancient literature. Once Nimi, king of Videha, was looking down at the street through an open window of the palace. A hawk was then seen flying up into the air, taking some meat from the meat market. The bird was molested by some othere birds which began to peck it with their beaks. It had to give up the piece of meat as their pecking was too much for it and the same piece of meat was then taken up by another bird which met with the same fate and dropped it and a third took it and was molested in the same way. Thereupon, the following thoughts arose in the king's mind:—"The possessor was unfortunate and the relinquisher was happy; sorrow befell a person who indulged in the pleasures of the senses but happiness was the lot of the man who renounced them; as he had sixteen thousand women he ought to live in happiness; but the pleasures of the senses should be renounced like the hawk relinquishing the morsel of flesh." Considering this, wise as he was, he realised the three properties of blessedness and gained spiritual illumination and reached the wisdom of a Paccekabuddha.'[38]

King Videha and King Bodhisattva of Gāndhāra

Another Jātaka story relates that Videha, king of Videha, and Bodhisattva, king of Gāndhāra, were on friendly terms though they never met each other. Once on the fast day of the full-moon, the king of Gāndhāra took the vow of the commands (a vow to keep the five moral precepts) and, sitting on a royal throne prepared for him, delivered before his ministers a discourse on the substance of the law. At that moment Rāhu was overshadowing the full moon's so that the moon's light became dim by an eclipse. The ministers told the king that the moon had been seized by Rāhu. The king observing the phenomenon thought that all the trouble came from outside; his royal retinue was nothing but a trouble and that it was not proper that he should lose his light like the moon seized by Rāhu. He then made over his kingdom to his ministers and took to a religious life and having attained transcendental faculty, he spent the rainy season in the Himālayan regions, devoting himself to the delight of meditation.

The king of Videha when he heard of the religious life of the king of Gāndhāra abdicated the throne of Mithilā and went to the Himālayan region and became a hermit. The two ex-kings lived together in peace and friendliness without knowing each other's antecedents. The ascetic of Videha waited upon the ascetic of Gāndhāra. One day they saw the moon' slight destroyed. The former asked the master (the ascetic of Gāndhāra) as to the cause of it. He was told by the master that all trouble came from outside like the trouble to the moon seized by Rāhu and that he (the master) taking the moon's orb seized by Rāhu as his theme, had left his kingdom and taken to a religious life. Whereupon Videha recognised the ex-king of Gāndhāra who had surely seen the good of a religious life and said that he had heard of it and had taken him as his ideal and left his kingdom to lead a religious life.[39]

King Makhādeva's Renunciation

We have already referred to the long life of King Makhādeva of Mithilā. The story of his renunciation may be summarised in a few words. One day he asked his barber to inform him when any grey hair on his head would be noticed by him. One day the barber saw a grey hair and placed it on the hand of the king who after seeing it became mortified and thought that his days were numbered. His eldest son was sent for and was asked to take charge of the sovereignty. The old king became a recluse and lived in a grove which was named Makhādeva's mango-grove. He developed very high spiritual powers and after death was reborn in the realm of Brahmā. Passing thence he became a king in Mithilā and once more became a hermit. He again came to the realm of Brahmā.[40]

King Sādhina's Story

Sādhina, a righteous king in Mithilā, kept the five virtues and observed the fast-day vows. The king's virtue and goodness were praised by the princes of Heaven who sat in the "Justice Hall" of Sakka. All the gods desired to See him. Accordingly, Sakka ordered Mātali to bring Sadhina to heaven in his own chariot. Mātali went to the kingdom of Videha. It was then the day of the full moon. Mātali drove his celestial chariot side by side with the moon's disc. All people kept on shouting, "See, two moons are in the sky." But the chariot came near them and they cried, "It is no moon but a chariot, a son of the gods it would seem. Surely the chariot is for our king, virtuous as he is." Mātali went to the king's door and made a sign that he (the king) should ascend the chariot. The king after arranging for the distribution of alms went away with Mātali. One-half of the city of gods and twenty-five millions of nymphs and a half of the palace of Vaijayanta were given by Sakka to Sādhina. The king lived there in happiness for seven, hundred years. But afterwards when his merits were exhausted, dissatisfaction arose in him and he did not wish to remain in heaven any longer. The king was carried to Mithilā where he distributed alms for seven days and on the 7th day he died and was reborn in the Heaven of Thirty-three.[41]

Story of King Suruci and his Consort Sumedhā

Suruci, king of Mithilā, had a wife named Sumedhā who was childless. Sumedhā prayed for a son. On the first of the fifteenth day of the month, she took the eight-fold sabbath vows (aṭṭhasilānī) against taking life, theft, impurity, lying, intoxicating liquors, eating at forbidden hours, worldly amusements, unguents and ornaments, and sat meditating upon the virtues in a magnificent room upon a pleasant couch.[42] Sakka in the guise of a sage came into the king's park and stayed at the window of the bedchamber of Sumedhā. She on learning from her companions that Sakka would give the boon of a son to a virtuous woman, entreated him to favour her with it. Sakka asked her to sing her own praises in fifteen stanzas which she did to his satisfaction. Afterwards she was blessed with a child.[43]

REFERENCES

1. The commentator of the Taittiriya Saṁhitā explains the adjective Vaidehī by Viśiṣṭa-deha-sambandhinī, 'having a splendid body' (see Vedic Index, Vol. II, p. 298 and Keith's Veda of black Yajus school, Vol. I, p. 138).
2. Śatapatha Brāhmana, S.B.E., Vol. XII. lut'ro. XLII-XLIII.
3. S.B.E., Vol. XII, p. 104. f.
4. Śatapatha Brāhmaṇa, trans, by Eggeling, S.B.E., XII pp. 104-106.
5. Described by Aśvaghoṣa as one who being a householder attained merit leading to final bliss.
6. Jātaka, Vol. I. p. 166 foil.
7. Viṣṇupurāṇa, p. 246 (Vaṅgavāsī edition).
8. *Rāmāyaṇa*, Bālakāṇḍam (Bombay edition), chap. 73.
9. *Rāmāyaṇa* (Vaṅgavāsī edition), i-3.
10. Mahāvaṁsa, Geiger's translation, p. 10,

11. Viṣṇupurāṇa, pt. Ill, Chap., XVIII, p. 217. (Vaṅgavāsī Edn.)
12. Bhaviṣyapurāṇa, "Nimeḥ putrastu tatraiva..purijanana sāmarthāl janakaḥ saca kīrtitaḥ."
13. P.T.S., Vol. II, p. 235.
14. Carmichael Lectures, 1918, pp. 58 & 59, Udayana is addressed as Vaidehīputta (S.V., Act. 6, p. 68, Gaṇapati Śāstrī's Edn.).
15. Rockhill, Life of the Buddha, pp. 63-64-
16. Jaina Sūtras, S.B.E., Vol. XXII, pt. I, p. 256.
17. Ibid., p. 264.
18. Arthaśāstra, translated by Shāmaśāstrī, p. 455.
19. Rhys Davids, Buddhist India, p. 26.
20. Jātaka (Cowell's edition), Vol III, p. 222.
21. Buddhist India, p. 37.
22. Beal's *Romantic Legend of Śākya Buddha*, p. 50.
23. Jātaka, Vol. Ill, p. 222.
24. Ibid., Vol. II, p. 27.
25. Beal's *Records of the Western World*, Vol. II, p. 78. n.
26. Dhammapāla's Paramatthadīpanī on the Theragāthā, pt. III, pp. 277-278.
27. Jātaka (Cowell). Vol. IV, p. 224.
28. Ibid., Vol. I, p. 31.
29. Majjhima Nikāya, Vol. II, Pt. I, pp. 133-134.
30. Jātaka, Vol. IV, pp. 198-205.
31. S.B.E., Vol. XLIX, pp. 161-201.
32. Jātaka. Vol. V, pp. 141-42.
33. Anargha Rāghava (Nirṇayasāgara edition), p. 117.
34. Beal. *Romantic Legend of Śākya Buddha,* p. 30.
35. Jātaka (Cowell), Vol. VI, p. 156.
36. Ibid., Vol. II, p. 27.
37. See my paper, "Taxila as a seat of learning in the Pāli Literature," J.A.S.B., Vol. XII, 1916. See also my "Historical Gleanings", p. I, foll.
38. Jātaka, Vol. III, p. 230.
39. Jātaka (Cowell's edition), Vol. III, pp. 232-223.
40. Jātaka (Cowell's), Vol. I, pp. 31-32. In the Makhādeva Suttaṁ (Majjhima Nikāya, Vol. II, pt. I, pp. 74-83) we find the same story with slight varistions. The king of Mithilā named Makhādeva was very righteous and used to perform his duties towards the Samaṇas, Brāhmaṇas, the

householders and the citizens. He used to observe the Sabbath on the 8th, 14th and 15th day of the lunar month. He told his barber to find out grey hairs. After many years, the barber found out grey hairs on his head and informed him. The other details are the same. Nimi a later king, was like Makhādeva. Indra with gods came to him and praised him very much. As soon as Nimi reached the Mote-Hall of the gods, he was received cordially by Indra- who again praised him in the midst of the assembly of gods. He was sent back to his kingdom in a celestial chariot.

41. Jātaka (Cowell), Vol. IV, pp. 224-27.

42. Ibid., pp. 198-205.

CHAPTER 4

THE MALLAS

The Mallas were a powerful people of eastern India at the time of Gautama, the Buddha. They are often Mentioned in the Budhist and the Jaina works.

The Country of the Mallas, and in the Mahābhārata

The country of the Mallas is spoken of in many passsages of a Buddhist work as one of the sixteen "great countries" (Mahājanapadas)[1]. It is also mentioned in the Sabhāparva of the Mahābhārata where we are told that the second Pāṇḍava, Bhīmasena, during his expeditin to East India conquered the chief of the Mallas besides the country of Gopālakakṣa and the Northern Kosala territories[2]. Amongst the peoples inhabiting the different countries in India, the Bhīṣmaparva mentions the Mallas along with such East Indian peoples as the Aṅgas, the Vaṅgas, and the Kaliṅgas.[3]

At the time we are speaking of, they appear to have been divided into two confederacies "one with headquarters at Pāvā, and the other with headquarters at Kuśīnārā" as we see from the Mahāparinibbāṇa Suttanta.[4] There is reason to believe that in the Buddha's time, Kuśīnārā was not a city of the first rank like Rājagaha, Vaisali or savatthi When the Lord expressed to Ānanda his desire to die at Kuśīnārā, Ānanda said to him, "Let not the Exalted one die in this little wattl-and daub town, in this town in the midst of the jungle, in this branch township........." The fact that tthe Buddha hastened to Kuśīnārā from Pāvā during his last illness proves that the jouney did not take him long; but the description in the Mahāparinibbāṇa Suttanta does not enable us to make any accurate estimate of the distance between the two cities of the Mallas. Kuśīnārā has been identified by Cunningham with the village of Kāsiā in the east of the Gorakhpur District and this view has recently been strengthened by the fact that in the stupa behind the Nirvāṇa temple, near this village, has been discovered a copperplate bearing the inscription (parini) rvāṇa-chaityatāmra-paṭṭa, or the copperplate of the parinirvāṇa-caitya. This identification appears to be correct, although the late Dr. Vincent A. Smith would prefer to place Kuśīnārā in Nepal, beyond the first range of hills.[6] Rhys Davids expresses the opinion that the territory of the Mallas of Kuśīnārā and Pāvā, if we may trust the Chinese pilgrims, was on the mountain slopes to the east of the Śākya land and to the north of the Vajjian confederation. but some would place their territory south of the Śākyas and east of the Vajjians.[7] It is a considerable distance from Kāsiā in the Gorakhpur district to Pāwāpurī of the Jainas in the Patna district and one so ill as the Buddha after his meal at the house of Cunda, was not likely to walk such a distance on foot. Therefore, Pāvā of the Buddhist books appears to have been distinct from Pāwāpurī and situated not very far from Kāsiā.

Anupiyā, another Malla town

The Cullavagga of the Vinaya Piṭaka mentions another town of the Mallas named Anupiyā[8] where the Buddha resided for some time. This Anupiyā may be the same as the mango-grove called Anupiya, where Gautama spent the first seven days after his renunciation, on his way to Rājaṛiha.[9]

Malla town—Uruvelakappa

A fourth town of the Mallas called Uruvelakappa is mentioned in the Aṅguttara Nikāya, where the Blessed One stayed for some time.[10] In its neighbourhood, there appears to have existed a wide forest called Mahāvana where the Buddha went alone for midday rest after his meal, and met the gahapati Tapussa.

Mallas—a Kṣatriya tribe—Vrātyas according to Manu

From the passage "The Exalted One was a Kṣatriya and so are we. We are worthy to receive a portion of the relics of the Exalted One. Over the remains of the Exalted One will we put up a sacred cairn, and in his honour will we celebrate a feast," it is evident that the Mallas belonged to the Kṣatriya caste and in the Mahāparinibbāṇa Suttanta[11] they are repeatedly addressed by the Buddha as well as by Ānanda and others as Vāseṭṭhas or Vāśisṭhas. The Mallas of Pāvā are also addressed as Vāseṭṭhas by the Buddha in the Saṅgīti Suttanta of the Dīgha Nikāya.[12] This shows that all the Mallas belonged to the Vaśiṣṭha gotra like the Licchavis. Like the Licchavis again, the Mallas are mentioned by Manu to have been born of a kṣatriya mother and of a kṣatriya father who was a vrātya, that is, who had not gone through the ceremony of vedic initiation at the proper age.

Political Organisation

According to Kauṭilya, the Mallas were a saṅgha or corporation of which the members called themselves rajas just as the Licchavis did and the commentator, Buddhaghoṣa, also calls them rājās.[13] A passage in the Majjhima Nikāya, in giving an illustration of saṅghas and gaṇas, mentions the Licchavis and the Mallas, showing that the Mallas were a typical example of a saṅgha-rājya.[14] The accounts givenabove show that the Mallas of Pāvā and Kuśīnārā had their respective Santhāgāras or Mote-Halls where all matters, both political and religious, were discussed, We have seen that a new council-hall called Ubbhaṭaka had been built by the Mallas of Pāvā but was still unused when the Buddha visited their city in the course of his peregrina tions, and it was there that they invited him to deliver his discourses to them. We have also seen the Mallas assembled and doing business in their Mote-Hall when Ānanda went to them with the message of the impending death of the Master and again, the Mallas assembled in the Santhāgāra to discuss the procedure to be followed in the disposal of the dead body, and afterwards to discuss the claims put forward by the various kṣatriya kings and peoples.

Malla Officers

In the Mahāpariṇibbāṇa Suttanta as given in the Dīgha Nikāya, there is the mention of a set of officers called Purisas[15] among the Mallas of Kuśīnārā, about whose functions we are quite in the dark. But Rhys Davids takes them to be a class of subordinate servants.[16]

The Mallas, a Martial race—but not unmindful of learning

It seems that the Mallas were a martial race and were devoted to such manly sports as wrestling.[17] It is probable that the word 'Malla' denoting a wrestler by profession was derived from the tribal name of this brave people. But it must not be thought that they neglected learning. We are told in one of the Buddhist texts that Bandhula, a son of a Mallian king of Kuśīnārā went to Taxila for education. There he sat at the feet of a great teacher along with Pasenadi of Kośala and Mahāli, a Licchavi prince of Vaiśālī. After completing his education he came back to his realm.[18]

Philosophical Speculation

The sojourn of the Mallian princes to Taxila was not altogether unfruitful because we find the Mallians discussing philosophy. Serious philosophical problems of sati, samādhi, viriya, saddhā, dukkha, etc., did not escape their attention as may be seen from the following incident : Bhadragakogāmaṇī, an upasaka, went to the Buddha and enquired of the cause of the arising of suffering and of the overcoming of suffering. The Buddha replied that he (Bhadragako) did not believe that the enquiry could be answered by exemplifications from past and future occurrences. So, the Buddha wanted to instruct him about it by means of the present happenings. The Lord said, "Is there any one in Uruvelakappa who if killed or imprisoned or injured or blamed produces trouble in your mind?" Gāmanī replied in the affirmative. The Buddha said, "What is the cause of it ? There must be some one here against whom if something be performed, the performance of that act surely produces trouble in your: mind." The Lord added, "The reason of this is that you have attachment towards that one and you have not attachment towards the other. Attachment is not the effect of this life but of the past life." The Buddha cleared his doubts as to his existence in the past. He further said, "There is attachment towards mother for the simple reason that he is born in her womb and for this he is troubled over her disease and death and thereby it is proved that there is a connection between this life and the next. Attachment is the root of our trouble and the uprooting of it is the uprooting of suffering."[19]

Living among the Mallas in Uruvelakappa, he told the Bhikkhus that the four indriyāni (saddhā, viriya, sati and samādhi) can be fully realised by the acquisition of sublime knowledge.[20]

Shortly before the passing away of the Lord while dwelling in the Śāla-grove of the Mallas at Kuśīnārā, he advised the Bhikkhus, among whom there must have been not a few Mallians, who were present, to bear in mind the following instruction, being ardent and strenuous:—"Vayadhammā saṁkhārā."[21] (All saṁkhāras are subject to decay.)

Early Religion

Before the advent of Jainism and Buddhism, the Mallas seem to have been caitya-worshippers like their neighbours, the Licchavis. One of their shrines called Makuta Bandhana, to the east of Kuśīnārā, is mentioned in connection with the death of the Buddha where his dead body was carried for cremation. There is. however, no indication of the kind of worship that was performed at this place.

Jainism

Jainism found many followers among the Mallas as among many other races of Eastern India. The accounts we get in the Buddhist Literature of the schism that appeared in the Jaina Church after the death of Mahāvīra amply prove this. At Pāvā the followers of Nigaṇṭha Nātaputta were divided after the death of their great Tīrthaṅkara. We find that there were both ascetics and lay devotees among these Jains for we read that on account of the disputations among the ascetics, "even the lay disciples of the white robe, who followed Nātaputta, showed themselves shocked, repelled and indignant at the Nigaṇṭhas."[22] These lay Jainas appear form this passage to have been draped in white robes, just as the Śvetāmbaras are at the present day. The Buddha as well as Sāriputta, one of the principal disciples, seems to have taken advantage of the schism that appears to have overtaken the Jaina church on the death of their founder for the propagation of the rival faith. In the Pāsādika Suttanta, we find that it is Cunda, the novice of Pāvā, who brings the news of the death of the great Tīrthaṅkara, Mahāvīra, to Ānanda at Sāmagāma in the Malla country and the latter at once saw the importance of the event and said, "Friend Cunda, this is a worthy subject to bring before the Exalted One. Let's go to him and tell him about it." They hastened to the Buddha who delivered a long discourse.[23]

Buddhism

Buddhism appears to have attracted many followers among the Mallas, some of whom like the venerable Dabba the Mallian, attained a high and respectable position among the brethren. We read in the Cullavagga,[24] "Now at that time the venerable Dabba the Mallian, who had realised Arhatship when he was seven years old, had entered into possession of every (spiritual gift) which can be acquired by a disciple; there was nothing left that he ought still to do, nothing left that he ought to gather up of the fruit of his past labour." On account of his virtues, he was appointed, after due election by the Buddhist saṅgha, a regulator of lodging places and apportioner of rations. He was so successful in the discharge of these duties which required a great deal of patience and tact that he was considered by the saṅgha to be possessed of miraculous powers. But there were some, like the followers Metteya and Bhummajaka, who became envious and set bhikkhunī Mettiyā and Vaddha, the Licchavi, to bring out his fall and expulsion from the saṅgha, but their evil intentions were discovered and the venerable Dabba the Mallian was exculpated from the charges brought against him.

Khaṇḍasumana, born in the family of a Malla rājā at Pāvā, entered the order and acquired six-fold Abhiññā.[25]

Once Buddha was in the country of the Mallas named Uruvelakappa. One day he asked Ānanda to stay there and himself left for Mahāvana to spend the day. While Ānanda was staying there, a householder named Tapussa probably a Mallian, came to him and told him that he was so much absorbed in the enjoyment of sensual pleasures that he was never averse to worldly life. He (the house-holder) further told him that even a young man was satisfied with the religion and teachings of the Lord. He asked him as to the cause of it. Ānanda took him to the Buddha while he was spending the day at Mahāvana. Ānanda having informed the Buddha, the Master said that such a state of things happened with him also before attaining enlightenment. He who has not seen and thought of the evil effect of sensual pleasures and he who has not thought of the fruition of emancipation cannot bend his mind towards emancipation. This is the cause of not being able to make oneself averse to worldly life. The Master continued that when he succeeded in seeing and thinking of the evil effect of sensual pleasures and of the fruition of emancipation, he realised the first stage of meditation. When he realised the first stage, the thinking of enjoyment ot sensual pleasures became a malady to him; when he realised the second stage, the first stage appeared trifling to him and so on up to the fourth stage. When he realised all the jhānas together with the āyatanas, his mind was bent upon nirvāṇa. Because of his realising the jhānas together with the āyatanas and the nirvāṇa and because of his thwarting the enjoyment of sensual pleasures, he was successful in being foremost in the Deva, Brahmā and the Māra worlds, amongst the Samaṇas and the Brāhmaṇas.[26]

Roja, a Mallian, asked Ānanda whether the Buddha would accept potherbs and meal from his hands. Accordingly, Ānanda asked the Lord whether presents would be acceptable. The

Lord replied in the affirmative. When Roja actually took those presents to him, the Lord asked him to hand them over to the bhikkhus. He did so and the bhikkhus were satisfied with them. Roja then sat on one side. When the Blessed One finished his meal, he 'taught, and incited, and conversed, and gladdened' him 'with religious discourse.' At last Roja rose from his seat and departed.[27]

Sīha was born in the country of the Mallas in the family of a rājā. As soon as he saw the Buddha, he saluted him and being attracted, he sat on one side. The Buddha noticing the trend of his thought, taught him the Norm. He entered the Buddhist order and spent his days in the forest but he could not practise concentration of mind. Seeing this, the Master advised him to cherish the good Norm within himself and to swiftly renounce the 'piled up lease of birth.' This advice of the Lord had a beneficial effect on him and he was able to develop insight and acquire saintship.[28]

The respect and veneration with which the Mallas looked upon the Buddha will appear from their solicitude for him when his last moment was approaching and also from the great liberality and magnificence with which they cremated the corpse and the care and consideration with which they treated the remains.

Honour to Mahāvīra and the Buddha, Buddha's discourse on his doctrine

It is remarkable that the Malla people were devotedly attached to the great founders of Jainism and Buddhism. We are informed by the Kalpa Sūtra that to mark the passing away of the Great Jīna, nine Mallakis or Malla chiefs were among those that instituted an illumination on the day of the new moon, saying, "Since the light of intelligence is gone, let us make an illumination of material matter."[29] The Saṅgīti Suttanta of the Dīgha Nikāya informs us that the Buddha, accompanied by five hundred followers, was travelling in the Malla country and came to Pāvā, the Malla capital.[30] There he dwelt in the Mango-grove of Cunda, the smith. Then a new Mote-Hall of the Pāvā Mallas named Ubbhaṭaka had just been built and had not been occupied by anybody. They invited the Buddha to this freshly built council-hall saying, "Let Lord, the Exalted One, be the first to make use of it. That it has first been used by the Exalted One will be for the lasting good and happiness of the Pāvā Mallas." At their request, the Buddha gave a discourse on his doctrine to the Mallas of Pāvā till late hour of the night "instructing, enlightening, inciting and inspiring them." They then went away and the Master 'laid himself down to rest.'

Parinirvāṇa

It was also at this Mallian city of Pāvā that the Buddha ate his last meal at the house of Cunda, the smith (kumāraputta), and he was attacked with dysentery. Being ill the Exalted One went to the rival Mallian city of Kuśinārā. When he felt that the last moment was fast approaching, he sent Ānanda with a message to the Mallas of Kuśīnārā who had then assembled in their Santhāgāra or Mote-hall for some public affair. On receipt of the news, they flocked to the Śāla grove with their youngmen, girls and wives, 'being grieved and sad and afflicted at heart.' The venerable Ānanda caused them 'to Honour to the Buddha's remains. stand in groups, each family in a group' and presented them to the Blessed One, saying, "Lord, a Malla of such and such a name with his children, his wives, his retinue and his friends humbly bows down at your feet." In this way he presented them all to him.[31] Then after his last exhortations to the assembled brethren to work out their salvation with diligence, he entered into parinirvāṇa.

Honour to the Buddha's Remains

They then met together in their council-hall to devise some means of honouring the earthly remains of the Lord in a suitable manner and carried them with music to the shrine of the Mallas, called the Makuṭa-bandhana, to the east of their city and they treated the remains of the Tathāgata as they would treat the remains of a king of kings (cakravarttī-rājā).[32] When at last the cremation was over, they put out the funeral pyre with water scented with all sorts of perfumes and collected the bones which they placed in their Mote-hall, surrounding them 'with a lattice work of spears and with a rampart of bows.'[33]

Among the various clans that pressed their claims for a share of the remains, were the Mallas of Pāvā for the reason that they had a separate principality. They sent a messenger to the Mallas of Kuśīnārā, saying:—"The Exalted One was a kṣatriya and so are we. We are worthy to receive a portion of the relics of the Exalted One. Over the remains of the Exalted One will we put up a sacred cairn, and in his honour, stūpas over the Buddha's relics. will we celebrate a feast." Both the Mallas of Pāvā and Kuśīnārā erected stūpas over their respective shares and celebrated feasts.

Dispute between the two neighbouring confederate clans—the Mallas and the Licchavis

The Mallas appear to have been usually on friendly terms with their neighbours, the Licchavis, with whom they had many ties of kinship, though, as was quite inevitable, there were occasional rivalries between the two states as the story of Bandhula shows. One day Bandhula, a Mallian general, drove his chariot to Vaiśālī, the capital of the Licchavis, passed the threshold of Mahāli, a Licchavi, with his wife Mallikā who wanted to go and bathe and drink water of the tank where the members of the king's families used to get water for the ceremonial sprinkling. Mahāli heard the clattering noise (rattling sounds) of the chariot and told the Licchavis of his apprehension of danger. The Licchavis guarded the tank well, spreading an iron net over it. The Mallian general came down from his chariot, put the guards to flight by means of his sword and burst through the iron network and in the tank bathed his wife and gave her water to drink; he then left the place with his wife in the chariot. The guards narrated the event to the Licchavis. The kings of the Licchavis being angry informed Mahāli of it. Mahāli asked them not to go further but to return.

Notwithstanding his advice, five hundred kings mounting their chariots set out to capture Bandhula who sped a shaft and it cleft the heads of all the chariots and passed right through the five hundred kings. Being wounded they followed him. He stopped his chariot and said, "I cannot fight with the dead." He then asked them to loosen the girdle of the first man, who, thereupon, fell dead before they could unfasten it. They were asked to go back to their homes and were ordered to instruct their wives and children to make necessary arrangements for their affairs and then drop their armours. They did so and all of them became lifeless.[34]

Independence crushed—dominions annexed

The Mallas who played an important part in the political and religious history of ancient india and who, as we have seen before, had an independent oligarchical republic, appear to have lost their independence at the hands of the ambitious monarch of Magadha, Ajātaśatru and their dominions were annexed to the empire gradually growing up in Magadha.[35]

REFERENCES

1. Aṅguttara Nikāya, see XLII, 4. etc., Vol. IV, p. 252
2. Vaṅgavāsī Edition, Vol. I, p. 241; Sabhā Chap. XXX, Śl. 3.
3. Vaṅgavāsī Edition, Bhīṣmaparva, Chap. IX, Śl. 46. p. 822.
4. Dīgha Nikāya, Vol. II, p. 165.
5. Cunningham, Ancient Geography of India , pp. 430-433.
6. V.A. Smith, Early History of India, p. I, 59, f. n. 5; Pargiter, J.R.A.S., 1913, p. 152.
7. Buddhist India, p. 26.
8. Cullavagga, VII, 1. I, Vinaya Texts, S.B.E., pt. III, p. 224.
9. Tasmim eva padese Anupiyaṁ nāma ambavanaṁ atthi: tattha sattāhaṁ pabbajjāsukhena vitināmetvā tiṁsayojanaṁ maggaṁ padasā gantvā Rājagahaṁ pāvisi. Introduction to the Jātakas, Faüsboll, Jātaka, Vol. I, pp. 65-66.
10. Evaṁ me sutam. Ekaṁ samayaṁ Bhagavā Mallikesu Viharati Uruvelakappaṁ nāma Mallikānaṁ nigamo." Saṁyutta Nikāya, pt. V, p. 238; Aṅguttara Nikāya, Vol. IV, p. 438.
11. Dialogues of the Buddha, pt. II, pp. 162 ff.

12. Dīgha Nikāya (P.T.S.), Vol. III, p. 209.
13. Dialogues of the Buddha, pt. III, p. 201.
14. Majjhima Nikāya, Vol. I, p. 231.
15. Dīgha Nikāya, Vol. II, p. 159.
16. Buddhist India, p. 21.
17. Jātaka (Cowell's Ed.) Vol. II, p. 65.
18. Faüsboll, Dhammapada (old edition), p. 211.
19. Saṁyutta Nikāya, pt. IV, pp. 327 foll.
20. Saṁyutta Nikāya pt. V, pp. 228-229
21. Saṁyutta Nikāya. pt. I, p. 18.
22. Dialogues of the Buddha, pt. III, p. 203.
23. Dialogues of the Buddha, pt. III, p. 112.
24. Vinaya Texts, pt. III, p. 4. foll.
25. Psalms of the Brethren, p. 90.
26. Aṅguttara Nikāya, Vol. IV, pp. 458-448.
27. Vinaya Text pt. II, S.B.E., Vol. XVII, p. 139.
28. Psalms of the Brethren, p. 80.
29. Jaina Sūtras, pt.I, S.B.E., XXII, p. 266. "Jaṁrayaniṁcaṇaṁ samaṇebhaga-aṁ Mahāvīre javasabbadukkhappahīṇe taṁrayaṇiṁcaṇaṁ navamllsi aṭṭhārasavi gaṇa rāyāṇo amāvasa evārābbayaṁ Posahavavāsaṁ paṭṭhavaiṁ Sugaesebhāvujjoyoe davujjoyaṁ karissāmo." (Kalpa sūtra, Dhanapat Singha's edition, p. 77.)
30. Dialogues of the Buddha, pt. III, p. 201.
31. Dialogues of the Buddha, II, pp. 162-164.
32. Ibid., p. 182.
33. Ibid., pp. 186-187.
34. Dhammapada, Faüsboll (old Ed.), pp. 218-220.
35. D.R. Bhandarkar, Carmicheal Lectures, 1918, p. 79.

CHAPTER 5

THE ŚĀKYAS

Importance of the Śākyas

The Śākyas have acquired a very great importance in Indian history owing to the Buddha having been born among them. Before the birth of the founder of Buddhism, they were comparatively little known, yet in the rugged fastness of the lower Himālayas, the Śākyas had built up a remarkable though not a very powerful principality at the time the great teacher was born. When there was a discussion, as the Lalitavistara [1] tells us, among the Devaputras in the Tuṣita heaven, as to which of the great royal families of India, the Bodhisattva should honour with his birth, no one mentioned the Śākyas. They pondered over the merits of all the sixteen Mahājanapadas in the whole of Jambudvīpa and analysed the claims of all the royal families that held up their heads high among the kṣatriyas of India at the time, but they found them all stained with one black spot or another. Among all these prominent kingly families of India, the Śākyas are not mentioned.[2] Being at a loss to find out a people worthy of claiming him as their congener, the Devaputras had at last recourse to the Bodhisattva himself and when at last, the Śākyas were chosen as the fortunate recipients of that great honour it was more on account of their purity and similar qualities, than any predominant political position.[3]

Accounts of their origin

The Śākyas of Kapilavastu claimed to be kṣatriyas. As soon

as they heard the news of the passing away of the Lord, they demanded a portion of the relics of the Buddha, saying, "Bhagavā amhākaṁ ñāti-seṭṭho,"[4] (The Blessed One was the chief of our kinsmen.) While all the other kṣatriya clans that claimed a portion of the ashes of the great teacher, did so on the basis of their belonging to the same caste ('Bhagavā pi khattiyo, mayam pi khattiyā'), in the case of the Śākyas, it was founded upon a closer relationship, that of consanguinity.

In the Sumaṅgala Vilāsiī

The origin of the Śākyas is traced back to King Okkāka, *i.e.,* Ikṣvāku. It is stated in the Sumaṅgalavilāsini that King Okkāka had five queens. By the chief queen, he had four sons and five daughters. After the death of the chief queen, the king married another young lady who extorted from him the promise to place her son upon the throne. The king thereupon requested his sons to leave the kingdom. The princes accordingly left the kingdom accompanied by their sisters and going to a forest near the Himālayas, they began to search for a site for building a city. In course of their search, they met the sage Kapila who said that they should build a town in the place where he (the sage) lived. The princes built the town and named it Kapilavatthu (Kapilavastu). In course of time, the four brothers married the four sisters, excepting the eldest one and they came to be known as the Śākyas. (Sumaṅgalavilāsini, pt. I, pp, 258-260.) The only grain of fact hidden in this fanciful story of the origin of the Śakyas seems to be that there was a tradition which traced their descent from King Okkāka or Ikṣvāku. Buddhaghoṣa in his great commentaries, though a very reliable guide as regards exposition and exegesis and the unravelling of metaphysical tangles, becomes quite the reverse when any point of history or tradition comes up. Here he accepts the wildest theories and takes as gospel truth even the most improbable stories, Sister-marriage was not in vogue in ancient India even in the earliest times of which we have any record, as the story of Yama and Yamī in the Ṛgveda amply demonstrates. If was a revolting idea to the Indians from the time of the Ṛgveda downwards. Yet we see that Buddhaghoṣa in the case of the Licchavis and again here in that of the Śākyas, tries to explain the origin by sister-marriage. Perhaps Buddhaghoṣa was actuated by the idea of purity of birth by a union between brothers and sisters as in the case of the Pharaohs of Egypt.

In the Mahāvaṁsa

The great Ceylonese chronicle, the Mahāvaṁsa, also traces the origin of the Śākyas to the same king Okkāka and goes further back to Mahāsammata of the same dynasty. We give here in full the geneology as given in the Mahāvaṁsa in the first twenty-four verses of Chapter II "Sprung of the race of king Mahāsammata was the Great Sage. For in the beginning of this age of the world there—was a king named Mahāsammata, and (the kings) Roja and Vararoja, and the two Kalyāṇakas, Uposatha and Mandhātar and the two, Caraka and Upacara, and Cetiya and Mucala and he who bore the name Mahāmucala, Mucalinda and Sāgara and he who bore the name Sāgaradeva ; Bharata and Aṅgīrasa and Ruci and also Suruci, Patāpa and Mahā-patāpa and the two Panādas likewise, Sudassana and Neru, two and two; also Accimā. His sons and grandsons, these twenty-eight princes whose lifetime was immeasurably (long), dwelt in Kusāvatī, Rājagaha and Mithilā. Then followed a hundred kings, and (then) fifty-six, and (then) sixty, eighty-four thousand, and then further thirty-six, thirty-two, twenty-eight, then further twenty-eight, eighteen, seventeen, fifteen, fourteen; nine, seven, twelve, then further twenty-five; and (again) twenty-five, twelve and (again) twelve, and yet again nine and eighty-four thousand with Makhādeva coming at the head, and (once more) eighty-four thousand with Kalārajanaka at the head and sixteen even unto Okkāka; these descendants (of Mahāsammata) reigned in groups in their due order, each one in his capital. The Prince Okkāmukha was Okkāka's eldest son; Nipuṇa, Candimā, Candamukha and Sivisaṁjaya, the great King Vessantara, Jāli, and Sīhavāhana and Sīhassara: these were his sons and grandsons. Eighty-two thousand in number were the royal sons and grandsons of King Sīhassara; Jayasena was the last of them. They are known as the Śākya kings of Kapilavatthu. The great King Sihahanu was Jayasena's son and Jayasena's daughter was Yasodharā. In Devadaha there was a prince name Devadhasakka, Aṅjana and Kaccānā were his two children. Kaccana was the first consort of Sīhahanu but the Sakka Añjana's queen was Yasodharā Anjana had two daughters, Māyā and Pajāpatī, and also two sons, Daṇḍapāṇi and the Sākiya Suppabuddha. But Sīhahanu had five sons and two daughters: Śuddhodana, Dhotodana, Sakka—, Sukka—and Amitodana, and Amitā and Pamitā; these were the five sons and two daughters. The royal consort of the Sakka Suppabuddha was Amitā; she had two children: Bhadda kaccānā and Devadatta. Māyā and Pajāpatī were Suddhodana's queens, and the son of the great King Suddhodan and of Māyā was our Conqueror.

Of this race of Mahāsammata, thus succeeding, was born, in unbroken line, the Great Sage, he who stands at the head of all men of lordly birth. The consort of the princes the Bodhisatta, was Bhaddakaccānā; her was Rāhula."[5] (The Mahāvaṁsa, Tr., Chap. II., pp. 10-12.)

In the Viṣṇu Purāṇa

There can be no doubt that King Okkāka in this geneology is none other than Ikṣvāku of the so-called solar dynasty of the Purāṇas. Comparing the names with those in the Paurāṇic list we find that the lists do not agree in every detail, yet there is an agreement with regard to some of the more prominent names. Thus, for example, in the long history of the solar dynasty given in the Viṣṇupurāṇa, pt. iv., we find many of the names in the Mahāvaṁsa list, like Māndhātā (Mandhātā Mv) Sagara (Sāgara Mv) etc. The Viṣṇupurāṇa states that King Bṛhadvala of this dynasty was killed in the Kurukṣetra war,[6] and next proceeds to trace the descent of King Śākya from this Brhadvala as given below :—

"I will now repeat to you the future princes of the family of Ikṣhwāku. The son of Bṛihadvala will be Bṛhat-kṣaṇa ; his son will be Urukṣepa ; his son will be Vatsa ; his son will be Vatsavyūha ; his son will be Prativyoma; his son will be Divākara ; his son will be Sahadeva ; his son will be Bṛhadaśva ; his son will be Bhānuratha ; his son will be Supratīka ; his son will be Marudeva ; his son will be Sunakṣatra ; his son will be Kimnara ; his son will be Antarikṣa; his son will be Suvarṇa; his son will be Amritajit; his son will be Bṛhadrāja ; his son will be Dharmin ; his son will be Kritañjaya ; his son will be Ranañjaya ; his son will be Sañjaya ; his son will be Śākya ; his son will be Śuddhodana ; his son will be Rāhula ; his son will be Prasenajit; his son will be Kṣhudraka ; his son will be Kuṇḍaka; his son will be Suratha; his son will be Sumitra. These are the kings of the family of Ikṣvāku, descended from Brihadvala. This commemorative verse is current concerning them : 'The race of the descendants of Ikṣvāku will terminate with Sumitra ; it will end, in the Kali age, with him.' "[7]

In the Mahāvastu

The source of the account given in the Mahāvaṁsa and the Sumaṅgalavilāsinī is not, however, the Purāṇas but such ancient Buddhistical works as the Mahāvastu. This latter work gives a detailed account of the foundation of Kapilavastu and the settlement of the Śākyas there. The marriage of sisters is given there and the Śākya family is traced there to Mahāsammata, as in the Mahāvaṁsa and the names of the kings that succeeded him, mostly agree in the two accounts, as will be seen from the Mahāvastu, which tells us that Kalyāṇa was the son of King Sammata. Kalyāṇa begot Rava. Rava begot Uposadha who begot Māndhātā. His sons, grandsons and all his descendants were kings by thousands. Later on Sujāta became king of the Ikṣvākus in the city of Sāketa. The Ikṣvāku King Sujāta had five sons, Opura, Nipura, Karaṇḍaka, Ulkāmukha and Hastikaśirṣa and he had five daughters, Suddhā, Vimalā. Vijītā, Jalā and Jalī. Sujāta had another son Jenta by name born of a concubine. Jenta's mother was called Jentī who gave all her services to Sujāta who became pleased with her.

Jentī was promised a boon by the king who told her, "Jentī, I will offer you a boon, whatever boon you pray for, I will grant it." She then began to speak, "Well, I shall first consult my parents and then I shall pray for a boon to your lordship." Her parents were thus informed, "The king has promised a boon. Then what boon is proper for me, which I shall pray for before the king." They then began to mutter whatever opinion they held, "Ask for an excellent village." There was one wandering nun present at that time, who was well-versed, skilled and intelligent. She said, "well Jentī, you are the daughter of a concubine. Your son will not inherit any property of his father, what to speak of a kingdom. These five princes are sons of a kṣatriya daughter. They will inherit their paternal kingdom as well as other things. You are promised a boon by the king. King Sujāta is a man of word. You ask the king for this boon: After banishing these five princes, please appoint my son Jenta as royal successor. After your death, my son will be the king of the great city of Sāketa. O king, give me this boon." Hearing this, Sujāta became much agitated in mind owing to the affection for those princes nor was he able to do anything but grant the boon. The king said to Jentī, "All right, let this boon be given." The gift of the boon that with the exile of the princes, the prince Jenta, son of the concubine, was to be installed as heir-apparent, was heard by the people of towns and villages. Then the people apprecia-ting the noble qualities of the princes became alarmed and said, "Wherever the princes will go, we shall follow them." It come to the ears of King Sujāta that many people of Sāketa were going to the place of exile along with the princes. He then issued the following proclamation:—"Whoever will go to the place of exile along with the princes, all the works done by him will be considered as works performed by the state and will be paid for from the royal treasury. Those whose works are performed with the help of elephants, horses, chariots, carriages, palan-quins or cars or oxen or buffaloes or goats or sheep, etc., will be considered as works done by the state and will be paid for by the royal treasury. For those who are going to the exile along with the princes, the royal treasury is open to them under royal orders, everybody gets what he asks for." Now, these princes along with many thousands of citizens, with a vast crowd, with thousands of chariots and carriages, went out of the city of Sāketa towards the north. They were cordially received by the king of Kāśī-Kośala. The princes were virtuous, well-reputed, peaceful and good companions. All the peple of Kāśī-Kośala were at heart-pleased with them. The people of Kāśī-Kośala said thus, "these princes; descendants of Kalyāṇa are religious. The king of Sāketa is true to the description given by the Buddha to Indra." The king of Kāśī-Kośala, however, became envious and drove out the princes from his kingdom. At the foot of the Himālayas there lived a sage Kapila, who was possessed of five kinds of supernatural knowledge and had attained the four kinds of meditation. He was strong and noble in mind. His hermitage was vast and was charming. It had fruits and flowers and it was adorned with good many plants and with a dense forest. The princes went to the dense forest and began to live there. Traders who went there came to the localities of Kāśi and Kośala.

The traders when asked by the people as to whence they came, replied that they had come from a certain part of the forest called Sākoṭavana. The people of Sāketa as well as the traders of Kośala visited the Sākoṭavana. Lest there be a defect in their clan (or impurity in their blood) they accepted their brides from among the sisters by the same mother. King Sujāta asked the ministers thus, "where do the princes live?" They replied, "They live in the Sākoṭavana at the foot of the Himālayas." Then the king asked the ministers, "Wherefrom they brought their wives ?" "They replied, "It was heard that for fear of a mixture of blood in them, they accepted their wives from among their own sisters by the same mother, so that there may not be any spoliation in their own race." The purohitas and the learned brahmins were then asked by King Sujāta whether such a custom was permissible. They replied, "Yes, O king, that can be done, laws permit it." Hearing this, the king being pleased said, "Still they are known as the Śākyas and along with the other Śākyas they are known as such." Then it came to the mind of the princes : "Shall we only live in the Sākoṭavana. Many people have come here. Let us build a town," The princes then went to the sage Kapila. Saluting him they said, "If you, Kapila, permit it, then we shall build a city here to be called after your name." The sage replied, "I can permit it if you make this hermitage a royal residence and then build a city." The princes promised to carry out his wishes. The hermitage was then given to them by the sage. The princes built a city after making the hermitage of the sage a royal residence. As the hermitage was given by Kapila the sage, it was known by the name of Kapilavastu which was prosperous, wealthy, peaceful, where alms were easily obtainable, where many people lived with their own families, being happy. The people of Kapilavastu were fond of trade and commerce. They were social and took part in festivities.

Of those five princes,Opura, Nipura,Karaṇḍaka, Ulkāmukha, Hastikaśīrsa, Opura was the eldest prince. He was elected King of Kapilavastu. Nipura was the son of King Opura and Karaṇḍaka was the son of King Nipura, Ulkāmukha was the son[8] of King Karaṇdaka, Hastikaśīrsa was the son of Ulkāmukha, Sinhahanu was the son of Hastikaśīrṣa. King Sinhahanu had four sons: Śuddhodana, Dhoutodana, Śuklodana, Amritodana and a daughter named Amitā (Mahāvastu, edited by Senart, Vol. I, pp. 348-52).

The story given in the Mahāvastu and the Śumaṅgalevilāsinī about the origin of the Śākyas by sister-marriage is referred to in the introduction to the Kunāla Jātaka. Here we observe that with regard to the Śākyas, the story of their origin exactly tallies with that in the Mahāvastu, but there is some difference in connection with the Koliyas. While the Mahāvastu says that they resided in a cave of a hill, the Jātaka story relates that they received the name *Koliya* for having resided in the hollow of a Kolī or jujube tree. As the story has a bearing on the question of origin of the two important tribes, we make an extract from it. There was a quarrel between the Śākya and Koliya cultivators who lived on opposite sides of the river Rohiṇi with regard to the right of water of the stream for use in irrigation. When words ran high they quarrelled.[9] The full description of the quarrel has been given in my account of the Koliyas.

The Śākyas are called in the Mahāvastu *ādityavandhus*[10] or people kin to the sun. This refers to their descent from the Solar dynasty to which the Ikṣvākus belonged. The Mahāvastu also speaks of King Śuddhodana as born in the Ikṣvāku family.[11] Another passage in the same work speaks of the Buddha as a Kṣatriya of the Ādityagotra and of the Ikṣvākukula, that is, born in the family of the Ikṣvākus who derived their descent from the sun.[12] The Lalitavistara also speaks of the Buddha as born in the royal family of Ikṣvāku (Lalitavistara, p. 112).

The Śākyas were Kṣatriyas of the Gotama gotra as is seen from the fact that the Buddha had the surname Gotama, while the Licchavis and Mallas who also belonged to the same race bore the gotra name of Vaśiṣṭha, and in the Pāli books while the latter are addressed as Vāseṭṭhas, the Buddha is addressed as Gotama, as in a formal conversation, people addressed each other by their gotra or family names in those days. We have shown elsewhere that the gotra of a Kṣatriya family was derived from the gotra name of the *purohita* or the family priest. This makes it evident that in an early age the Śākyas had adopted the Gotamas as their purohita.

The Gotama-gotra is described in the Pāli books as occupying a very high position among the gotras, no doubt from its association with the founder of Buddhism: for example, the Suttavibhaṅga[13] mentions the Gotamagotta as an example of a high gotra.

Kapilavastu, capital of the Śākyas

We have seen how the Mahāvastu accounts for the name of the capital of the Śākyas: "Because it was given them to live (vastu) by the Ṛṣi Kapila, therefore it acquired the appellation of Kapilavastu."—thus says the Mahāvastu. But the name is also spelt otherwise. It is also called Kapilavaśtu, that is, the vastu or place of residence of the Sage Kapila. The Lalitavistara calls it also Kapilavastu and sometimes Kapilapura (p. 243) or Kapilāhvayapura (p. 28,etc.) and these names are also found in the Mahāvastu (Vol. II, p. II, line 3). The Divyāvadāna also connects Kapilavastu with the Sage Kapila. Thus we read, "A prince is born among the Śākyas on the slope of the Himālayas, on the bank of the river Bhāgīrathī not far from the hermitage of the Ṛṣi-Kapila,"[14] and generally the town is spoken of as Kapilavastu[15] but sometimes it is referred to as Kapilavastu[16] also. In the Buddhacarita also the city is described as Kapilasya-vastu.[17]

Kapilavastu is said to have been surrounded by seven walls according to the Mahāvastu (Vol. II, p. 75).

A clue to the identification of Kapilavastu is furnished by the discovery of the famous Rummindei Pillar which marks the site of the ancient Lumbini garden, the traditional scene of Śākyamuni's birth. Dr. Smith is inclined to identify the Śākya capital which lay not far from the Lumbinigrāma with Pipprāwā in the north of the Basti district on the Nepalese frontier.

The celebrated Chinese pilgrim, Fā-Hien, who visited India early in the fifth century A.D., says that white elephants and lions infested the neighbourhood of Kapilavastu, against which the people had to be on their guard.[18] The country was thinly populated. He noticed towers at Kapilavastu set up in various places, *viz.:* where prince Siddhārtha left the city by the eastern gate, where his chariot was made to turn back to the palace, where his horoscope was cast by the sage Asita, where the elephant was struck by Nanda and others, where the arrow going thirty li in south-easterly direction; penetrated into the earth and produced a fountain of water which quenched the thirst of travellers in later generations, where Śuddhodana was met by his son when the latter had acquired supreme wisdom, where five hundred Śākya converts honoured Upāli and where the children of the Śākyas were massacred by King Viḍūḍabha.[19]

Later on, Hiuen Tsang who visited India in the seventh century A.D., narrates that Kapilavastu, the country of the Śākyas, was about four thousand li in circuit. The royal precincts built of brick were within the city measuring fourteen or fifteen li round.[20]. He says that long after the passing away of the Buddha, topes and shrines were built in or near Kapilavastu.[21] The villages were few and desolate. The monasteries (saṁghārāmas) which were then in ruins were more than one thousand in number. There still existed a saṁghārāma near the royal precincts which contained 30 (3000 according to one text) followers who read 'the little vehicle of the Sammatiya school.' There were two deva temples where different sectarians worshipped. There were some dilapidated foundation walls, the remains of the principal palace of King Śuddhodana, above which, a vihāra (monastery) was built containing a stūpa of the king. Near it, was a foundation in ruins representing the sleeping palace of Queen Mahāmāyā. Above it, a vihāra was built containing a figure of the queen. Close by, stood a vihāra where the Bodhisatta entered the womb of his mother. A stūpa was built to the north-east of 'the palace of spiritual conception' of the Bodhisatta.[22] To the north-west of the capital, a stūpa was built where King Viḍūḍabha massacred the Śākyas.[23] The cultured land was rich and fertile. The climate of the country was bracing.

Śākya Villages

According to Dr. Rhys Davids, there were villages round the rice fields and the cattle roamed about in the outlying forest. The jungles which were occasionally resorted to by robbers divided one village from another.[24]

Other Śākya Towns

Mention is made of several other Śākya towns besides Kapilavastu, *viz.*, Chātumā, Sāmagāma, Ulumpā, Devadaha, Sakkara, Sīlāvatī, and Khomadussa. (The Cambridge History of India p. 175.) The last mentioned city was so called on account of its abundant produce of linen cloth.[25]

People : their Characteristics.

It is stated in the Jātaka that the Śākyas were a haughty people. They were so very haughty that they did not do obeisance to Siddhārtha on the ground that he was younger in age. But they were afterwards made to do so on seeing a miracle performed by him.[26] Hiuen Tsang saw them obliging in manners.[27] They did not kill any living thing, 'not even a black beetle.'[28] Cattle and rice supplied their only means of livelihood.[29] The Śākya peasants enjoyed rights in common.[30]

Social Customs

The Tibetan Buddhist books as translated by Rockhill (Life of the Buddha, p. 15) relate that the Śākya law allowed a man one wife only. This law is rather remarkable inasmuch as from the Vedic age downwards, polygamy was in vogue in India, and this was so, specially among the Kṣatriyas who were rich and powerful. We may, however, account for the existence of this law among the Śākyas on the ground of their special constitution and position. The Śākyas were a small tribe and very haughty and proud of their birth. They would not give away one of their girls in marriage even to such a powerful prince as Pasenadi of Kosala. Among such a people, marriage was generally confined within the tribe itself, and as such, the number of marriageable girls being limited, many adult males would have to go without a wife, if polygamy prevailed. Hence, naturally the law had grown up among them limiting the number of wives to only one. But that the Śākyas had no objection to polygamy as such on religious or other grounds, is quite clear from the fact narrated by the same Tibetan works, that the rigorous provision of the law was relaxed in the case of Śuddhodana, the father of the Buddha; in consideration of a great public service rendered by him when a young prince, in subduing the hillmen of the Pāṇḍava tribe, he was allowed to have two wives by the Śākyas who must have assembled in their Santhāgāra to express their gratitude in this way to the heroic prince, who before this, could not marry two wives, though two girls, Māyā and Mahāmāyā had been offered by their father, Suprabuddha.

The Lalitavistara seems to suggest that Śuddhodana had a crowded harem, when it says that Māyādevī was the chief queen of Śuddhodana, being at the head of a thousand ladies.[31] But this appears to be a mere poetic exaggeration, because the Pāli books speak of only two wives of the king. Prince Siddhārtha also had only one wife according to all accounts, and according to the Lalitavistara itself even the hand of this girl was not granted to him though a prince, until he could satisfy the proud Śākya father, of his knowledge of the śilpas or arts by an open exhibition of skill in warfare as well as the finer arts. The Lalitavistara thus makes Daṇḍapāṇi, the father of Gopā, reply to the purohita sent by king Śuddhodana, "The honourable prince has been reared at home among luxuries. This, however, is our family custom that a girl is to be made over to one proficient in the arts (śilpas) and not to one ignorant of them. The prince has no knowledge of the śilpas, nor is he acquainted with the methods of fighting with the sword, the bow or other weapons. How can I then make over the girl to the prince?"[32] The same reply is given in the Mahāvastu (II, 73) by Mahānāma, the father of Yaśodharā when Śuddhodana demands his girl as a bride for the young prince. Then the work goes on to narrate how he stood easily first in a tournament in which five hundred Śākya youngmen took part. The wife of Siddhārtha is named Yaśodharā in the Mahāvastu and her father is called Mahānāma.[33]

How proud and aristocratic the Śākyas were when asked to give away their daughters in marriage to any one outside their clan will appear from the following story of King Pasenadi of Kosala who wanted to have the proud distinction of having a Śākya girl as his consort. Thus, goes on the Jātaka commentary:— "At Sāvatthī in the house of Anāthapiṇḍika there was always unfailing food for five hundred Brethren, and the same with Visākhā and the king of Kosala. But in the king's palace, various and fine as was the fare given, no one was friendly to the Brethren. The result was that the Brethren never ate in the palace, but they took their food and went off to eat it at the house of Anāthapindika or Visākhā or some other of their trusted friends.

One day the king said, 'A present has been brought: take this to the Brethren,' and sent it to the refectory. An answer was brought that no Brethren were there in the refectory. 'Where are they gone ?' he asked. They were sitting in their friends' houses to eat, was the reply. So, the king after his morning meal came into the Master's presence, and asked him, 'Good Sir, what is the best kind of food ?' 'The food of friendship is the best, great king,' said he; 'even sour rice-gruel given by a friend becomes sweet.' 'Well, Sir, and with whom do the Brethern find frendship ?' 'With their kindred, great king, or with the Śākya families.' Then the king thought, what if he were to make a Śākya girl his queen-consort. then the Brethren would be his friends, as it were with their own kindred.

So rising from his seat, he returned to the palace, and sent a message to Kapilavatthu to this effect: 'Please give me one of your daughters in marriage, for I wish to become connected with your family.' On receipt of this message the Śākyas gathered together and deliberated :'We live in a place subject to the authority of the king of Kosala; if we refuse a daughter, he will be very angry, and if we give her, the custom of our clan will be broken. What are we to do ?' Then Mahānāma said to them, 'Do not trouble about it. I have a daughter, named Vāsabhakhattiyā. Her mother is a slave woman, Nāgamuṇḍā by name she is some sixteen years of age, of great beauty and auspicious prospects, and by her father's side noble. We will send her, as a girl nobly born.' The Śākyas agreed, and sent for the messengers, and said they were willing to give a daughter of the clan, and that they might take her with them at once. But the messengers reflected, 'These Śākyas are desperately proud in matters of birth. Suppose they should send a girl who is not of them, and say that she is so. We will take none but one who eats along with them.' So they replied, 'Well, we will take her, but we will take one who eats along with you.'

The Śākyas assigned a lodging for the messengers, and then wondered what to do. Mahānāma said: 'Now do not trouble about it; I will find a way. At my meal time bring in Vāsabhakhattiyā drest up in her finery; then just as I have taken one mouthful, produce a letter, and say, My Lord, such a king has sent you a letter; be pleased to hear his message at once.'

They agreed; and as he was taking his meal they drest and adorned the maid. 'Bring my daughter,' said Mahānāma, 'and let her take food with me.' 'In a moment,' said they, 'as soon as she is properly adorned,' and after a short delay they brought her in Expecting to take food with her father, she dipt her hand into the same dish. Mahānāma had taken one mouthful with her, and put it in his mouth; but just as he stretched out his hand for another, they brought him a letter, saying, 'My lord, such a king has sent a letter to you: be pleased to hear his message at once.' Said Mahānāma, 'Go on with your meal, my dear,' and holding his right hand in the dish, with his left took the letter and looked at it. As he examined the message the maiden went on eating. When she had eaten, he washed his hand and rinsed out his mouth. The messengers were firmly convinced that she was his daughter, for they did not divine the secret.

So Mahānāma sent away his daughter in great pomp. The messengers brought her to Sāvatthī, and said that this maiden was the true-born daughter of Mahānāma. The king was pleased, and caused the whole city to be decorated, and placed her upon a pile of treasure, and by a ceremonial sprinkling made her his chief queen. She was dear to the king, and beloved."[34]

From the above account, it is evident that the Śākyas contracted their marriages within their own tribe and even their ruling house did not enter into matrimonial relations with any of the numerous princely houses in northern India. Thus while the royal houses of Kośala, Magadha and Videha did marry with each other, we do not hear of the Śākya people entering into such relations with any outsiders. When the marriage of Prince Siddhārtha was decided upon at the council of five hundred Śākya elders, the latter did not go out to find a suitable princess from among the many ruling families, but they proceeded to select a bride for him from among themselves. This clannish custom among the Śākyas gave rise perhaps to the idea that they married their sisters as we have seen when speaking of their origin. But this seems to have been tauntingly spoken of them by their rival tribes, like the Koliyas.

The Śākyas had a peculiar custom that when a child was born, it was carried to the temple of Īśvaradeva to be presented to the God. The temple contained a stone image of the God in the posture of rising and bowing. (Watters on Yuan Chwang, Vol. II., p. 13.)

Position of Women

The women appear to have enjoyed a greater amount of independence and free thinking among the Śākyas than among the peoples of the plains perhaps owing to the same scarcity of women that forced them to enact a law prohibiting multiple marriages. This is evidenced by the fact that the Śākya ladies were the first to come out of their hearth and home and embrace the hardy life of nuns in order to ensure the emancipation of their souls. Even the Master who always evinced a solicitude for not violating the usual social customs, was not willing to ordain them. But the importunities of the Śākya ladies prevailed at last, and the Master, though unwilling, had to yield. Thus, according to all Buddhist accounts, the Śākya ladies were the first to cut themselves off from the world, and to institute the order of nuns, the foster-mother of the Buddha taking the lead. Thus we read—"Now at that time the Blessed Buddha was staying among the Śākyas in Kapilavatthu, in the Nigrodhārāma. And Mahāpajāpatī the Gotamī went to the place where the Blessed One was, and on arriving there, bowed down before the Blessed One, and remained standing on one side. And so standing she spake thus to the Blessed One :

'It would be well, Lord, if women should be allowed to renounce their homes and enter the homeless state under the doctrine and discipline proclaimed by the Tathāgata.'

'Enough, O Gotamī! Let it not please thee that women should be allowed to do so.'

[And a second and a third time did Mahā-pajāpatī the Gotamī make the same request in the same words, and receive the same reply.]

Then Mahā-pajāpatī the Gotamī sad and sorrowful for that the Blessed One would not permit women to enter the homeless state, bowed down before the Blessed One, and keeping him on her right hand as she passed him, departed thence weeping and in tears.

Now, when the Blessed One had remained at Kapilavātthu as long as he thought fit, he set out on his journey towards Vesālī; and travelling straight on he, in due course arrived thereat. And there at Vesālī the Blessed One stayed, in the Mahāvana, in the Kūṭāgāra Hall.

And Mahā-pajāpatī the Gotamī cut off her hair, and put on orange-coloured robes, and set out, with a number of women of the Śākya clan, towards Veśālī; and in due course she arrived at Veśālī, at the Mahāvana, at the Kūṭāgāra Hall. And Mahā-pajāpatī the Gotamī, with swollen feet and covered with dust, sad and sorrowful, weeping and in tears, took her stand outside under the entrance porch.

And the venerable Ānanda saw her so standing there, and on seeing her so he said to Māhā-pajāpatī: 'why standest thou there, outside the porch, with swollen feet and covered with dust, sad and sorrowful, weeping and in tears ?'

'Inasmuch, O Ānanda, as the Lord, the Blessed One, does not permit women to renounce their homes and enter the homeless state under the doctrine and discipiine proclaimed by the Tathāgata.'

Then did the venerable Ānanda go up to the place where the Blessed One was, and bow down before the Blessed One, and take his seat on one side. And, so sitting, the venerable Ānanda said to the Blessed One:

'Behold, Lord, Mahā-pajāpatī the Gotamī is standing outside under the entrance porch, with swollen feet and covered with dust, sad and sorrowful, weeping and in tears, inasmuch as the Blessed One does not permit women to renounce their homes and enter the homeless state under the doctrine and discipline proclaimed by the Blessed One. It were well, Lord, if women were to have permission granted to them to do as she desires.'

'Enough, Ānanda! Let it not please thee that women should be allowed to do so.'

[And a second and a third time did Ānanda make the same request, in the same words, and receive the same reply.]

Then the venerable Ānanda thought:' The Blessed One does not give his permission, let me now ask the Blessed One on another ground.' And the venerable Ānanda said to the Blessed One:

'Are women, Lord, capable—when they have gone forth from the household life and entered the homeless state, under the doctrine and discipline proclaimed by the Blessed One—are they capable of realising the fruit of conversion, or of the second Path, or of the third Path, or of Arahatship ?'

'They are capable, Ānanda.'

'If then, Lord, they are capable thereof, since Mahā-pajāpatī the Gotamī has proved herself of great service to the Blessed One, when as aunt and nurse she nourished him and gave him milk, and on the death of his mother suckled the Blessed One at her own breast, it were well, Lord, that women should have permission to go forth from the household life and enter the homeless state, under the doctrine and discipline proclaimed by the Tathāgata.'

'If then, Ānanda, Mahā-pajāpatī the Gotamī take upon herself the Eight Chief Rules, let that be reckoned to her as her initiation.'

Then the venerable Ānanda, when he had learnt from the Blessed One these Eight Chief Rules, went to Mahā-pajāpatī the Gotamī and [told her all that the Blessed One had said].

'Just Ānanda, as a man or a woman, when young and of tender years, accustomed to adorn himself, would, when he had bathed his head, receive with both hands a garland of lotus flowers, or of jasmine flowers or of atimuttaka flowers, and place it on the top of his head; even so do I, Ānanda, take upon me these Eight Chief Rules, never to be transgressed my life long.'

Then the venerable Ānanda returned to the Blessed One, and bowed down before him, and took his seat, on one side. And, so sitting, the venerable Ānanda said to the Blessed One: 'Mahā-pajāpatī the Gotamī, Lord, has taken upon herself the Eight Chief Rules, the aunt of the Blessed One has received the upasampadā initiation.'

'If, Ānanda, women had not received permission to go out from the household life and enter the homeless state, under the doctrine and discipline proclaimed by the Tathāgata, then would the pure religion, Ānanda, have lasted long, the good law would have stood fast for a thousand years. But since, Ānanda, women have now received that permission, the pure religion, Ānanda, will not now last so long, the good law will now stand fast for only five hundred years. Just, Ānanda, as houses in which there are many women and but few men are easily violated by robber burglars; just so, Ānanda, under whatever doctrine and discipline women are allowed to go out from the household life into the homeless state, that religion will not last long. And just, Ānanda, as when the disease called mildew falls upon a field of rice in fine condition, that field of rice does not continue long; just so, Ānanda, under whatsoever doctrine and discipline women are allowed to go forth from the household life into the homeless state, that religion will not last long. And just, Ānanda, as when the disease called blight falls upon a field of sugarcane in good condition, that field of sugarcane does not continue long; just so, Ānanda under whatsoever doctrine and discipline women are allowed to go forth from the household life into the homeless state, that religion does not last long. And just, Ānanda, as a man would in anticipation build an embankment to a great reservoir, beyond which the water should not overpass; just even so, Ānanda, have I in anticipation laid down these Eight Chief Rules for the Bhikkhunīs, their life long not to be overpassed.'" [Vinaya Texts, S.B.E., Vol. xx., pt. iii, pp. 320-326, 1, 2, 3, 4, 1st. para, and paras 5 and 6.]

Education

There was a technical college of the Śākyas in the mango grove. The translators on the authority of the Sumaṅgalavilāsinī, the commentary on the Dīgha Nikāya by Buddhaghoṣa, say, "It was a long terraced mansion made for the learning of crafts."[35] The learning of one or other of the arts was incumbent upon every Śākya youth, otherwise no father would give his daughter in marriage to an idler or ignoramus, as we see from the reply received by King Śuddhodana when he proposed for a bride for the young Prince Siddhārtha. There was also a school for archery at Kapilavastu where the Śākyas were trained.[36] The Śākyas being a kṣatriya tribe devoted to warlike pursuits, and surrounded as they were, by warlike tribes on all sides, the school of archery was necessarily a flourishing institution. The Lalitavistara describes in detail the various sciences and arts beginning with the arts of writing that the young Siddhārtha had to learn. But the whole description, as will be seen, is that of an ideal school which the poet pictured to his imagination, basing the account, no doubt, on the condition of education in India at the time the poet lived. There is nothing in it that might be called particularly Śākya.

Influence of the Buddha's teachings on the Śākyas

The minds of the Śākya royal princes and nobles were so

enlightened by the Buddha that they were able to realise "the perfect fruit of righteousness."[37] Nandupananda and Kuṇḍadana two principal nobles, and other persons of the Śākya clan became recluses.[38] Upāli, son of Atalī, followed their example. Then the other princes and the sons of the chief minister renounced the world.[39] At the request of the Buddha many Śākyas became recluses.[40] They were well provided for.[41] The life of the Śākya recluse was so attractive that Sumaṅgala (reborn in a poor family) became a hermit. They were respected for their simplicity of life.[42] They used to shave their heads, put on yellow robes and carry the alms-bowl.[43] Seldom could they find time to sleep as they had too many duties to attend to.[44] There was a residence at Kapilavastu provided by the community for recluses of all schools.[45]

Buddha and Tissā

Some of the Śākya ladies that left the world and adopted the life of the female ascetic have left behind them poems and songs that are preserved in the Psalms of the Sisters. At the time of the Buddha Gautama,Tissā was born at Kapilavastu among the Śākyas. She renounced the world with Mahā-pajāpatī Gotamī and became spiritually so developed that she attained Arahatship.[46]

Buddha and Abhirūpanandā

Abhirūpanandā was the daughter of Khemaka, the Śākya. She was called Nandā the Fair for her great beauty and amiability. Her beloved kinsman, Carabhūta, died on the day on which she was to choose him from amongst her suitors. She had to leave the world against her will. Though she entered the Order, she could not forget that she was beautiful. Fearing that the Buddha would rebuke her, she used to avoid his presence. The Buddha knew that the time had come for her to acquire knowledge and asked Mahāpajāpatī Gotamī to bring all the Bhikkhunīs before him to receive instruction. Nandā sent a proxy for her. The Buddha said, "Let no one come by proxy." So she was compelled to come to him. The Buddha by his supernatural power conjured up a beautiful woman who became transformed into an old and fading figure. It had the desired effect and she became an Arahat.[47]

Buddha and Therī Mittā

Mittā, born in the royal family of the Śākyas at Kapilavastu, left the world with Mahāpajāpatī Gotamī. After the necessary training, she soon attained Arahatship (saint-ship).[48]

Buddha and Therī Sundari Naṇdā

Sundarī Nandā was born in the royal family of the Śākyas. She was known as the beautiful Nandā. Thinking about the fact that her elder brother, her mother, her brother, her sister and her nephew had renounced the world, she too left it. Even after her renunciation, she was obsessed with the idea of her beauty and would not approach the Lord lest she should be reproached for her folly. The Lord taught her in the same way as he did in the case of Nandā the Fair. She listened to the Master's teachings and enjoyed the benefit of the fruition of the first stage of sanctification. He then instructed her, saying, "Nandā, there is, in this body, not even the smallest essence. It is but a heap of bones covered with flesh and besmeared with blood under the shadow of decay and death." Afterwards she became an Arahat.[49]

Government

The administrative and judicial business of the Śākya clan were carried out in their santhāgāra or Mote-Hall at Kapilavastu. (Buddhist India, p. 19.) A young Brahmin named Ambaṭṭha who went to Kapilavastu on business, had the opportunity of visiting the Mote-Hall of the Śākyas where he saw the young and the old seated on grand seats.[50] The santhāgāra is spoken of as saṁsthāgāra in the Mahāvastu and the Lalitavistara and we find there that five hundred Śākyas usually took their seats in the Hall. Thus, the Mahāvastu describes how thirty-two princes, the sons of a Śākya girl and Rājā Kola of Benares, came to settle in Kapilavastu (Śākyānām samudācāra), they presented themselves before the Śākya council (Śākyapariṣā or Śākyapariṣad) where sat together five hundred Śākya leaders to transact some important business. A new Mote-Hall of the śākyas was raised at Kapilavastu when the Buddha was dwelling at the Nigrodhārāma in the Mahāvana which was close to it. At their request, the Buddha inaugurated the hall and a series of ethical discourses lasting the whole of the night, were delivered by him, Ānanda and Moggallāna.[51]

The Lalitavistara also gives the same number, five hundred as the number of the members of the Śākya council. Thus we are told that when the young Siddhārtha was seated in the council hall (saṁsthāgāra) with the Śākyas in council assembled, then the Śākya elders urged upon the king the advisability of getting the prince married early in order that he might not get out of the world and that he might become a great sovereign (cakra-varttī). Thereupon King śuddhodana asked them to look for a suitable bride. Upon this, the Lalitavistara asserts, the five hundred Śākyas said each of them that his own girl was beautiful and was a fit mate for the prince.[52] From these two stories it appears clear that the number of members in the Śākya council was fixed at five hundred. The pariṣad or council of the Licchavis appears to have been larger, but the system of administration seems to be very much the same, though there was this great difference that while at Vaiśālī everyone called himself a rājā, at Kapilavastu people had a distinct headman called the rājā. That King Pasenadi of Kosala should marry one of the daughters of the Śākya chiefs, was decided in the council. Among the Śākyas, there was only one chief who bore the title of rājā, and was elected by the people. According to Dr. Rhys Davids, he ñad to preside over the sessions and when no sessions were held, he had to conduct the business of the state. Once Bhaddiya, a young cousin of the Buddha, took the title of rājā and Śuddhodana was styled a rājā, although he was a simple citizen, Śuddhodana the Śākiyan.[53] In the opinion of Dr. Rhys Davids, all the important places had a Mote-Hall "or pavilion covered with a roof but with no walls in which to conduct their business." The local affairs of the villages were conducted in open assembly, consisting of the householders, "held in the groves ......which formed so distinctive a feature of each village in the long and level alluvial plain."[54] In the time of the Chinese travellers, Fā-Hien, Sung-Yun and Hiuen Tsang there was no central government at Kapilavastu. There existed a congregation of priests and about ten families of laymen.[55] Each town appointed its own ruler and there was no supreme ruler.[56]

Dr. D.R. Bhāndārkar says that kula or clan sovereignty was prominent among the Śākyas. Kula, which was more extensive than the family, was the lowest, political unit amongst the political saṁghas. To quote his words, kula "denotes not simply the domination of a chief over his clan but also and principally his supremacy over the territory occupied by that clan." The Śākya country was governed by one ruler but was not solely occupied by the Śākyas, there were brahmins, artisans and traders.[57]

The Śākyas and their Neighbours

It appears from the Mahāvastu (Vol. II, p. 76) that Koliya and Licchavi youngmen also showed their prowess at the tournament held to test the knowledge of Prince Siddhārtha before his marriage. It seems that the Koliyas and the Licchavis were on terms of close relationship with the Śākyas. The Koliyas, as we have seen, were of kindred origin and the Licchavis from their living in the country to the south-east of the Śākya territory, most probably often became intimate with the Śākyas.

The Śākyas and Kośala

The Kośala country bordered on the region occupied by the Śākyas and there were mutual jealousies between the two peoples that often developed into war. Thus we are told that the Śākyas became the vassals of King Pasenadi of Kosala who received homage from them and they treated him in the same way as the king treated the Buddha. (Dialogues of the Buddha, pt. III., p. 80.) The Tibetan books have preserved a story of the Kośala king who visited the capital of the Śākyas. Once Pasenadi, king of Kosala, carried away by his horse reached

Kapilavastu alone, and roaming' about hither and thither, came to the garden of Mahānāman. Here he saw the beautiful Mallikā who was well versed in the śāstras and asked her as to whose garden it was and was told that it belonged to Śākya Mahānāman. He then got down and wanted some water to wash his feet with. She brought it. Again she was asked to bring some water with which to wash his face and she brought it and the king washed his face with it. Afterwards he wanted some water to drink which was brought for him in a leaf-cup. Then she was requested by the king to rub his feet which she willingly did. Hardly, had she touched his feet when he fell asleep. She thought that the king might have enemies and she closed the gate when the cries of 'open' were heard by her from a multitude of people who wanted to rush in. She did not open the gate. The king awoke and asked her what the matter was. She told him what she did. Her shrewdness and wisdom were admired by the king. Coming to know that she was a slave girl of Mahānāman, he went to her master and expressed his desire to marry her. The master agreed and the king took her with him in great pomp to Śrāvastī. But the king's mother was highly displeased as her son had married a slave girl. When Mallikā went to pay respects to her and touched her feet, she at once fell asleep. When she awoke, she thought that such a touch could not but be of a maiden of noble birth, worthy of the family of Kośala. At that time Pasenadi had a wife named Varśikā, famous for her beauty, besides Mallikā, well known for her wonderful touch. Shortly afterwards, a son was born to Mallikā who was called Virudhaka or the high-born.[58] This story is nothing but a Tibetan version of the story of Pasenadi and Vāsabhakhattiyā.

We have already seen how Pasenadi wished to establish a connection with the Buddha's family by marriage and wanted to marry one of the daughters of the Śākya chiefs. The Śākyas afterwards decided that it was beneath their dignity to marry one of their daughters to the king of Kośala.[59] A girl named Vāsabhakhattiyā, a daughter by a slave girl of one of their leading chiefs, Mahānāman, was sent by the Śākyas to the king.

But King Pasenadi had great admiration for the Buddha who was a Śākya. The king went to him and rubbed his feet out of devotion to him. He further said, "Worldly life is full of civil strifes-as people have not yet realised the Dharma of the Tathāgata."[60]

Viḍūḍabha, the son of Pasenadi and Vāsabhakhattiyā, when he came of age, found out that the Śākyas had deceived his father Pasenadi by giving him a daughter of a slave girl to marry. He resolved to take revenge upon them. Viḍūḍabha, therefore, wanted to get possession of the throne for himself, and with the aid of his commander-in-chief, Dīrgha Cārāyana or Dīgha Kārāyana, he deposed his father who fled with his life from Śrāvastī, the Kośala capital; he set out for Rājagaha, the Magadhan capital. "It was late when he came to the city, and the gates were shut and lying down in a shed, exhausted by exposure to wind and sun, he died there." (Jātaka, Vol. IV, p. 96.) After ascending the throne, Viḍūḍabha invaded the Śākya country, took their city and slew many of them without any distinction of age or sex.

Having annihilated the Śākyas, five hundred Śākya girls were taken by him for his harem to celebrate the victory. The girls who were full of rage and hatred said that they would never submit to the king. They abused him and his family. On hearing this, the king was enraged and gave orders to kill them. The officers, according to the orders of the king, cut off their hands and feet and threw them into a ditch. The girls sought the aid of the Buddha who saw their distress and ordered a Bhikkhu to go to them and to preach before them the most profound doctrine of the Buddha. They having heard the instructions of the Buddha, attained "purity of the eyes of law." They then died and were all re-born in heaven.[61] Viḍūḍabha himself is said to have perished by a sudden flood along with numerous Kośalan followers.

There is a different version of the above account stated in the Viḍūḍakāvadānaṁ of the Avadānakalpalatā.[62] According to it, Viḍūḍaka slaughtered seventy-seven thousand Śākyas and stole one thousand boys and girls. One day when he was eulogising his own prowess in his court, the stolen Śākya girls said, "Why is this pride when death is inevitable to a man bound by action?" The king heard this and became angry and ordered his men to cut off the hands of the girls.

Rhys Davids says that the motives which led Viḍūḍaka to attack and conquer the Śākyas were most probably similar to the political motives which afterwards persuaded Ajātaśatru to attack and conquer the Licchavis of Vaiśālī.[63] We think that the only reason of Viḍūḍabha's invading the Śākya country and massacring a large number of the Śākyas was that they when asked by his father King Pasenadi to give him a Śākya girl, deceived him (Pasenadi) by sending Vāsabhakhattiyā, a girl of low birth.

It is stated in the Mahāvaṁsa Ṭīkā that during the lifetime of the Buddha, some Śākyas being oppressed by Viḍuḍabha, fled to the Himālayas where they built a beautiful city which was known as the Moriyanagara (Mauryanagara) on account of the spot always resounding with the cries of peacocks.[64] The Buddhisis hold that Aśoka and the Buddha were of the same family as the former was descended from Candragupta who was a son of the queen of one of the kings of Moriyanagara.[65]

REFERENCES

1. Lefmann, Lalitavistara, pp. 20-22.
2. "Te Bodhisattva Devaputtrāsca sarvasmiṁ Jambudvīpe ṣoṛaśajanaadesu yāni kāniciduccoccāni rājakulāni tāni sarvāni vyavalokayantaḥ (tāni) sarvāni sadoṣ āṇyarākṣaḥ." (Lalitavistara, edited by Lefmann, pp. 22-23.)
3. Lalitavistara, edited by Lefmann, pp. 26-27.
4. Dīgha Nikāya (P.T.S.), Vol. II, p. 165.
5. Mahāsammatarājassa vaṁsajo hi mahāmuni
   Kappādismiṁ hi rājāsi Mahāśammatanāmako,
   Rojo ca Vararojo ca tathā Kalyāṇaka duve,
   Uposatho ca Mandhātā Carakopacarā duve,
   Cetiyo Mucalo ceva Mahāmucalanāmako,
   Mucalindo Sagaro ceva Sāgaradevanāmako,
   Bharato Aṅgiraso ceva Rucī ca surucī pi ca,

6 Patāpo Mahāpatāpo Panada ca tathā duve,
Sudassanā ca Nerū ca tathā eva duve duve
Accimā cāti rājāno tassa puttapaputtakā
Asaṁkheyyāyukā ete aṭṭhavīsati bhūmipā
Kusāvatiṁ Rājagahaṁ Mithilaṁ cāpi āvasuṅ,
Tato sataiṁ ca rājāno chapaññāsa ca saṭṭhi ca
Caturāsīti sahassāni chattiṁsā ca tato pare,
Dvattiṁsa aṭṭhavisaṁ ca dvāvīsati tato pare
Aṭṭhārasa sattarasa paṇṇarasa catuddasa
Nava satta dvādasaṁ ca pañcavisa tato pare,
Pañcavīsaṁ dvādasaṁ ca dvādasaṁ ca navāpi ca,
Caturāsīti sahassāni Makhādevādīkā pi ca
Caturāsīti sahassāni Kalārajanakādayo,
Solasa yāva Okkākā paputtā rāsito ime
Visuṁ visuṁ pure rajjaṁ kamato anusāsisuṁ,
Okkāmukho jeṭṭhaputto Okkākassāsi bhūpati,
Nipuṇo Candimā Candamukho ca Sivisaṁjayo
Vessantaro mahārāja Jālī ca Sīhavahano
Sīhassaro ca iccete tassa puttapaputtakā.
Dve asīti sahassāni Sīhassarassa rājino
Puttapaputtarājāno, Jayaseno tadantimo.
Ete Kapilavatthusmiṁ Sākyarājāti vissutā.
Sīhahanu mahārājā Jayasenassa atrajo,
Jayasenassa dhītā ca nāmenāsi Yasodharā.
Devadahe Devadahasakko nāmāsi bhūpati,
Añjano cātha Kaccānā āsuṁ tassa sutā duve.
Mahesī cāsi Kaccānā rañño Sīhahanussa sā,
Āsi Añjauasakkassa mahesī sā Yasodharā.
Añjanassa duve dhītā Māyā cātha Pajāpatī
Puttā duve Daṇḍapāṇi Suppabuddho ca Sākiyo.
Pañca puttā duve dhītā āsuṁ Sīhahanussa tu:
Suddhodano Dhotodano Sakkasukkāmitodano,
Amitā Pamitā cāti, ime pañca imā duve.
Suppabuddhassa Sakkassa mahesī Amitā ahu,
Tassāsuṁ Bhaddakaccānā Devadatto duve sutā.
Māyā Pajāpatī ceva Suddhodanamahesiyo,
Suddhodanamahārañño putto Māyāya no jino.
Mahāsammatavaṁsaṁhi asaṁbbinne mahāmuni
Evaṁ pavatte saṁjāto Sahbakhattiyamuddhani.
Siddhatthassa Kumārassa bodhisattassa sā ahu
Mahesī Bhaddakaccānā, putto tassāsi Rāhulo."

(Mabāvaṁsa, Edited by W. Geiger, pp. 12-14.)

6 Viṣṇupurāṇa, pt. IV., Chap. IV, Verse 48.

7. H.H. Wilson, Viṣṇupurāṇa, Vol. IV, Chapter XXII, pp. 167-172.

8. It will be observed that Opura, Nipura, Karaṇḍaka, Ulkāmukha and Hastikaśirṣa are represented as sons of King Sujāta in a former passage of the Mahāvastu. Here the relationship between each prince and the one mentioned next is represented as that of father and son. We do not vouch for the historical accuracy of the Mahāvastu.
9. Jātaka, Vol. V, p. 219.
10. "Yo so vādityavandhunām Śākyānāṁ paramomuniḥ." (Mahāvastu. II, p. 303.)
11. "Śuddhodanassa rāgño Ikṣvākujassa putro Māyāya Śākyakalanandijanano śākyobhūtśākyasukumāro." (Mahāvastu, III, p. 247.)
12. Ādityagotra tejasvī Ikṣvākukulasambhavo jātītaḥ kṣatriyo agro Bhagavāṁ agrapudgalo." (*Ibid.*, III, p. 246.)
    Dr. H.C. Ray Chaudhuri points out (Political History of Ancient India, p. 48) that in the Sutta-Nipāta, the Buddha refers to his people as "Ādiccas by family, Sākiyas by birth."
13. Suttavibhaṅga, Pācittiya II, 2, Vinaya-Piṭaka, Oldenberg, Vol. IV, p. 6.
14. Divyāvadāna, p. 548, lines 20-32.
15. *Ibid.*, pp. 90, 390.
16. *Ibid.*, p. 67.
17. Buddhacarita, Book I, Verse 2.
18. Travels of Fā-Hien and Sang-Yun, by S. Beal, pp. 88-98.
19. Travels of Fā-Hien by S. Beal, pp. 85-87.
20. S. Beal's *Records of the Western World*, Vol. II, pp. 13-14.
21. Watters on Yuan Chawang, Vol. II, p. 4.
22. Beal's Records of the Western World, Vol. II, pp. 14 15.
23. *Ibid.*, Vol. II, p. 12.
24. Buddhist India, pp. 20-21.
25. The Book of the Kindred Sayings, pt. I, p. 2-3.
26. Jātaka (Cowell), Vol. VI, pp. 246-247.
27. S. Beal's Records of the Western World, Vol. II, p. 14.
28. Rockhill, Life of the Buddha, p. 117.
29. Rhys Davids, Buddhist India, p. 20.
30. *Ibid.*, p. 20.
31. Śuddhodanassa pramadā pradhānā nārīsahasreṣu hi sāgraprāptā." Lalitavistara, p. 28.
32. Lalitavistara, pp. 243 ff.
33. Mahāvastu, II, 48.
34. Jātaka (Cowell), Vol. IV, pp. 91-92.
35. Dialogues of the Buddha, Vol. IV, pt. III, p. III. f. n.
36. Waiters, On Yuan Chwang, Vol. II. p. 13.
37. S.B.E. Vol. XIX, p. *226*.
38. *Ibid.*, pp. 226-227.
39. *Ibid.*, p. 227.
40. *Ibid.*, pp. 226-227.

41. Psalms of the Brethren, p. 81.
42. Ibid., p. 47.
43. Mricchakoṭika, Act VIII, pp. 1215-126. (Jīvānarnda Vidyasāgara's edition.)
44. Chārudatta, Act III, p. 53.
45. Buddhist India, p. 20.
46. Psalms of the Sisters, pp. 12-13.
47. Ibid, pp. 22-23.
48. Ibid, p. 29.
49. Ibid, pp. 55-57.
50. Dialogues of the Buddha, I, p. 113.
51. Buddhist.India, p. 20.
52. Lalitavistara; Edited by Lefmann, p. 136 (line 10) to p. 137 (line 10).
53. Buddhist India, p. 19.
54. *Ibid.*, p. 20.
55. S. Beal's Travels of Fā-Hien and Sung Yun, pp. 85-87.
56. S. Beal, Records of the Western World, Vol. II, p. 14.
57. Carmichael Lectures, 1918, pp. 162-164.
58. Rockhill, Life of the Buddha, pp. 75-77. According to Pāli canonical literature, Virudhaka was the son of Pasenadi by another wife named Vāsabhakhattiyā who was given in marriage to Pasenadi by the Śākyas.
59. Rhys Davids, Buddhist India, p. 11.
60. Majjhima Nikāya (P.T.S.), Vol. II, pt. I, pp. 118-124.
61. Beal's Records of the Western World, Vol. II, pp. 11-12.
62. 11th Pallava, Avadānakalpalatā (Bibliotheca Indica series).
63. Buddhist India, pp. 11-12.
64. Mahāvaṁsa Ṭīkā, (Ceylonese edition) pp. 119-121.
65. S. Bēal's Records of the Western World, Vol. I, Introduction, p. xvii.

CHAPTER 6

THE BULIS, THE KOLIYAS, THE MORIYAS, THE BHAGGAS, THE KĀLĀMAS[1]

Five Minor Clans

Besides the clans of which some account has been given in the previous chapters, there are a few others occasionally referred to in the Buddhist texts. particularly in the Book of the Great Decease. They may be enumerated as follows:—

1. The Bulis of Allakappa.
2. The Koliyas of Devadaha and Rāmagāma.
3. The Moriyas of Pipphalivana.
4. The Bhaggas of Suṁsumāra Hill.
5. The Kālāmas of Kesaputta.

"There are," as Dr. Rhys Davids points out, "several other names of tribes of which it is not yet known whether they were clans or under monarchical government. We have only one instance of any tribe, once under a monarchy, reverting to the independent state. And whenever the supreme power in a clan became hereditary, the result seems always to have been an absolute monarchy, without legal limitations of any kind."[2]

Their claim to kṣatriya rank. Their solicitude for he remains of the Buddha

The five clans or tribes mentioned above are mere passing shadows in early Buddhist records, there being hardly any data for an historical account of them. The Book of the Great

Decease[3] mentions the Bulis of Allakappa, the Koliyas of Rāmagāma and the Moriyas of Pipphalivana, along with the Licchavis of Veśālī, the Śākyas of Kapilavatthu and others, as so many distinct kṣatriya clans or corporations, claiming shares of the bodily remains of the Buddha Gautama on the ground that like the deceased master they were all of the kṣatriya caste. The message sent by each of these clans to the Mallas of Kuśinārā is as follows:—"The Blessed One belonged to the soldier caste, we too are of the soldier caste. We are worthy to receive a portion of the relics of the Blessed One. Over the remains of the Blessed One will we put up a sacred cairn and in their honour, will we celebrate a feast."[4] The claimants are said to have obtained their respective shares of relics, which they enshrined with customary ceremonies. The Bulis of Allakappa and the Koliyas of Rāmagāma had the good fortune to obtain one share each of the bodily remains while the Moriyas of Pipphalivana had to be satisfied with a share of the ashes as they were rather late in sending their messenger to Kuśinārā. One of their descendants—a Moriya of Pāṭaliputra—was more fortunate. The existing Buddhist traditions all agree in bearing out the fact of redistribution of the relics of the Buddha in the time of King Aśoka Moriya (Maurya) with the exception of those enshrined at Rāmagāma by the Koliyas. The legend from the Aśokāvadāna which has been summarised by late Dr. Vincent Smith is as follows:—"The Avadāna story is that when King Aśoka desired to distribute the sacred relics of the body of Buddha among the eighty-four thousand stūpas erected by himself, he opened the stūpa of the Urn, wherein King Ajātaśatru had enshrined the cremation relics collected from seven of the eight original stūpas. The eighth, that at Rāmagāma, was defended by the guardian Nāgas, who would not allow it to be opened. The relics thus withdrawn from the stūpa of the Urn, were distributed among eighty-four thousand stūpas, 'resplendent as the autumn clouds,' which were erected in a single day by the descendant of the Mauryas."[5] A similar legend can be gathered from the Sinhalese chronicles and other late Pāli works, particularly Buddhaghoṣa's commentary[6] on the Mahāparinibbāṇa Suttanta. The evidence of the Pāli Canonical texts themselves amply corroborates the truth of the later legends barring certain details which have a special importance of their own. The epilogues attached to the Book of the Great Decease and the Buddha-vaṁsa prove that the sacred relics bf Buddha's body were, after their re-distribution, enshrined all over northern India from Gandhāra to Kaliṅga.[7]

The Bhaggas

In the Bhīṣmaparva of the Mahābhārata, mention is made of the Bhargas along with other tribes, *e.g.*, the Andhras, the Kirātas, the Kośalas, the Gāndhāras, the Sauvīras, the Sindhus, and so forth (9th chapter, p. 822). The Bhaggas of the Suṁsumāra Hill have been casually referred to in some suttas of the Majihima and the Saṁyutta Nikāyas.[8] There can be no doubt about the fact that the Suṁsumāra Hill was used as a fort. It was situated in a deer park at Bhesākalāvana. In the life time of the Buddha, Prince Bodhi, son of Udena, ruled over the Bhaggas, apparently as his father's viceroy. He became one of the followers of the Buddha.[9] When the Buddha was amongst the Bhaggas, the householder, Nakulapitā, went to him and spoke to him thus, "I have become old and wearied, let the Lord admonish me and instruct me for my eternal happiness." He afterwards became one of the devotees of the Master at Bhesakaḷāvana.[10]

The Kālāmas

As regards the Kālāmas of Kesaputta, our information is very meagre. There is but a bare mention of them in the Nikāyas. No doubt they existed at the time of the Buddha as a distinct tribe or people. Probably their home or seat of government was in a mountain fastness, not far from the upper Gangetic valley. We are quite in the dark about their origin and other particulars. We must bear in mind that in ancient India, the tribe lent its name to the place of its settlement, that is to say, the tribal name became local. The word 'Kesaputta' should be taken in its plural form, denoting the land of the Kesaputtas. The etymology of the name indicates that the tribe traced its descent from the Kesins, a tribe connected with the Pañcālas.[11] In the Mahāparinibbāṇa Suttanta,[12] and other Buddhist texts, ancient and modern, we are introduced to a renowned religious teacher named Ālāra Kālāma (Sanskrit, Arāḍa Kālāma). One caravan merchant named Pukkusa, a young Mallian, was a disciple of Ālāra Kālāma. Much emphasis was laid by Pukkusa on the spiritual attainments of Kālāma. He said that his preceptor's ecstatic trance was so very deep and profound that a long train of heavily laden carts passed by him but he did not perceive them.[13] Ālāra Kālāma might have been a Haṭhayogin. Buddhaghoṣa says that he was called Ālāra because he was a Dighapiṅgala or a hermit of long standing, Kālāma being his family name.[14] It would seem clear that Ālāra Kālāma came of the Kālāma tribe or that he was in some way connected with it. The Buddhist texts represent the Kālāmas as worshippers of the Buddha Gautama who was before his enlightenment, a disciple of Kālāma, a renowned teacher of philosophy.[15]

The Koliyas

The Sumaṅgalavilāsinī (pp. 260-262) states that the eldest of the five daughters of Okkāka by the chief queen contracted leprosy (kuṭṭharoga). The four sons of Okkāka, who were brothers of the eldest daughter, apprehending that if they lived with her, they might contract the disease, took her on the pretext of going to a garden, to a forest and there confined her in an underground closet. At that time, Rāmā, king of Benares, got leprosy and being detested by his wives and relations, left the kingdom, entered the forest and there eating leaves and fruits of wild trees, was soon cured of the disease and began to live in the forest. One night he heard the voice of the woman and in the morning, going in the direction of the voice, found the princess in the underground closet. He cured her by means of those leaves and fruits by which he himself was cured and married her. He then built a town in the forest removing a big Kola tree. Inasmuch as the town was built on the site of the

Kola tree, it came to be called Kolanagara and the descendants of the king came to be known as Koliyas.

The Mahāvastu tells us that a daughter of a certain Śākya noble who was handsome and endowed with all good qualities, was attacked with leprosy. The physicians were treating her but the disease was incurable. They prescribed ointments and laxative medicines for her. Sores appeared all over the body. The people began to hate her. She was taken by all the brothers in a palanquin to a spot close to the Himālayas. They dug out a subterranean room and she was left there with abundance of food and water. They put planks to block the path leading to the interior of the cave and the doors were closed and they put a big heap of dust in front of the cave and then they returned to Kapila vastu. She living in that stuffy room in the heat of the cave, was cured of leprosy. Her body became altogether soreless and she resumed her former beauty. A tiger got scent and it came towards her. Having got the scent of a human being, the tiger began to throw off the heap of dust. Not far from the cave lived a royal sage named Kola who was possessed of five supernatural knowledges and had attained the four meditations. His hermitage was full of vegetables, flowers and fruits. It was very charming. The sage while wandering hither and thither in the vicinity of the hermitage, came to the cave where the Śākya girl lived. The tiger threw off the heap of dust with its legs, leaving only the plank. The tiger saw the sage who compelled it to leave that spot and go away. As the sage saw the tiger throwing off the dust, curiosity arose in his mind. Then the plank having been removed by the sage, the door of the cave was opened. The Śākya girl was seen in all her great beauty. The sage asked, "Well lady, who are you ?" She replied, "I am a woman and I am the daughter of a certain Śākya of Kapilavastu. Having fallen a victim to leprosy, I have been left here to spend the rest of my life." Seeing the exquisite beauty of the Śākya girl, he became very much attached to her. Coming in contact with the Śākya girl the sage lost the power of meditation and his supernatural knowledge. He then went to the hermitage along with the Śākyagirl who lived in the hermitage with the sage Kola. Sixteen pairs of twin sons were born to them. Thirty-two sons of the sage were beautiful and had plaited hairs. The sons of the sage, when they grew up, were sent to Kapilavastu by their mother who said to them thus, "Sons, go to the city of Kapilavastu where live my father and your maternal grandfather. There the sons of such and such persons are your maternal uncles and they are Śākya nobles and your relations. They will provide you with means to maintain yourselves." She trained them thus in the manners of the Śākyas, "You will approach a Śākya gentleman in this way. This is the proper way to salute. In this way you should sit down." Having trained them in the manners of the Śākyas, they were allowed to go. They saluted their parents, went round them and then went away. They in course of time reached Kapilavastu. They entered Kapilavastu with their beautiful appearance. The vast crowd seeing the sons of the sage received them and said, "These sons of the sage are beautiful and have plaited hairs." They went to the Mote-Hall of the Śākyas surrounded by a vast crowd. Five hundred Sākyas assembled in the Mote-Hall for some business. They approached the Śākya assembly in the way they were taught by their mother. The Śākya assembly became astounded to see the Śākya manners in them. The Śākya assembly asked the sons of the sage thus, "Where-from do you come ?" Being instructed they answered thus, "We are sons of Kola, the royal sage, who has his hermitage somewhere at the foot of the Himālayas. Our mother is the daughter of a certain Śākya." Hearing them, the Śākyas became pleased. Their maternal grandfather, who was one of the leading Śākyas and whose lineage was noble, was still alive. The royal sage Kola gave his eldest son, the kingdom of Benares and he went out of the kingdom for ordination. The Śākyas were then very glad to learn that they were born of the royal sage and not of persons of inferior rank. They said, "They must also be Śākyas. They belong to the same caste to which we belong. Let them be given Śākya girls and appointments." They were given Śākya brides, cultivable lands and villages. As the princes were born of the sage Kola, they were known as Koliyas. (Mahāvastu, Vol. I, pp. 352-355.)

It is stated in the Introduction to the Kunāla Jātaka that the Koliyas used to dwell in the Kola tree (Kolarukkhe). Hence they came to be called 'Koliyas' or dwellers in 'jujube' (Kolī) trees (Jātaka, Faüsboll, V, p. 413).

From the Thera-Gāthā (Verse 529, p. 56), it appears that the territories of the Śākyas and the Koliyas lay side by side and the river Rohiṇī formed the boundary between these two clans. *("Passantu tam Sākiyā Koliyā ca pacchāmukhaṁ Rohiṇi-yaṁ tarantaṁ.")*

Feud between the Koliyas and the Śākya

The river Rohiṇī flowed between the territories of the Koliyas and the Śākyas. Both the tribes used water of the river for cultivation and they had the river confined by a single dam. In the month of Jeṭṭhamula, when the crops began to droop, the Koliya and the Śākya labourers assembled together. Then the people of the Koliya said, "Should this water be drawn off on both sides, it will not prove sufficient for both us and you. But our crops will thrive with a single watering; give us then the water." The people of Kapilavatthu said, "When you have filled your garners with corn, we shall hardly have the courage to come with ruddy gold, emeralds and copper coins and with baskets and sacks in our hands, to hang about your doors. Our crops too will thrive with a single watering; give us the water." "We will not give it," they said. "Neither will we," said the others. As words thus ran high, one of them rose up and struck another a blow, and he in turn struck a third and thus it was that what with interchanging blows and spitefully touching on the origin of their princely families they increased the tumult. The Koliya labourers said, "Be off with your people of Kapilavatthu, men who like dogs, jackals, and such like beasts, cohabited with their own sisters. What will their elephants and horses, their shields and spears avail against us ?" The Śākya labourers replied, "Nay, do you, wretched lepers, be off with your children, destitute and ill-conditioned fellows, who like brute beasts had their dwelling in a hollow jujube tree (Kolī). What shall their elephants and horses, their spears and shields avail against us?" So, they went and told the councillors appointed to such services and they reported it to the princes of their tribes. Then the Śākyas said; "We will show them how strong and mighty are the men who cohabited with their sisters," and they sallied forth, ready for the fray. And the Koliyas said, "We will show them how strong and mighty are they who dwelt in the hollow of a jujube tree," and they too sallied forth ready for the fight.

Another version of the story is this:—"When the female slaves of the Śākyas and Koliyas came to the river to fetch water, and throwing the coils of cloth that they carried on their heads upon the ground, were seated and pleasantly conversing, a certain woman took another's cloth, thinking that it was her own; and when owing to this a quarrel arose, each claiming the coil of cloth hers, gradually the people of the two cities, the serfs and the labourers, the attendants, headmen, councillors and viceroys, all of them sallied forth ready for battle." Now, it was at eventide that they would be sallying forth, ready for the fray. At this time the Blessed One came to the spot from Sāvatthī, sat cross-legged in the air between the two hosts. The Śākyas could recognise him and at once threw down their arms with the words, "Let the Koliyas slay us or roast us alive." The Koliyas too on seeing the Buddha acted in the same way. The Lord instructed them, quelled the feud and brought about a reunion. (Jātaka, Cowell's edition. Vol. V, p. 219 foll.)

The Mahāvastu tells us that there was a Koliya prince who was a rival to Gautama Buddha in the art of arrow shooting but he was defeated along with others. (Edited by Senart, Vol. II, pp. 76-77.)

The Udāna tells us that the daughter of the king of the Koliyas (Koliyadhītā) named Suppavāsā who remained pregnant for seven years, was terribly suffering from labour-pains for seven years. She thought that the Buddha and his disciple after undergoing such sufferings, were freed from them and she further thought that there was Nibbāṇa but there was no such pain in it. She requested her husband to go to the Buddha who was then dwelling at Kuṇḍi and inform him of it. The Buddha being informed desired that she should give birth to a healthy son without any pain. As soon as the Buddha expressed such a desire, she gave birth to a healthy son without pain. The husband returned home and found Suppavāsā with a healthy son. Suppavāsā again requested "her husband to go to the Buddha and invite him with his followers to her house for seven days and her husband was also instructed by her to inform the Buddha of her easy delivery of a son. The Buddha accepted the invitation and he was sumptuously fed in her house. Sāriputta who also went to her house asked the son, "Are you all right? Have you any want? Are you free from suffering?" The son answered, "I had to live for seven years in a jar of blood." Suppavāsā was greatly pleased seeing her son talking with Sāriputta. The Buddha asked her whether she would desire to have any more sons. She expressed her desire to have seven such sons. The Buddha then left her (Udāna, P.T.S., pp. 15-18).

According to some, the name, the Koliyas of Rāmagāma, indicates that the tribe came originally from the same ethnic group as the Koliyas of Devadaha. According to Cunningham, Rāmagāma (Rāmagrāma) is identical with Deokāli.[16] There are no historical data for ascertaining the political relations of the Koliyas of Rāmagāma (Rāmagrāma) with the Śākyas.

It is stated in the Mahāparinibbāṇa Suttanta of the Digha Nikāya that the inhabitants of Rāmagāma belonged to the serpent race.[17]

The Moriyas

The Mahāvaṁsa commentary[18] furnishes us with some interesting information about the origin of the Moriyas of

Pipphalivana and their connection with the Maurya rulers of Magadha. We are told that there are theories about the derivation of the name Moriya. According to one theory, the name is derived from 'modiya' meaning pleasing or delightful. The Moriyas were a people who lived in a delightful land. According to the other, the name is connected with 'mora' peacock. The people came to be known as Moriyas from the fact that the place, where they founded their city, always resounded with the cries of peacocks. It is said that some of the Śākya princes, being hard pressed by Prince Viḍūḍabha, the ambitious and cruel usurper of the throne of Kośala, fled to the Himālayan region where they built a new city round a lake in the forest tract abounding in pepul trees.

The above legend about the origin of the Moriyas of Pipphalivana cannot be accepted as a historical fact. When the Moriyas are introduced to us in the Book of the Great Decease, they are contemporaries and powerful rivals of the Śākyas of Kapilavatthu or Kapilavastu. Moreover, Viḍūḍabha's invasion of Kapilavatthu and the carnage committed upon its citizens took place, if the tradition is at all to be believed, shortly before the demise of the Buddha. There may be some truth in the implied suggestion that the Moriyas were, in some way, connected with the Śākyas of Kapilavatthu. With the advance of ethnological researches, it may be found that the matrimonial alliance of the Śākyas with the neighbouring hill peoples brought some new tribes into existence. Further, the Mahāvaṁsa commentary traces the origin of the Maurya rulers of Magadha to the Moriyas of Pipphalivana. Candagutta, the founder of the Maurya dynasty, was born of the chief queen of the Moriyan king of Pipphalivana. This account conflicts with the evidence of Viśākhadatta's Mudrārākṣasa where Candragupta is represented as a Vṛṣala,[19] a person of low birth, an illegitimate son of the last Nanda king by a śūdra woman named Murā. How far Viśākhadatta's account represents the true state of things, is a controversial point. But there are many instances where such misconception of history resulted from a conjectural etymology of personal and dynastic names. It appears that the royal family of the Nandas was connected by matrimonial alliance with the Moriyas of Pipphalivana, and this may derive some support from the fact that in earlier and later times, the rulers of Magadha found it necessary to establish friendly relations, through marriage, with the neighbouring clans, *e.g.*, the Licchavis of Vaiśālī and the Videhans of Mithilā.

It seems certain that the minor clans had much in common with those dealt with in the previous chapters. Their social customs, religious beliefs, laws and administrative systems, were, in all likelihood, the same. It is left to the future historian of India to decide how far the clans under review were instrumental in colonising Bengal, Bihar and Assam.

REFERENCES

1. I have derived substantial help from Dr. B.M. Barua while engaged in writing this chapter.
2. T.W. Rhys Davids, Buddhist India, p. 23.
3. Digha Nikāya, II, p. 164 foll.
4. Buddhist Suttas, S.B.E., Vol. XI, p. 132.
5. Vincent Smith, Aśoka, 2nd edition, pp. 251-252.
6. Sumaṅgala-vilāsinī, Burmese edition, pt. II, p. 183, foll.
7. Dīgha-Nikāya, II, p. 167. The Buddhavaṁsa and the Cariyāpiṭaka, J.P.T.S., 1882, p. 68.
8. Majjhima Nikāya, Vol. I, pp. 332-338 ; Vol. II, pt. I, pp. 91-97. Saṁyutta Nikāya, pt. IV, p. 116; *Ibid.*, pt. III, pp. 1-5.
9. Bodhirājakumāra Sutta, Majjhima Nikāya, Vol. II, p. 91. Faüsboll, Jātaka, Vol. III, p. 157.
10. Saṁyutta Nikāya, pt. III, pp. 1-5.
11. Vedic Index, Vol. I, p. 468.
12. Dīgha-Nikāya, Vol. II, pp. 130-131.
13. Buddhist Suttas, S.B.E., Vol. XI., p. 76.
14. *Ibid.*, p. 75. f.n.
15. Kern, Manual of Indian Buddhism, p. 18.
16. Cunningham, Ancient Geography of India, p. 423.
17. Dīgha Nikāya (P.T.S., Vol. II, p. 167.
18. Mahāvaṁsa Ṭīkā (Sinhalese Edition), pp. 119 foll.
19. Act III, pp. 134-136, 141-143, etc.

CHAPTER 7

THE MADRAS[1]

The Madras in Vedic Times

The Madras are an ancient kṣatriya tribe of the Vedic times. They are not mentioned in the early Vedic Saṁhitās but the Vaṁśa Brāhmaṇa of the Sāmaveda mentions an ancient Vedic teacher, Madragāra Śauṅgāyani from whom, as we shall see in the chapter on the Kāmbojas, Aupamanyava, the Kāmboja, received the Vedic lore. From the name Madragāra, scholars infer[2] that Śauṅgāyani belonged to the Madra tribe, and this very fact that Vedic learning had spread so much among the Madras as to give one of them a respected position in the list of ancient teachers, shows that the Madras belonged to the Vedic Aryandom before the age of the Brāhmaṇas. Their Vedic learning in the Brāhmaṇa times is testified to by the Śatapatha Brāhmaṇa where we find that sages of Northern India, most probably of the Kuru-Pañcāla district, repaired to the Madra country to receive their education in Vedic learning. In the Bṛhadāraṇyaka-Upaniṣad,[3] Uddālaka Āruṇi told Yājñavalkya, "We dwelt among the Madras in the houses of Paṭañcala Kāpya, studying the sacrifice." And, again, Bhujyu Lāhāyani said, "We wandered about as students, and came to the house of Paṭañcala Kāpya."[4] These facts prove unmistakably that the Madras held a high place among the Vedic people.

In the Aitareya Brāhmaṇa (VIII. 14.3), we find the mention of a section of the Madra people, the *Uttara,* or the northern *Madras* who lived beyond the Himālayas *(pareṇa Himavantaṁ)* in the northern regions close to the Uttara-Kurus ; Uttara-Madra is supposed by scholars[5] to have been located in Kashmir.

Location and Early References

In the Rāmāyaṇa we read that Sugrīva sent monkies to the Madrakas and other tribes in quest of Sītā.[6] In the Viṣṇupurāṇa mention is made of Madra along with Arāma, Pāra sīka and others.[7] In the Matsya Purāṇa, Madra is mentioned along with Gāndhāra, Yavana and others.[8] In the same Purāṇa, reference is made to King Aśwapati of Śākala in the kingdom of the Madras.[9] Madda is not mentioned in the list of sixteen mahājanapadas in the Buddhist literature. Some suppose that Madda was also called Vāhlika.[10] The Madras held the central parts of the Punjab.[11] The country they occupied lay between the Rāvi and the Chenāb.[12] They appear in the epic to have occupied the district of Sialkot between the rivers Chenāb and Rāvi (Cambridge History of India, Ancient India, pp. 549-550). India is, according to one description, divided into nine divisions (nava khaṇḍā). This was the description first given by the astronomers, Parāśara and Varāhamihira and it was also adopted by the authors of several of the Purāṇas. According to this arrangement, Madra was the chief district of the north.[13] In the Bṛhatsaṁhitā of Varāhamihira, mention is made of the Madra tribe.[14] It is evident from the Allahabad Pillar Inscription that Madra lay by the side of the territory of the Yaudheyas.[15] The Madra kingdom is mentioned in the Bhīṣmaparva of the Mahābharata.[16] Pāṇini mentions it in his grammar (II. 3. 73; IV. 4. 67). Its capital was Śāgala or Śākala in which form the name occurs in the Mahābhārata (ii. 1196, viii. 2033). Śākala has been identified by General Cunningham with Sangla-wala-Tiba, to the west of the Rāvi (Ancient Geography of India, p. 180). Cunningham holds that Śākala is still known as Madradeśa or the district of the Madras, which is said by some to extend from the Bias to the Jhelum but by others only to the Chenāb.[17] T.W. Rhys Davids says that Cunningham thought that he (Cunningham) had found the ruins of it; but no excavations have been carried out, and the exact site is still therefore uncertain. It lay about 32° N by 74° E.[18]

Chinese Account

It appears from *Hwui-lih* that the pilgrim Hiuen Tsiang went to Śākala.[19] The old town of Sakala (She-ki-lo), according to the great pilgrim, is about 20 li in circuit. Although its walls are thrown down, the foundation is still firm and strong. In the midst of it a town of about 6 or 7 li in circuit has been built.[20] There is in Śākala a Saṅghārāma with about one hundred priests who study the little vehicle. In old days Vasubandhu (Shi-t'sin) Bodhisatta composed in this place the treatise called Shing-i-tai (Paramārthasatya Śāstra). By the side of the convent of the stūpa about 200 feet high, on this spot the four former Buddhas preached the law, and here again are the traces of their walking to and fro. To the north-west of the Saṅgnārāma, 5 or 6 li is a stūpa, about 200 feet high built by Aśoka-rāja. Here also the four past Buddhas preached. About 10 li to the north-east of the new capital, we come to a stūpa of stone about 200 feet in height built by Aśoka.[21]

Description of Śākala in the Miilndapañho

The Milindapañho gives a splendid description of the Madra capital. There is a great centre of trade called Sāgala, the famous city of yore in the country of the Yonakas. Sāgala is situated in a delightful country well-watered and hilly, abounding in parks and gardens, groves, lakes and tanks, a paradise of rivers and mountains and woods. Wise architects have laid it out. Brave is its defence, with many strong towers and ramparts, with superb gates and entrance archways and with the royal citadel in its midst, white-walled and deeply moated. Well laid out are its streets, squares, cross roads and market places. Its shops are filled with various costly merchan-dise. It is richly adorned with hundreds of alms-halls of various kinds and splendid with hundreds of thousands of magnificent mansions. Its streets are filled with elephants, horses, carriages and foot passengers, frequented by the group of handsome men and beautiful women and crowded by men of all sorts and conditions, brāhmaṇas, nobles, artificers and servants. They resound with cries of welcome to the teachers of every creed and the city is the resort of the leading men of each of the different sects. Shops are there for the sale of Benares muslin, of Koṭumbara stuffs and of other cloths of various kinds, and sweet odours are exhaled from the bazars where all sorts of flowers and perfumes are tastefully set out. Jewels are there in plenty and guilds of traders in all sorts of finery display their goods in the bazars that face all quarters of the sky. So full is the city of money and of gold and silver ware, of copper and stone ware, that it is a mine of dazzling treasures. And there is laid up there much store of property and corn and things of value in warehouses, foods and drinks of every sort, syrups, and sweetmeats of every kind. In wealth it is the rival of Uttara-Kuru and in glory it is as Ālaka mandā, the city of Gods.[22] Its inhabitants are prosperous and rich.[23]

Caste

According to the evidence borne by the Sanskrit Epics and Pāli Jātakas, the Madras were kṣatriyas belonging to the warrior caste.[24] and entered into matrimonial alliance with the kṣatriya dynasties of the Gangetic kingdoms. The great Kuru king, Pāṇḍu married the Madra princess, Mādrī, as we shall show below, and besides, from the Ādiparva of the Mahābhārata, we learn that Parīkṣit married Mādravatī and Janamejaya and others were born to him by her.[25]

The Jātakas bear ample testimony to the fact that the Madra princesses were sought in marriage by the great kṣatriya houses of northern India. Thus, we read in the Kusa-Jātaka : The King of Madda had seven daughters, "of extraordinary beauty, like to nymphs of heaven." The eldest of them was called Pabhāvatī. Rays of light streamed forth from her person. King Okkāka sent his emissaries to the Madda king. They told the Madda king that their king had a son, the bold prince Kusa, to whom he had intended to make over his kingdom, and had sent them to ask him (Madda king) to give his daughter Pabhāvatī in marriage to his son. The Madda king was glad 'thinking an alliance with so noble a king would be an auspicious one.' He consented. King Okkāka with a great retinue set out from Kusāvatī and in course of time reached the city of Sāgala. He was received with great honour. Pabhāvatī was then given in marriage to Kusa, son of King Okkāka. The two kingdoms, Madda and Kusāvatī were thus united by matrimonial alliance.[26]

The same story of the union of Prince Kuśa of the great Ikṣvāku family with a Madra princess, is also told in the Mahāvastu-Avadāna with some variations. At Benares, the Mahāvastu tells us, there was a king named Kuśa who belonged to the Ikṣ vāku family. One day he approached his mother, Alindādevī and asked her to bring for him the most beautiful bride. The ministers in quest of a beautiful girl, reached the city of Kānyakubja in the kingdom of Śūrasena where the Madra king, Mahendra ruled. They saw one day his beautiful daughter and thinking her to be the best possible selection, they approached her father who readily consented to give her in marriage to king Kuśa of Benares. But king Kuśa's appearance was repulsive and he had many defects in his body. His wife Sudarśanā discovered the defects in him and with the permission of her mother-in-law, she left Benares for Kānyakubja. In the meantime king Kuśa returning to his palace could not see his beloved wife. He left the kingdom leaving his brother Kuśadruma in charge of it and he at once started for Kānyakubja. Kuśa reached the palace of his father-in-law and tried by various means to get favour from his wife, *e.g.*, by preparing garlands, by making earthen pots, ornaments but all such things were rejected by Sundarśaṇā. He then entered the kitchen of the king as a cook and prepared an excellent soup. The king after taking the soup enquired of the cook-and praised him much. In the meantime seven kṣatriya kings of the neighbouring countries came to win the married daughter of the Madra king but they were refused. Then Kuśa by his own power drove away all the seven kings and after saving his father-in-law's kingdom, he came back to his own kingdom with his wife. The Madra king, Mahendra, being advised by his son-in-law, Kuśa, gave his seven daughters in marriage to the seven kings who came to attack him and thereby the Madra king strengthened his position (Mahāvastu, Vol. II, p. 440 foll.).

From the Kāliṅga-Bodhi Jātaka we observe that even a prince of the royal house of Kāliṅga in the far east sought the hand of a princess of the Madra country. In the kingdom of Madda and in the city of Sāgala, a daughter was born to the king of Madda. It was foretold that the girl should live as an ascetic but her son would be an universal monarch. The kings of India heard of this prediction and surrounded the city. The king of Madda could not give his daughter in marriage to one of them to incur the wrath of others. So, he fled to a forest with His wife and daughter. In this forest lived Prince Kāliṅga. One day while the prince was coming out of the river, a flower-wreath caught in his hair. The prince thought that the wreath must have been made by a tender young girl. He began to search for her. So, deeply in love he journeyed up the Ganges until he heard her singing in a sweet voice, as she sat on a mango-tree. The prince came there and learnt from her that she was a khattiyā. He told her that he was also of the warrior caste. They repeated to each other their secrets. The princess then came down and returning home told her parents everything a bout the son of the king of Kāliṅga. They consented to give her to the prince. The prince married the girl. A matrimonial alliance was thus established between the king of Madda and the king of Kāliṅga.[27] In the Chaddanta Jātaka we find that the royal houses of Benares and Madra were allied with each other through matrimony. Subhaddā, the daughter of the chief queen-consort in the Madda kingdom was given in marriage to the king of Benares.[28] Candādevī, the daughter of the king of the Maddas, was the chief queen of a Kāśīrājā who had no sons. The king asked her to pray for a son. The queen was devoted to good work and used to lead a purely virtuous and religious life. Through the power of her piety, Sakka granted her prayer and in due course she pleased the crown and the country with a son.[29] The great Ceylonese chronicle records an alliance between a Madra princess and a prince of eastern India. We are told that in Sīhapura, on the death of King Sīhavāhu, his son Sumitta became king. He married the daughter of the Madda king and had three sons by her.[30]

Constitution and Customs

The Madras, according to the Arthaśāstra of Kauṭilya, were a corporation of warriors and lived by the title of a rājā (Rāja-śabdopajīvinah).[31] The Mahābhārata tells us that it was a custom of the Madras to give their daughters in marriage on taking a fee (śulka). This was their family custom.[32] The marriage proposal was first made by the bridegroom's party to the bride's party. When Pāṇḍu, the Kuru prince, won the hand of Kuntī, the daughter of a Bhoja king in a Svayaṁvara (the ceremony of a woman choosing her husband), Bhīṣma wished to have him married once again. Then he set out with ministers, old brahmins and sages and came to the city of the Madra king named Śalya of the Vālhika dynasty. He asked the king to give his sister in marriage to Pāṇḍu. The Madra king said, "O great-minded one: matrimonial relation with your family is always desirable but we have a family custom that we should give girls in marriage on taking a fee (śulka). I cannot ignore that custom." Bhīṣma consented and gave to the Madra king much wealth as fee for the bride and the Madra king too decorated his sister with various ornaments and gave her to Bhīsma. Bhīṣma brought her to Hastināpura. In an auspicious moment the marriage ceremony was performed. Mādrī became the wife of Pāṇḍu.[33] Two sons were born to her and they were named Nakula and Sahadeva.[34]

Legendary History—The Story of Śalya, king of the Madras

In the great epic, we have further details of Śalya, the heroic king of the Madras. On the eve of the Kurukṣetra war, messengers were sent to him for help by Yudhiṣṭhira. The Madra king, when he learnt from the messengers that King Yudhiṣthira had welcomed him, set out with his brave sons and a huge army. His army went on occupying the space of half a yojana, with various weapons, decorated with dress and ornaments. Duryodhana heard of this and intending to win the powerful alliance of the Madra sovereign, received him on the way. In order to give him a suitable ovation, he arranged many meetings, amusements, festivities, etc. He caused many good wells, lakes and water-places to be dug. Śalya was highly pleased with him and asked him to pray for his boon. Duryodhana played for his help in the ensuing Kurukṣetra war. King Śalya consented, but on reaching the field-of battle, he said everything to Yudhiṣṭhira who said, "You should not break your promise, but I have a prayer which you will have to fulfil. When Karṇa and Arjuna will fight, you will, in the capacity of Karṇa's charioteer, protect Arjuna." King Śalya agreed to do this.[35] He then came to Duryodhana with his entire army consisting of 109,350 foot, 65,610 horses, 21,870 chariots and 21,870 elephants to help him.[36] He had a golden plough in front of his chariot.[37]

Early in the morning, before going to fight, the kings after bathing and wearing white garments, and offering sacrifices in the fire and taking up their weapons, went to fight. The Madra king, Śalya, went to the battle, being guided by Duryodhana.[38] There he guarded the left side of the army of Dhṛtarāṣṭra,[39] Being defeated by the Pāṇḍavas, Duryodhana piteously appealed to Madrarājā to stop the activity of King Yudhiṣṭhira. The Madra king went towards Yudhiṣṭhira in a chariot. King Yudhiṣṭhira attacked his army. King Yudhiṣṭhira cast ten arrows that struck him in the breast and Nakula and Sahadeva pierced him with seven arrows. The Madra king, Śalya, pierced each of them with three arrows and again with sixty arrows he pierced Yudhisṭ hira. Thus, when Yudhisṭhira and the two sons of Mādrī were tired by the Madra king, Bhīṣma came there and began to fight vehemently.[40] At last the Madra soldiers were killed by Arjuna in the Kuruksetra war.[41]

The legend of Sāvitrī and Satyavān so popular all over India, is connected with the Madra country. In the Vanaparva of the Mahābhārata we read that there was a Madra king named

Aśvapati who observed many vows to have children. He worshipped Sāvitrī who later on appeared before him. He asked for the boon of having children. A daughter was afterwards born to him by his chief queen, Mālavī. This daughter was named Sāvitrī who grew up and selected Satyavān as her husband, Nārada objected by saying that Satyavān would not live long and hence she should not choose him as her husband but Sāvitrī resolved to marry him. Shortly afterwards Satyavān died on her lap. Yama came to take away the dead body. Sāvitrī followed Yama and at last she succeeded in winning the boon of getting back her dead husband. She actually got back her departed husband. It is also stated there that Sāvitrī had one hundred sons and her father Aśvapati too had the like number of sons. (Mahābhārata—Vanaparva, Chaps. 291-298, pp. 509-523, Mahārājā of Burdwan's edition.)

Authentic History

In the city of Śākala, Alexander found the second Paurava king, whose dominions he annexed to the satrapy of his relation and rival, the great Paurava, who ruled over the adjacent territory between the Jhelum and the Chenāb. We may conclude then that the kings of the Madras claimed to be Pūrus and that their dominions together with their capital, Śākala, twice passed under the sway of the Yavanas—under Alexander and under his successor, Menander. At a later date, in the early part of the sixth century A.D., Śākala became the capital of the Hūṇa conqueror, Mihirakula.[42]

In the course of the two or three centuries following the death of the founder of Buddhism, the religion had spread to the extreme west of India from the north-eastern districts, no doubt specially owing to the powerful proselytising zeal of the great Maurya Emperor Aśoka. We find Menander (Milinda) a powerful Greek king, ruling over the country, becoming a convert to Buddhism. Milinda was the king of Sākala or Sāgala. He was, to quote the words of the Milinda-Pañho, learned, eloquent, wise and able, a faithful observer and that at the right time, of all various acts of devotion and ceremony enjoined by his own sacred hymns concerning things past, present and future. He knew various arts and sciences, holy tradition and secular law; the Sāṅkhya, Yoga, Nyāya and Vaiśeṣika systems of philosophy; arithmetic, music, medicine, the four Vedas, the Purāṇas and the Itihāsas, astronomy, magic, causation and spells, the art of war; poetry and conveyancing. In a word, he knew all the nineteen kinds of śilpas or Sippas. (Arts and Sciences.)[43] During his reign, the people knew of no oppression since all their enemies and adversaries had been put down. He had lively discussions with Nāgasena on various topics, *e.g.* continuous identity, re-birth, ego, etc., which are all embodied in a Pāli Buddhist work, the Milinda-Pañho.

Even before this King Sākala seems to have come under Buddhist influence.

In the records of the early Brothers and Sisters also, we find mention of some of them coming from the Madra country, Bhaddā Kapilānī was born in the family of a Brahmin of the Kesiya clan at Sāgala, which, according to the Apadāna, was a capital of the Maddas or Madras. She with her husband obtained ordination and afterwards became a Therī. (Psalms of the Sisters, p. 48.) It is stated in the Theragāthā that the. same lady was born as a chief wife of the Kosiya-gotta Brahmin at Sāgala in the kingdom of Madda. (Psalms of the Brethren, p. 359.)

The Madras used to pay taxes to Samudra Gupta as we learn from the fact that Samudragupta's imperious commands were fully gratified by the Madras and others giving all kinds of taxes and obeying his orders and coming to perform obeisance.[44]

From the records of the travels of the great Chinese pilgrim Hiuen Tsang, we get a fairly detailed account of the political activities in North-western India about the time that he came, and from his account also, the Huns under Mahirakula appear to have been in possession of the Madra country. Some centuries ago, we read in his records, there was in the town of Sākala, a king named Mo-hi-lo-kiu-lo (Mahirakula), who established his authority in this town and ruled over India. He was of quick talent and naturally brave. He subdued all the neighbouring provinces without exception. In his intervals of leisure he desired to examine the law of the Buddha, and he commanded that one among the priests of superior talent should wait on him. But none of the priests ventured to attend to his command. At this time there was in the king's household an old servant who had been a monk for a long-time and had made a name for his eloquence and ability to enter on discussion. He was sent to the king to answer his questions. The king was enraged and lost his respect for the priesthood. He ordered his men to destroy all the priests through the five Indies, to overthrow the law of the Buddha and to leave nothing remaining.

Bālāditya-rājā, king of Magadha, heard of the cruel persecution and atrocities of Mahirakula and refused to pay tribute after strongly guarding the frontiers of his kingdom. When he heard that Mahirakula was marching against him, he fled to the islands of the sea. His soldiers too followed him. Mahirakula left his army to the charge of his younger brother and himself embarked on the sea to attack Bālāditya but was captured by the soldiers of Bālāditya.

Mahirakula overcome with shame at his defeat covered his face with his robe. He was brought to the presence of Bālāditya's mother at whose request he removed his mantle and showed his face. King Bālāditya, as ordered by his mother, gave Mahirakula in marriage to a young maiden. Mahirakula came back to his kingdom but found his brother on the throne. He then went to Kashmir where he was received with honour by the king. After some years he succeeded in killing the king and placing himself on the throne. Then he plotted against the kingdom of Gāndhāra. He killed all the members of the royal family and the chief minister, overthrew the stūpas, and destroyed the saṅghārāmas: Then he took the wealth of the country he had destroyed, assembled his troops and returned.[45] The Chinese traveller also adds that he caused the demolition of one thousand six hundred topes and monasteries and put to death nine koṭis of lay adherents of Buddhism.[46]

It appears that the kingdom of Madra continued till the ninth century A.D., when we find the Madras as the allies of Dharmapāla, the monarch of Bengal, who with the assent of the Madras and other northern powers dethroned Indrarāja, the king of Pañcāla.[47]

REFERENCES

1. Mr. H.C. Ray has contributed a paper to the J.A.S.B., (New series, Vol. XVIII, 1922, No. 4), on the same subject, but my chapter was written independently for this volume and it contains some matters not noticed in Mr. Ray's monograph.
2. Vedic Index, II, p. 123.
3. Bṛhadāraṇyaka-Upaniṣad, iii. 7, 1, S.B.E., 15, 132.
4. Br. Upaniṣad, iii, 3, i, S.B.E., 15, 127.
5. Zimmer, Altindisches Leben, p. 102.
6. Rāmāyaṇa (Griffith's translation) Additional Notes, p. 43.
7. Second-Aṅka-, Chap. 3, 17.
8. Matsya Purāṇa, Chap, pp. 114, 41.
9. *Ibid.*, Chap, p. 208, Śl. 5.
10. N.L. Dey, Geographical Dictionary, p. 49.
11. Early History of India, V.A. Smith, p. 286.
12. N.L. Dey, Geographical Dictionary, p. 49. J.R.A.S., 1897, p. 889.
13. Cunningham, Ancient Geography of India, pp. 5-6.
14. Kern, Bṛhatsaṁhitā, p. 92.
15. R.C. Majumdar, Corporate Life in Ancient India, p. 272.
16. Bhīṣmaparva, Chap. IX, p. 822.
17. Cunningham, Ancient Geography, p. 185.
18. Buddhist India, p. 39.
19. S. Beal's Records of the-Western World, Vol. I, p. 166, f. n. 5.
20. *Ibid.*, Vol. I, p. 167.
21. *Ibid.*, Vol. I, p. 172.
22. Questions of Milinda (S.B.B.), pt. I, pp. I-3.
23. Records of the Western World, Vol. I, p. 167.
24. Jātaka (Cowell), Vol.IV, pp. 144 145.
25. Ādiparva, Chap. 95, p. 105.
26. Jātaka (Cowell), Vol. V, pp. 146-147.
27. Jātaka (Cowell), Vol. IV, pp. 144-145.
28. Jātaka, Vol. V, p. 22.
29. Jātaka, Vol. VI, p. 1.

30. Mahāvaṁsa, translated by Geiger, p. 62.
31. Kauṭilya, Arthaśāstra, p. 455.
32. Mahābhārata, Ādiparva, Chap. 113, p. 119.
33. *Ibid.*, 113, p. 119.
34. *Ibid.*, Chap. 95. p. 105.
35. Mahābhārata, Udyogaparva, Chap. VIII, pp. 633-634.
36. *Ibid.*, Chap. XIX, pp. 641-642.
37. *Ibid.*, Droṇaparva, Chap. 103, p. 1064.
38. *Ibid.*, Udyogaparva, Chap. XIX, p. 807.
39. Bhīṣmaparva, Chap. LI, pp. 924-925.
40. Mahābhārata, Bhīṣmaparva, Chaps. CV-CVI, p. 974.
41. *Ibid.*, Karṇaparva, Chaps. V-VI, pp, 1167-1169.
42. Cambridge History of India, pp. 549-550.
43. The Questions of King Milinda (S.B.E.) pt. I, p. 6.
44. Corpus Inscriptionuṁ Indicarum, Vol. III. p. 14. Gupta Inscriptions, Texts and Translations.
45. S. Beal's Records of the Western World, Vol. I, pp. 165-172.
46. Watters, On Yuan Chwang, Vol. I, p. 289.
47. V.A. Smith's Early History of India, p. 39.

CHAPTER 8

THE KĀMBOJAS

The Kāmbojas in theVedic Literature

The Kāmbojas appear to have been one of the early Vedic tribes. The earliest mention occurs a list of ancient Vedic teachers given in the Vaṁśa Brāhmaṇa of the Sāmaveda where we find one of the teachers in the line to be Kāmboja Aupamanyava, that is, Kāmboja, the son of Upamanyu. (Vaṁśa Brāhmaṇa, edited by Puṇḍit Satyavrata Sāmaśramī) We are told that the sage Ānandaja received the Vedic learning from Śāmba, the son of Śarkarākṣa and also Kāmboja, the son of Upamanyu. We do not know under what circumstances Ānandaja received the Vedic lore from two teachers, as one teacher is the usual rule, and we can only be certain that they must have been very special. From the order in which the names are given, Śāmba appears to have been the first teacher and later the Kāmboja teacher must have been approached, perhaps because the latter was marked by some special pre-eminence in Vedic learning. We lay stress on this fact as it shows that the Kāmbojas, in early Vedic times, must have been a Vedic Indian people and not Iranian as has been supposed by several scholars. Coming back to the list of Vedic teachers we meet again with an important fact, *viz.*, that both the teachers of Ānandaja, Śāmba Śārkarākṣ a and Kāmboja Aupamanyava, had received their own education in Vedic lore from the same sage, *viz.*, Madragāra Śauṅgāyani, whose name itself shows, as scholars have pointed out (Vedic Index, I, p. 138) that he belonged to the Madra people. This connection between the Madras and the Kāmbojas is but natural, as they were close neighbours in the north-western part of India.

The Kāmbojas are not mentioned in the Ṛgveda, but indirect evidence may justify the assumption that they were included among the Vedic Aryans in the Ṛgvedic era. A sage Upamanyu is mentioned in a hymn of the Ṛgveda (Ṛgveda I. 102, 9), as Ludwig has pointed out (Translation of the Ṛgveda, III, 113), and it is not quite unreasonable to conjecture that he may have been the father of the Kāmboja teacher mentioned in the Vaṁśa Brāhmaṇa list. A possible connection like this is suggested by Zimmer (Alt-indisches Leben, p. 102). Whatever may be the value of these cenjectures, the fact stands out without any possible doubt that a sage from among the Kāmboja people, had found a place in the list of the great ancient teachers by whom the Vedic lore was kept up and handed on, and there is no room for any hesitation in saying that the Kāmbojas in Vedic times formed an important section of the Vedic Indian people.

The Kāmbojas in the Nirukta

The next important mention of the Kāmbojas is in a passage of Yāska's Nirukta 'which shows that they spoke a dialect of the Vedic tongue differing in some respects from the standard language which in Yāska's time was apparently the language of the Madhyadeśa, the region about the Ganges-Jumna Doab. Yāṣka points out that the verb '*Śavati'* was used in its original radical meaning of 'going,' among the Kāmbojas, while only a derivative from the same root, *viz. Śava,* was used in the standard dialect in which the verbal significance had gone out of use. This has been supposed to support a non-Indian and Iranian connection of the Kāmbojas, but without any valid reason. The Kāmbojas appear from Yāska's remarks to have been a vedic people who had retained the original radical sense of an ancient verb amongst them, while it was lost among other sections of the same people separated from them by geographical barriers.

Sir George Grierson holds that without discussing the

correctness of the statement that Śava has a connection with Śavathi, we can gather from this that Yāska thinks that the Kāmbojas were, not Aryans and that they spoke Sanskrit but with dialectic variations of vocabulary. Śavathi does not occur in Sanskrit at all but it is an Iranian word. There is the old Persian—Vsiyar—and the Avesta Nsav, Śavaite, to go. To sum up, Sir George is of opinion that the Kāmbojas, a barbarous tribe of North-western India, either spoke Sanskrit with an infusion of Iranian words to which they gave Indian inflexions or else spoke a language Partly Indo Aryan and partly Iranian.[2]

Yāṣka also attempts, though we must say with indifferent success, a philological explanation of the name Kamboja. He connects the word with *Kambala, 'a* blanket.' He says that the Kāmbojas are so called, because they were *Kambalabhojas,* that is, were characterised by the use of *Kambalas* or blankets, which they certainly had to do on account of the great cold in the north-western highlands that they occupied. Yāska again looks for a root from which to derive the word Kamboja, and he found the root *Kam,* which might be requisitioned to offer a derivation, and he suggests that the Kambojas may have been so called because they were *Kamanīyabhojas* or 'enjoyers of pleasant things,' and adds that a *Kambala* is a pleasant thing; there can be no..doubt that the warm blanket, *Kambala,* was a pleasant thing to a people living in a rigorous climate like the Kāmbojas, but scholars will always doubt how far Yāska has been successful in establishing a philological relationship of the root *Kam* with the word *Kambala and* of these two again with the tribal designation, Kāmboja.

The Kāmbalas or blankets manufactured by the Kāmbojas are referred to in the Mahābhārata which tells us that at the great Rājasūya sacrifice, the Kāmboja king presented to Yudhiṣṭhira "many of the best kinds of skins, woollen blankets, blankets made of the fur of animals living in burrows in the earth, and also of cats—all inlaid with threads of gold;"[3] and again, we read a little earlier, 'The king of Kamboja sent to him hundreds and thousands of black, dark and red skins of the deer called *Kadali* and also blankets *(Kāmbalas)* of excellent texture."[4]

The Name also Applied to the Kamboja king

The next mention, chronologically speaking, of the Kāmboja people is that made by Pāṇini. A sūtra of Pāṇini (iv. i. 175) has Kambojal=luk, which, says Dr. D.R. Bhāndārkar, lays down that the word Kamboja denotes not only the Kamboja country or the Kamboja tribe but also the Kamboja king. But then there are other words which are exactly like Kāmboja in this respect but which Pāṇini has not mentioned. Kātyāyana is, therefore, compelled to supplement the above sūtra with the Vārtika, Kambojādibhyo=lug—vachanam Choḍādyarthaṁ. This means that like Kamboja, the words Choḍa, Kaḍera and Kerala denote each not only the country and the tribe but also the king.[5]

Location of Kamboja

T.W. Rhys Davids says that Kamboja was a country in the extreme north-west of India with Dvārakā as its capital.[6] Dr. S.K. Aiyangar agrees with T.W. Rhys Davids in fixing the Kamboja capital at Dvārakā, and places it in the territory answering to the modern Sindh and Gujarat.[7] Dr. P.N. Banerjee too in his Public Administration in Ancient India assigns Kāmboja to a country near modern Sindh with its capital at Dvārakā.[8] In Dhammapāla's commentary on the Peta-vatthu, Dvārakā occurs along with Kamboja but it is not distinctly stated there that it is the capital of Kamboja.[9] V.A. Smith seems to place the Kāmbojas among the mountains either of Tibet or of the Hindu Kush.[10] Smith further says that the Kāmbojas or Kāmbojas are supposed to have spoken an Iranian tongue. (Early History of India, p. 184 and p. 184, f.n.) According to McCrindle, Kamboja was Afghạnisthan, the Kaofu (Kambu) of Hiuen Tsiang. (MeCrindle, Alexanders Invasion, p. 38.) Mr. R.D. Banerjee refers to a Kamboja or Cambodia on the east side of Samatata.[11] But it can hardly be our Kamboja mahājanapada which is invariably associated with Gāndhāra. Dr. D.R.

Bhāndārkar holds, "It is very difficult to locate Kamboja. According to one view, they were a northern Himālayan people, and according to another, the Tibetans. But in our period, they were probably settled to the north-west of the Indus and are the same as Kambujiya of the old Persian inscriptions. Their capital is not known."[12] In the Vedic Index it is stated that they were settled to the north-west of the Indus and were the Kambujiya of the old Persian inscriptions as Dr. Bhāndārkar points out. According to Sir Charles Eliot, the Kāmbojas were probably Tibetans.[13] In another volume of the same work, Sir Charles calls them an ambiguous race who were perhaps the inhabitants of Tibet or its border lands. Mr. Foucher in his Iconographie Bauddhique points out that the Nepalese tradition applies the name Kambojadeśa to Tibet.[14] In the opinion of Sir George Grierson, the Kāmbojas were a north-western tribe frequently mentioned in the Sanskrit literature.[15] Doubtful would be the attempt to connect Cambyses (O.P. Ka (m) būjiya) with the frontier people of Kamboja.[16] Dr. H C. Ray Chaudhuri points out that from a passage of the Mahābhārata we learn that a place called Rājapura was the home of the Kāmbojas (Mahābhārata, VII, 4-5, "Karṇa Rājapuraṁ gatvā Kamboja nirjitāstvayā."). The association of the Kāmbojas with the Gāndhāras enables us to identify this Rājapura with Rājapura of Hiuen Tsang (Watters, Yuan Chwang, Vol. I, p. 284), which lay to the south or south-east of Punach. (Political History of India from the accession of Parikshit to the coronation of Bimbisāra, p. 77.) We quite agree with Dr. Ray Chaudhuri in identifying the Kamboja mahājanapada with Rājapura.

Pāṇini belonged to the north-western quarter of India and hence had an accurate knowledge of the customs and dress of the Kāmbojas. The Mayuravyaṁsakādi—gaṇa of Pāṇini speaks of the Kāmbojas as muṇḍas or shaven-headed. Apparently the Kāmbojas were in the practice of shaving their heads clean, as would also appear from a passage quoted by Raghunanadana from the Harivaṁśa and pointed out by Max Müller. "The Śakas (Scythians) have half their head shorn, the Yavanas

(Greeks?) and Kāmbojas the whole, that the Pāradas (inhabitants of Paradene) wear their hair free, and the Pahlavas (Persians) wear beards."[17]

Kamboja—a great Janapada of Ancient India

Coming to the Pāli Buddhist literature we find the Kamboja country spoken of in many places in the canonical text as one of the sixteen great states (mahājanapadas) that were most prominent in India about the time that the Buddha flourished. Kamboja is one of the sixteen mahājanapadas mentioned in the Aṅguttara Nikāya of the Sutta Piṭaka. The Nikāya says that the merit acquired by one observing the eight precepts is worth sixteen times more than the sovereignty over any one of these mahājanapadas.[18]

The People of Kamboja—a Kṣatriya Tribe

In the Harivaṁśa, we find that the people of Kamboja were formerly kṣatriyas. It was Sagara who caused them to give up their own religion (Harivaṁśa, 14). If we read the verses 43 and 44 of Chapter X of the Manusaṁhitā, we find that the following tribes of kṣatriyas, namely, the Kambojas, the Śakas, the Yavanas and so forth have been gradually degraded to the condition of Śūdras on account of their omission of the sacred rites and of their not consulting the Brāhmaṇas. This shows that the Kāmbojas were kṣatriyas who were degraded to the state of Śūdras because they neglected the Brahmins.[19] The Arthaśāstra of Kauṭilya states that the corporations of warriors (kṣatriyaśreṇī) of Kāmboja and some other countries lived by agriculture, trade and wielding weapons (Vārtāśāstropajivin). From this statement also, it is clear that the Kāmbojas were kṣatriyas.[20]

The Kamboja Horses

The horses of Kamboja were famous throughout all periods of Indian history. In the Sumaṅgalavilāsinī, Kamboja is spoken of as the home of horses (Kambojo assānaṁ āyatanam).[21] The Great Epic is full of references to the excellent horses of

Kāmboja. In the Sabhāparva we read that the king of Kāmboja presented to Yudhiṣṭhira three hundred horses of variegated colours, speckled like the partridge and having fine noses like the *śuka* bird.[22] In the great battle fought on the field of Kurukṣetra, the fast and powerful horses of Kamboja were of the greatest service. Thus, we read in the account of the fifth day's battle that when Arjuna was pressing the Kuru army very hard and fear had struck the soldiers, 'the great fast running horses coming from the Kāmboja country' rendered great help to the Kauravas.[23] On the eighth day Irā vān, the great Nāga hero and son of Arjuna, delivered a fierce attack against the Kaurava army with a very large force of cavalry *(hayasādi)* mounted on the best horses of the Kāmbojas.[24] Again in the Droṇaparva we read that "Studs of the Kāmboja breed beautiful to look at and decked with the feathers of the śuka bird, bore Nakula,"[25] and Dhṛṣṭaketu, the king of the Cedis, "was carried by horses of Kāmboja breed and of variegated hue."[26] Other princes on the field were also "borne by fleet studs of the best Kāmboja breed."[27] In the Karnaparva also we find mention of a chariot drawn by horses of the best Kāmboja breed.[28] The Sauptikaparva again tells us that Kṛṣṇa was borne in a chariot drawn by horses of the best Kāmboja breed decked with garlands of gold.[29]

The Jaina Uttarādhyayana Sūtra tells us that a trained Kambojian horse exceeds all other horses in speed and no noise can frighten it.[30] In the Campeyya Jātaka we read that a king of Kāśī was requested by a nāga king to visit the nāgabhavana. The king ordered to yoke well-trained Kamboja horses to the royal chariot.[31] Viṣṇuvardhana, the real founder of Hoysala greatness, who later on became ruler of Mysore, had Kamboja horses and he made the earth tremble with the tramp of his Kamboja horse.[32] In the copper-plate of Devapāladeva discovered at Monghyr, we find it stated in connection with the conquest of Devapāla that young horses returned to Kamboja and were much delighted to see their beloved ones.[33] Again in the Mahāvastu, a Mahāyāna Buddhist work, we find that a king ordered his ministers to get ready the decorated royal chariot yoked by well-trained excellent horses of Kamboja to see the abodes of the nāgas.[34] All these go to show that Kambojian horses were excellent and fast runners. No doubt they were very much liked in ancient times. As stated above, the best Kamboja horses were so trained that no noise could frighten them. The Aṭṭhakathā on the Kunāla Jātaka furnishes us with the interesting piece of information that the Kambojas were in the habit of capturing horses in .the forest by tempting them with acquatic vegetables which they besmeared with honey. They used to enclose a space with fences having a door. When the horses used to come to drink water at the place where it was available, they were tempted by the smell of honey, and greedily took these acquatic vegetables. They then used to go to the arena, taking the grass besmeared with honcy. When the horses entered the arena, they were caught by the Kāmbojas. (Jātaka, Vol. V, p. 446.)

In the Raghuvaṁśa, Kālidāsa makes Raghu meet the Kāmbojas after defeating the Hūṇas on the bank of the Vaṅkṣū or the Oxus. We read there that the Kāmbojas being unable to meet the prowess of Raghu bowed low before him just as their walnut trees were bent down on account of Raghu's elephants being tied to them. An immense treasure including excellent horses was offered as tribute to Raghu by the Kāmbojas, but even this did not rouse the pride of this king of Kośala.[35] We are told by Kālidāsa that after defeating the Kāmbojas, Raghu mounted the Himālayas; he must, therefore, have met them on his return journey homewards from the banks of the Oxus, where, as we have seen, he had vanquished the Hūṇas.

Legendary Accounts in the Mahābhārata

Among the kṣatriya tribes in the great Epic the Kāmbojas occupy a prominent place. In the geographical enumeration of the peoples of India, the Kāmbojas are placed in the north. (Mahābhārata, Bhīṣmaparva, Chap. 9.) They were the allies of Duryodhana and by their bravery, and especially the prowess of their king, Sudakṣiṇa, they rendered great service to the Kuru side in the long drawn battle at Kurukṣetra. Sudakṣiṇa was one of the few *Mahārathas* or great heroes on the field.

Drupada advised Yudhiṣṭhira to send messengers to the Kāmbojas and other tribes on the western frontiers for their assistance,[36] but the Pāṇḍavas do not appear to have succeeded in obtaining their alliance. Duryodhana was more successful, perhaps through the powerful influence of the Gāndhāras, whose king was his grandfather on the mother's side and whose Prince Śakuni was one of the most prominent actors in the Kuru-Pāṇḍava episode. We find Ulūka, the messenger sent by Duryodhana to the Pāṇḍavas on the eve of the great battle, reporting to them the vaunt of Duryodhana whether the Pāṇḍavas could master courage to fight him, allied as he was with the Kāmbojas and other northern people,[37] among others. Duryodhana in his message, when finally summing up, also gives an important place to the Kāmbojas by placing them side by side with the greatest heroes on his side: thus he says that his immense army, "with Bhīṣma as the current which cannot be crossed, with Droṇa as the alligator which cannot be approached, with Karṇa and Śalya as a swarm of small fishes and Kāmboja as the mouth giving out flames" was a veritable ocean.[38]

In the enumeration of great heroes on the Kuru-side, Bhīṣma extols the prowess of the Kāmboja king, Sudakṣiṇa, of whom he says, "In my opinion Sudakṣiṇa of Kāmboja is equal to one Ratha and he will fight in the battle with the enemy desiring the success of your objects. The prowess of this lion among the chariot-warriors exerted on your behalf, O best among kings, will be seen by the Kurus in battle as equal to that of Indra himself. The best of the chariot-warriors under him are strikers with fierce force. The Kāmbojas, O great king, will cover the land like a swarm of locusts."[39]

When the Kaurava army took up their position on the field, the Kāmbojas occupied the van of Duryodhana's army along with the home forces of the Pauravas themselves. We are told, "The Pauravas, the Kaliṅgas and the Kāmboja, with their king, Sudakṣiṇa and Kṣemadhanvā and Śalya took up their positions in front of Duryodhana."[40]

When the fight thickened round Bhīṣma, Sudakṣiṇa, the king of the Kāmbojas, was in the thickest of the battle and fought the Pāṇḍava heroes when they made their onset. Sañjaya thus describes the fight, "O great king, Śrutakarmā attacked in that battle the great chariot-warrior, the mighty Sudakṣiṇa the king of the Kāmbojas. O king of kings, Sudakṣiṇa wounded that great chariot warrior, the son of Sahadeva, but he could not make him waver; he stood as the Maināka-mountain. Thereupon, Śrutakarmā in great anger covered the great chariot-warrior of the Kāmbojas with countless arrows and mangled him in many parts of his body."[41]

On the third day of the fight, when Bhīṣma arrayed his army in the *Garuḍavyūha*, the Kāmbojas occupied the tail or the hinder part,[42] and on the sixth day's fight they stood occupying the place at the head of the Makaravyūha, arrayed by Bhīsma.[43] On the seventh day, they took up their position in their thousands by the side of Trigarta.[44]

After the fall of the great Bhīṣma when the reins of the Kuru army were placed in the hands of Droṇa, the Kāmbojas with Śudakṣiṇa at their head, were by his side[45] with their powerful horses.

When Droṇa arrayed the Kuru army in a *Garuḍavyūha* the Kāmbojas were placed by him at the neck (grīvā).[46] Afterwards when Arjuna after the fall of his son, put forth his best energy and fought for all that he was worth to carry out his oath of taking the life of Jayadratha whom he took to be mainly responsible for the slaughter, then the Kāmboja Prince Sudakṣ iṇa with the battalions of the Kāmbojas stood in his way and delivered a fierce attack.. Sudakṣiṇa fought a duel with Arjuna and for once threw him into a swoon, but finally was overpowered and killed by him. The verses that describe him as he lay slain on the field of battle are interesting and testify to the opulence of the Kāmbojas and the soft and rich woollen clothes manufactured by them. Thus we read: "Thereafter the heroic Sudakṣhiṇa, the son of the Kamboja king rushed against that slayer of foes, *viz.*, Phalguna, being borne by fleet studs. At him, O Bharata, Pṛthā's son shot seven arrows, which penetrating through that hero, entered the surface of the earth. Pierced deep by those sharp arrows shot from the *Gāṇḍīva* bow, he in turn pierced Arjuna in battle with ten shafts furnished with the feathers of the Kanka bird. He once more pierced Vasudeva's son with three and Pārtha with five arrows, then, O Sir, Pṛthā's son bursting open his bow, cut down his standard; and the son of Pāṇḍu pierced him with a couple of *vallas* of exceeding sharpness: He also having pressed Pṛthā's son with three such arrows uttered a fierce yell. Thereafter, the brave Sudakṣiṇa inflamed with rage hurled at the wielder of the *Gāṇḍīva* bow, a lance, dreadful, tied with bells and made wholly of iron. Having reached that mighty car-warrior Arjuna, that lance blazing like a mighty meteor and emitting scintillations of fire, penetrated through him and then fell down on the ground. Pierced deep with that lance, Arjuna was overwhelmed with a swoon. Then in an instant, that highly puissant hero recovering soon enough began to lick the corners of his mouth. Then Pārtha of inconceivable prowess pierced Sudakṣiṇa and his steeds, standards, bow and charioteer with ten *nūrācas* furnished with the feathers of the Kaṅka bird. And with innumerable other arrows he rendered the latter's chariot useless and cut it to pieces. The son of Pāṇḍu then with an arrow of exceeding sharpness pierced on the chest of Sudakṣiṇa; the Kamboja ruler whose purpose and prowess had both been baffled. Then with his armour shattered, trembling in all his limbs, with his crown and *Aṅgadas* falling off, that hero fell with head downwards like a flagstaff loosened from the socket. Like a charming Karnikara tree in the spring growing gracefully on the top of a hill, with beautiful branches, lying on the grove when uprooted by the tempest, the prince of the Kāmbojas lay on the bare ground deprived of life, though accustomed to sleep on the most precious bed. Adorned with precious ornaments, graceful, possessing eyes of coppery hue, wearing round the head, a tiara of gold radiant like the flames of fire the mighty armed Sudakṣiṇa, the prince of the Kāmbojas, felled by Pārtha with his arrows, and lying dead on the ground, appeared beautiful like a charming hill with a flat summit. Then beholding Srutayusha and the prince of the Kāmbojas slain in battle, all the soldiers of your son's army began to fly in all directions."[47]

In the fierce battle that took place the same day, when Sātyaki, urged by Yudhiṣṭhira, was proceeding in the track of Arjuna, the Kāmbojas stopped him. Here we are told, "Yuyudhāna emerging out of the divisions of the Bhojas, quickly proceeded against the strong host of the Kāmbojas. There he was opposed by many a heroic chariot-warrior; in consequence whereof, Sātyaki of unbaffled prowess, could not move even one step forward."[48] Then we are told that Sātyaki slew thousands of the Kāmbojas, and "making a havoc among the Kāmbojas who were unconquerable in battle,"[49] he passed through the immense army of the Kāmbojas and made his advance.[50]

Again when Karṇa took up the helm of the Kuru army, the Kāmbojas were there taking an active part, by the side of Karṇa,[51] and Sudakṣiṇa's younger brother who had apparently taken the lead among the Kāmbojas after the valiant prince's death, also laid down his life in the Kuru cause.[52] Even after this prince's death, we hear of the Kāmbojas still delivering an attack on Arjuna.[53]

When Śalya was at last placed in command of the remnant of the Kaurava host, we are told that the Kāmbojaṣ had been slain,[54] yet it appears that their immense host had not been exterminated, for we are told that when Śalya arrayed the army in a vyūha, Aśvatthāmā brought up the rear surrounded by the Kāmbojas.[55]

Besides these we hear in the Ādiparva of the Mahābhārata

of a king named Candravarma who ruled in the kingdom of the Kāmbojas.[56]

We thus find the Kāmbojas leading a very large powerful army to the field of Kurukṣetra and laying down their lives like valiant kṣatriyas as they were. Afterwards it appears from the later sections of the Mahābhārata, *viz.*, the Śānti and Ānuśāsanika parvas, that their country had been overrun by barbarous hordes, so that the ancient kṣatriya population was overwhelmed and absorbed by the new-comers and we find the Kāmbojas ranked with the Yavanas and looked upon as one of the barbarous peoples. Thus, a verse in the Śāntiparva enumerates the Kāmbojas along with many peoples that were not included among the Indo-Aryan Society[57] and in another chapter they are placed among the barbarous peoples of the Uttarāpatha or the northern regions.[58] The Anuśāsanaparva speaks of the Kāmbojas as having been degraded to the rank of śūdras for want of Brāhmaṇas in their country.[59] All these passages show that the Kāmbojas in later times, no doubt, by admixture with barbarous hordes, were losing their Indo-Aryan culture and touch with Brahmanical society, and coming to be regarded as outside the Indo-Aryan social organisation when these two *parvas* or sections were added to the great Epic.

Legendary Accounts of Kamboja in the Rāmāyaṇa

In the Ādi Kāṇḍa of the Rāmāyaṇa, Chap. 58, we read that the Kāmbojas were created at the request of Vaśiṣṭha by the divine cow Śavalā (20-24). The Kiṣkindhyā Kāṇḍa (Chap. 43) tells us that Sugrīva sent a monkey named Sutavala to northern India in search of Kamboja and other countries. (11-12.)

In the Purāṇa and the Harivaṁśa

The Vāyu Purāṇa informs us that after killing the Haihayas, King Sagara was engaged in totally annihilating the Kāmbojas, Śakas, Yavanas, Pahlavas and so forth. Being oppressed by Sagara, all of them secured the help of Vaśiṣṭha. King Sagara who was true to his promise, listening to the word of his spiritual guide, Vaśiṣṭha, set the Kāmbojas free after having completely shaven their heads. (Vaṅgavāsī Edition, Chap. 88.) It is stated in the Harivaṁśa that the Ikṣvāku King Vāhu was dethroned by Kāmbojas and others. (Chaps. 13, 14.)

In the Buddhist Works

In the Jātakas we read that the Kāmbojas were a north-western tribe who were supposed to have lost their original Aryan customs and to have become barbarous.[60] In the Bhūridatta Jātaka we find that many Kāmbojas who are not Ariyas hold that the people are purified by killing insects, flies, snakes, frogs, bees, etc. This is undoubtedly a false dharma.[61] It is stated in the Sāsanavaṁsa that in the two hundred and thirty-fifth year of the Parinibbāṇa of the Buddha, Mahārakkhita them went to the Yonaka province and established the Buddha's Sāsana in Kāmboja and other places.[62] Uttarājīva thera went to Ceylon with a sāmanera named Chapada who studied the Tripiṭaka and obtained full ordination there. He then desired to return to Jambudīpa but he thought thus, "I shall be put to inconvenience if I do not perform Vinaya Kammam with the Bhikkhus of Jambudīpa and hence I should take with me four bhikkhus who are well versed in the Tripiṭaka." He took four bhikkhus with him, among whom may be mentioned Tāmalinda thera, son of the king of Kāmboja, and sailed back to Jambudīpa.[63] Sirīhaṁsya came from Kāmboja and conquered the city of Ratanapura. He thought, "Bhikkhus being without wife and son, train pupils and bring them up and thus their families grow. If they turn their attention to worldly affairs, they will be able to conquer kingdoms, therefore, I should kill the bhikkhus now." In a field in the forest named Toṅ-bhī-luḥ, he erected many pandals in which he invited all the mahātheras of Jeyyapura, Vijayapura and Ratanapura with their many disciples. There he caused them to sit and killed them surrounding them with his army consisting of elephants, horses, etc. About three thousand bhikkhus were slain by him and many books were burnt and many shrines were demolished.

Relations of Kamboja with the Maurya and Pāla Empires

In Rock Edict XIII of Aśoka, we read that the true conquest, *i.e.*. the conquest of the law of piety or duty has been won by His Sacred Majesty Aśoka in his own dominions among the Kāmbojas, the Greeks and so forth (V.A. Smith, Aśoka, p. 186.) V.A. Smith says that King Aśoka sent missionaries to the nations on the borders of his empire, *viz.*, the Kāmbojas, the Yavanas and so forth with the object of converting them to his faith.[65] The fifth Rock Edict of Aśoka tells us that Censors were created by Aśoka for the establishment of the law of piety, for the increase of the law and for the welfare and happiness of the Kāmbojas, Gāndhāras and others living on the western frontier of Aśoka's dominions.[66] V.A. Smith sums up that true conquest consists in the conquest of men's hearts by the law of piety or duty. Aśoka won such conquests in his dominions among the Kāmbojas and others. In tact, the Kāmbojas and others hearing Aśoka's ordinance based on the law of duty and his instruction in that law, practise and will practise that law.[67]

In the ninth century A.C. the Kāmbojas are said to have been defeated by Devapāla[68] the great king of the Pāla dynasty of Bengal. But during the latter part of the tenth century, the tables were turned and the rule of the Pāla kings of Bengal was interrupted by the Kāmbojas, who set up one of their chiefs as king.[69] In a certain place called Vānagārh in Dinājpur, mention is made of a certain king of Gauḍa born in the Kamboja family. It is probable that during the reign of Devapāladeva, the Kāmbojas first attempted to conquer Gauḍa, but were, at that time defeated.[70] Mr. R.P. Chanda supposes that in the middle of the tenth century A.D., the Kāmbojas of the Himālayas again attacked North-Bengal and the present inhabitants of North Bengal, *viz.*, Koch, Mech and Pāliā were descended from them.[71] The Kamboja rulers were expelled by Mahīpāla I, the ninth king of the Pāla line, who is known to have been reigning in A.D. 1026 and may be assumed to have regained his ancestral throne about A.D. 978 or 980.[72]

REFERENCES

1. "Śavatirgatikarmā Kamvojeṣveva bhāṣyate Kamvojāḥ Kamvalabhojāḥ Kamaniyabhojāvā Kamvalaḥ Kamanīyo bhavati Vikāramasyāryeṣu bhaṣyante śava iti." (Nirukta, II. 8.)
2. J.R.A.S., 1911, pp. 801-802.
3. Mahābbārata, Sabhāparva, Chap. 51, 3. "Aurṇān vailān Vārṣadaṁśān jātarūpa pariṣkritān prāvārājinamukhyāṁśca Kāmbojaḥ pradadau bahūn."
4. Mahābhārata, Sabhāparva, Chap. pp. 48, 19.
5. Dr. D.R., Bhāndārkar, Carmichael Lectures, 1918, pp. 6-7.
6. Buddhist India, p. 28.
7. S.K. Aiyangar, Ancient India, p. 7.
8. p. 56.
9. Paramatthadīpanī on the Petavatthu, P.T.S., p. 113; vide also my "The Buddhist Conception of Spirits, p. 81 foll.
10. Early History of India, p. 184.
11. Vāṅgālār Itihāsa, Vol I, p. 95.
12. D.R. Bhāndārkar, Carcichsel Lectures, 1918, pp. 54-55.
13. Hinduism and Buddhism, Vol. I, p. 268.
14. *Ibid.*, p. 134.
15. J.R.A.S., 1911, pi 891.
16. The Cambridge History of India, Ancient India, p. 334. f. n.
17. A History of Ancient Sanskrit Literature by Max Müller (Published by the Pāṇini office) p. 28.
"Arddhaṁ Śakānāṁ śiraso muṁdayitvā Vyasarjayat
Yavauānāṁ śiraḥ sarvaiṁ Kambojānāṁ tathaivaca
Pāradā muktakeśāśca palhavāḥ śmaśrudhārinaḥ
Niḥsvādhyāyavaṣaṭkārāḥ kritāstena mahātmanā."
18. Aṅguttara Nikāya, Vol. I, p. 213, *Ibid.*, Vol. IV, pp. 252-256, etc.
19. Bühler, Laws of Manu S.B.E., p. cxiv.
20. Arthaśāstra Translated by Shāma Shāstrī, p. 455.
21. Vol. I, p. 124.
22. Mahābhārata, Sabhāparva, Chap. 51, 4.
23. *Ibid.*, Bhīṣmaparva, Chap. 71, 13.
24. *Ibid.*, Chap. 90, 3.
25. Mahābhārata, Droṇaparva, Chap, 22, 7.
26. *Ibid.*, Chap. 22, 22, 23.
27. *Ibid.*, Chap. 22, 42.
28. *Ibid.*, Karṇaparva, Chap. 38, 13.
29. *Ibid.*, Sauptikaparva, Chap. 13, 12.

30. Jaina Sūtras, S.B.E., pt. II, p. 47.
31. Jātaka, (Faüsboll), Vol. IV, p. 464.
32. S.K. Aiyangar, Ancient India, p. 236.
33. R.D. Banerjee, Vāṅgālār Itihāsa, pp. 179-180.
34. Vol. II, p. 185.
35. Raghuvaṁśa, Chap. IV, Verses 69-70.
36. 'Kāmvojā riṣīkā ye ca paścimānupakāśca ye'—Mahābhārata, Udyogaparva, 18.
37. 'Udīcya Kātnbojaśakaiḥ Khaśaiśca'—Mahābhārata, Udyogaparva, Chap. 160, 25.
38. "Bhīṣmavegaṁaparyantaṁ Droṇagrāhadurāsadaṁ Karnasalyajhaṣāvartaṁ Kambojavaḍavā mukhaṁ"—Mahābhāiata, Chap. pp. 160, 40.
39. "Sūdakṣiṇastu Kāmbojo Ratha ekaguṇo mataḥ
Tavārtha sidhimākāṅkṣau yotsyate samare paraiḥ,
Etasya Rathasirhhasya tavārthaṁ rājasattama.
Parākramaṁ yathendrasya drakṣanti Kuravo yudhi
Etasya Rathavamśe hi tigmavegahprahārinaḥ
Kāmbojānāṁ Mahārāja salabhānāmivāyatīḥ."
(Udyogaparvaṁ, Chap. 165, 1-3.)
40. "Tasya Pauravakāliṅga kāmbojāḥ sasudakṣiṇāḥ, Kṣemadhanvā ca Śalyaśca tasthuḥ pramukhato Rathāḥ"
(Mahābhārata, Bhīṣmaparva, Chap. 17, 26-7.)
41. "Sudakṣiṇantu rājendra Kāmbojānāṁ tnahārathaṁ
Śrutakarmā parākrāntamabhyadravata saṁjuge
Sudakṣiṇastu samare sāhadeviṁ mahārathaṁ
Viddhvā nākampayata vai Maināka miva parvataṁ
Śrutakarmā tataḥ kruddhaḥ Kāmbojānāṁ mahārathaṁ
Śarairvahubhi-rānarcchaddāryanniva sarvaśaḥ."
(Mahābhārata, Bhīṣinaparva. Chap. 45, 66-68.).
42. Mahābhārata, Bhīṣmaparva, Chap. 56. 7.
43. *Ibid.*, Chap. 75. 17.
44. *Ibid.*, Chap. 87. 10.
45. "Teṣīṁ prapakṣāḥ Kāmbojāḥ Sudakṣiṇa puraḥ sarāḥ Yajuraśvairmahāvegaiḥ śakāśca Yavanaiḥ saha." (Mahābhārata, Droṇaparva, Chap. 7. 14)'
46. Śakā Yavanakāmbojāstathā haṁsapathāśca ye grivāāyāṁ surasenastu daradā Madrakaikayāḥ. (*Ibid.*, Droṇaparva, 19. 7.)
47. The Mahābhārata (M.N. Dutta), Droṇaparva, Chap. XCII, p. 136, Verses 61-75.
48. Mahābhārata, Chap. III, 59-60.
49. 'Kāmbojasainyaṁ vidrāvya durjayaṁ yudhi-Bhārata'—Mahābhārata.
Droṇapatva, 119. 51.

50. "Jalasaudhārṇavaṁtīrttvā Kāmbojānāaca vāhinīṁ" —*Ibid.*, Chap. 118, 9.
51. Mahābhārata, Karṇaparva, Chap. 46, 15.
52. Mahābhārata, Karṇaparva, Chap. 56.
53. *Ibid.*, Chap. 88.
54. *Ibid.*, Śalyaparva, Chap. I, 26.
55. *Ibid.*, Śalyaparva, Chop. 8, 25.
56. *Ibid.*, Ādiparva, Chap 67.
57. *Ibid.*, Śāntiparva, Chap. 65, 14.
58. Mahābhārata, Śāntiparva, Chap. 207, 43-44.
59. *Ibid.*, Ānuśāsanika-parva, Chap. 33, 21.
"Śakā Yavanakāmbojāstāstāḥ Kṣatriyajātayaḥ
Vṛṣalatvaṁ parigatā Brāhmaṇānāmadarśayāt."
60. Jātaka (Cowell), VI, p. 110, f.n.
61. Faüsboll, Jātaka, Vol. VI, pp. 208 and 210.
62. Sāsanavaṁsa (P.T.S.), p. 49. "Sāsane pana pañcatiṁsādhike dvivassasate sampatte Mahārakkhitathero Yonakaraṭṭhaṁ gantvā Kamboja....ādīsu anekadısu raṭṭhesu sāsauaṁ pa'ṭiṭṭhāpesi.
63. *Ibid.*, p. 40.
64. Sāsanavaṁsa, (P.T.S.).p. 100.
65. V.A. Smith, Aśoka, p. 168.
66. *Ibid.*
67. V.A. Smith, Ancient and Hindu India, p. 96.
68. R.D. Banerjee, Vaṅgālār Itihāsa, p. 182.
69. V.A. Smith, Early History of India, p. 309
70. R.D. Banerjee, Vaṅgālār Itihāsa, p. 184.
71. *Ibid.*, p. 205.
72. V.A. Smith, Early History of India, p. 399.

CHAPTER – 9

THE GĀNDHĀRAS

Gāndhāra formed an integral part of India since the earliest epoch of Indo-Aryan civilisation. The Gandhāris or the people of Gandhāra are mentioned in the hymns of the Ṛgveda itself. Gāndhāra occúrs in the other Vedas, and in the Epics and the Purāṇas as well as in the Buddhist books. In the days of Aśoka and some of his successors, Gāndhāra was one of the most flourishing seats of Buddhism.

Location of Gāndhāra

The country was on the north-western frontiers of India in the neighbourhood of the Madras, Kāmbojas and similar other tribes, but there are some differences of opinion among scholars with regard to the exact boundaries of the region known as Gāndhāra in ancient India. The Gāndhāra country, says Smith, was equivalent to the north-west Punjab and the adjoining regions (V.A. Smith, Aśoka, p. 170). Mr. Rapson, on the authority of Herodotus, has pointed out in his Ancient India, a distinction between the Gāndhārians and the Indians. He says that the Gāndhārians have been described by Herodotus as bearing bows of reed and short spears, and the Indians as being clad in cotton garments and bearing similar bows with arrows tipped with iron (Ancient India, p. 87). Rhys Davids in his Buddhist India (p. 28) says that Gāndhāra (modern Kāndahār) was the district of Eastern Afghanisthan and it probably included the northwest of the Punjab. In Geiger's Mahāvaṁsa we read that Gāndhāra comprises the district of Peshawar and

Rawalpindi in the Northern Punjab (Geiger, Mahāvaṁsa, p. 82, n. 2). Dr. S.K. Aiyangar holds that Gāndhāra is eastern Afghanis than between the Afghan mountains and a little way east of the Indus. (Ancient India, p. 7.) According to Dr. D.R. Bhāndārkar, Gāndhāra included the western Punjab and Eastern Afghanisthan. Its capital was Takṣaśilā where ruins are spread near Sarāīkālā in the Rawalpindi district in the Punjab (Carmichsel Lectures, 1918, p. 54). The country of Gāndhāra lies along the Kabul river between the Khoaspes (Kunar) and the Indus. Ptolemy makes the Indus the eastern boundary of the Gandari. It is the Kiantolo of Hiuen Tsang, the Kundara Gandaridse of Strabo and other ancient Greek geographers. In the Ain-i-Akbari it forms the district of Pukely lying between Kashmir and Attok. Gāndhāra, says Mr. N.L. Dey, comprised the modern districts of Peshawar and Hoti Murdan or what is called the Eusofzai country, where discoveries were made of excellent Buddhist architecture and sculpture of the time of Kaniṣhka *i.e.,* of the first century of the Christian era (N.L. Dey, Geographical Dictionary, p. 23). The boundaries of Gāndhāra may be described as Lamghān and Jalālābād on the west, the hills of Swāt and Bunir on the north, the Indus on the east and the hills of Kālabāgh on the south (Cunningham, Ancient Geography, p. 48). Undoubtedly Gāndhāra forms a most important link connecting India with the west as Mr. Rapson points out (Ancient India, p. 81). We agree with Mr. Rapson when he says that it holds a unique position among all the countries of India from the fact that its history may be traced with remarkable continuity from the times of the Ṛgveda even down to the present day. (Ancient India, pp. 81-82.) In the Cambridge History of India, we are told that Gandhāra and Gandhāri may certainly be interpreted as referring to the districts of Peshawar and Rawalpindi, north-east from Kabul. A part of these districts has belonged rather to Iran, than to India in historic times, but it is equally impossible to deny or to minimise the role they have played in India's development ever since the remote age when the tribal ancestors of the present

Hindus occupied them on their way into their later established home (p. 321). According to Strabo, the country of the Gandarai, which he calls Gandaritis, lay between the Khoaspes and the Indus, and along the river Kophes. The name is not mentioned by any of the historians of Alexander, but it must nevertheless have been known to the Greeks as early as the times of Hekataios who, as we learn from Stephanos of Byzantion, calls Kaspapyros, a Gandaric city. Herodotus mentions the Gandarai. There was some difference of opinion about the position of the Gandarioi. Rennell placed them on the west of Baktria in the province afterwards called Margiana while Wilson took them to be the people south of the Hindukush, from about the modern Kandahar to the Indus, and extending into the Punjab and to Kashmere. There is, however, no connection between the names of Gandaria and Kandahar (Ancient India as described by Ptolemy—McCrindle, pp. 115-116). Cunningham relying on the narratives of the Chinese pilgrims gives the boundaries of Gāndhāra which they call Kien-to-lo: on the west Lamghān and Jalālābād, on the north the hills of Swāt and Bunir, on the east the Indus and on the south the hills of Kālabāgh. (Ancient India as described by Ptolemy—McCrindle, p. 116.) In some books, the name "Cave country" was applied to Gāndhāra. (Watters on Yuan Chwang, Vol. I, p. 200.)

From the observations about the location of Gāndhāra and the mention of the country in Indian literature as we shall show below, it appears that the boundaries of the country varied at different periods in its history, so that its eastern and western frontiers must have changed from time to time. At one time it appears to have included the Afghan District round Kandahar, but afterwards it receded to the mountains on the Indian frontier.

Gāndhāra in Vedic Literature

In the Ṛgveda the long wool of the sheep reared by the Gandhāris is referred to by Lomaśā, the Queen of king Bhāvya or Bhāvayavya, who, according to the Ṛgveda itself, ruled on the banks of the Sindhu or the Indus; she says to her husband, "I am covered with down like a ewe of the Gandhārins." (Ṛgveda I, 126, 7; Wilson's Translation, ii, p. 78.) From the facts that the verse is brought in very abruptly and that it is in a metre different from the rest of the hymn in which it occurs, Wilson observes that it "is probably a fragment of some old popular song" *(Ibid.,* p. 19). This would, therefore, attribute a knowledge of the Gandhāris to the Vedic Aryans in very ancient times.

A hymn in the Atharvaveda consigns Takman or fever to the Gāndhāris along with other people like the Mūjavants, the Aṅgas and the Magadhas; the Gāndhāris and the Mūjavants belonged to the north whereas the Aṅgas and the Magadhas were in the east, and it is rather peculiar that all these people should be mentioned together. The authors of the Vedic Index explain it by noting that "the latter two tribes are apparently the Eastern limit of the poet's knowledge, the two former the northern." (Vedic Index, I, 219.) In the Brāhmaṇa literature also we find mention of this people. The Chāndogya Upaniṣad in giving an example, thus goes on: "As one might lead a person with his eyes covered away from the Gāndhāras, and leave him then in a place where there are no human beings; and as that person would turn towards the east, or the north, or the west, and shout, 'I have been here with my eyes covered, I have been left here with my eyes covered,' and as thereupon some one might loose his bandage and say to him, 'Go in that direction, it is Gāndhāra, go in that direction'; and as thereupon having been informed and being able to judge for himself, he would by asking his way from village to village arrive at last at Gāndhāra, in exactly the same manner does a man, who meets with a teacher to inform him, obtain the true knowledge. For him there is only delay so long as he is not delivered (from the body); then he will be perfect." Max Müller observes in this connection, "The Gāndhāras but rarely mentioned in the Ṛgveda and the Aitareya Brāhmaṇa, have left their name in Kandaroi and Candahar, The fact of their name being evidently quite familiar to the author of the Upaniṣad might be used to prove either its antiquity or its northern origin." (S.B.E., I, p. 105) But here he is wrong as will be evident from a glance at the context. The author is without doubt referring to a country where he or his countrymen were likely to meet with some difficulty owing to ignorance of the Gāndhāra district and he is apparently speaking of a region at some distance from his own place of residence.

The Aitareya Brāhmaṇa (VII, 34) mentions Nagnajit, a king of Gāndhāra among the Vedic teachers who propagated the Soma-cult, so that it is evident that Gandhāra or Gāndhāra was not outside Vedic Aryandom, but must have been included in it. This is placed beyond doubt by the fact that in the Śatapatha Brāhmaṇa (viii, 1, 4, 10) also we find a king of Gāndhāra, Svarjit Nāgnajita or Nagnajit being quoted though without approval on a point of ritual. His opinion is treated with scant respect as he was merely a *Rājanya-vandhu,* that is, one belonging to the princely order, and not a Ṛṣi. But this King Nagnajit is treated with great regard and respect in later literature from the great Epic downwards, and in a technical book on painting he is regarded as the originator of that art (Dokumente der Indischen Kunst, Erstes Heft, Malerei, des Citra Lakṣaṇa edited by Berthold Laufer).

Coming down to the next period of Vedic literature, *viz.*, the period of the Sūtras, we find that the people of Gāndhāra were very familiar to the Vedic Aryans. Thus we find them in the Śrauta-Śūtras of Baudhāyana, Āpastamba, and Hiraṇyakeśi along with other Aryan peoples of the east and the west (Baudhāyana Śrauta Sūtra, xxi, 13, Āpastamba Śrauta Sūtra, xxii, 6, 18, Hiraṇyakeśī Śrauta Sūtra, xvii, 6),

Legends about Gāndhāra in the Mahābhārata

In the Ādiparva of the Mahābhārata we find that there was a king named Suvala in the kingdom of Gāndhāra. Dhṛtarāṣṭra, the king of the Kurus, married his daughter Gāndhārī and it is well-known to us that 100 sons were born to her. (Mahābhārata,

Chap. 63, p. 72.) Dwāpara appeared on earth as Śakuni, son of King Suvala of Gāndhāra. (Ādiparva, Chap. 67, pp. 77-79.) A princess of Gāndhāra was one of the wives of Ajamīḍha who was the originator of the family of the Kurus. Gāndhāra, it is said, was named after this Gāndhārī. (Ādiparva, Chap. 95, p. 105.) In the same Parva we find that Bhīṣma said to Vidura thus, "Vidura, I know that it is advisable to accept as wives, the daughters of King Suvala and King Madra." It is heard later that Bhīṣma sent the proposal of marriage of Dhṛtarāṣṭra with Gāndhārī, to Suvala who accepted the proposal. Then Suvala came with Śakuni and Gāndhārī to Dhṛtarāṣṭra and went back home after giving Gāndhārī in marriage to Dhṛtarāṣṭra. (Chap. 10, p. 118.)

In the Sabhāparva we learn that the king of Gāndhāra, Suvala, came to Yudhiṣṭhira as soon as he heard the news of the Rājasūya sacrifice. (Chap. 34, p. 245.) In the Bhīṣma parva mention is made of Gāndhāra amongst many countries. (Chap. 9, p. 822.) We read that Śakuni, the Gāndhāran prince, stood in front of the army with many other warriors. (Chap. 16, pp. 827-828.) In the same parva we find that the Gāndhāran prince, Śakuni followed Duryodhana with his alpine army. (Chap. 28, pp. 830-831.) The same parva states that the Gāndhāran King Śakuni guarded Droṇācārya. (Chap. 51, p. 924.) In the Droṇa-parva it is mentioned that Karṇa brought Gāndhāra under the sway of Duryodhana. (Chap. 4, p. 997.) In the Udyogaparva we find that King Yayāti sent his son Yadu to exile in Gāndhāra because he began to disregard his kṣatriya superiors and became puffed up on account of his strength. (Chap.149, p. 771.)

In the Aśvamedhaparva we read that Arjuna went to Pañcanada (the Punjab.) There he had a hard fight with the son of Śakuni, the king of Gāndhāra. Many Gāndhāran soldiers were killed by Arjuna who saved the life of Śakuni's son. The Gāndhāran army fled because they could not stand against him. Then the wife of Śakuni appeared before Arjuna with many good articles and begged his pardon. Arjuna then invited the son of Śakuni to attend the Aśvamedha sacrifice and left for Hastināpura. (Chaps. 83-84, pp. 2093-2094.) On the field of Kurukṣetra, the Gāndhāras, led by their prince Śakuni, made up a strong and powerful division of the Kuru army. When at the commencement of the battle on the first day Duryodhana came out in procession at the head of his vast army, the Gāndhāra King Śakuni with his contingent of hill troops *(Pārvatīyaiḥ),* surrounded him on all sides *(Bhīṣmaparva,* XX, 8). This shows that the warriors hailing from the hills of Gāndhāra were the most trusty of his soldiers, so that they formed the body-guard of the monarch. After the battle had well begun, five Gāndhāra princes with all their troops engaged the five Kekaya brothers with their army *(Ibid.,* 46, 76). In the second day's fight the Gāndhāras with Śakuni at their head defended Bhāradvāja Droṇa *(Ibid.,* Ch. 51, 14). On the third day, when the fight was at its thickest, then two great heroes on the Pāṇḍava side, Sātyaki and Abhimanyu, with a large division of the army, made a fearful onset against the heroic Gāndhāras led by their princes and at the very first onrush the Sauvala or Gāndhāra princes succeeded in breaking up Sātyaki's chariot, so much so that Sātyaki saved himself with difficulty by precipitously running into the chariot of Abhimanyu and the two heroes had to go through the fight in the same chariot *(Ibid.,* Ch. 58, 7-10). On the fifth day, the Gāndhāras along with the Kāmbojas, Madras and other peoples of the north-western frontier made an onset against Arjuna under the lead of Śakuni *(Ibid.,* Ch. 71, 13-17). In the eighth day's fight when Arjuna's son, Irāvān, with an intrepid army of soldiers mounted on powerful horses, was working a great slaughter of the Kaurava forces, then the Gāndhāra princes, six brothers of Śakuni, made an advance on fast horses of their country and essayed to stop the tide of Irāvān's great rush. The cowardly Śakuni tried his level best to persuade them to desist from this imprudent advance, but his younger brothers had a higher idea of their duties on the field and rushed to the spot where Irāvān was making a dreadful havoc with his cavalry. They with their horses surrounded Irāvān and lor a moment the son of Arjuna seemed to be in danger but the latter got the better of the Gāndhāra princes by clever manoeuvres and the young men all lay dead on the field *(Ibid.,* Ch. 90).

After Bhīṣma's fall when Droṇa, as Commander-in-Chief, arrayed the Kaurava forces in the Garuḍa-vyūha, Gāndhāras were placed in the rear (Droṇaparva, Ch. 20). Two other brothers of Śakuni also led their forces against Arjuna himself and beset him from all sides with their fierce Gāndhāra troops, but five hundred of them laid down their lives and when the chariot of one of them was cut to pieces by Arjuna, both the brothers fought in the same chariot and showed considerable prowess, but ultimately met with death in the hands of Arjuna. On their death Śakuni, dreadfully incensed, tried to defeat Arjuna by clever tricks (Māyāyuddha) but finding them useless against the great hero, fled from the field like a coward and the great speed of the excellent horses of his country saved his life *(Ibid.,* 29, 2-27).

When Abhimanyu, the valiant son of Arjuna had his chariot broken by the combined onset of the Kaurava heroes, then Kālikeya, a Gāndhāra leader of the family of Suvala (Suvala-dāyāda) met him but he with seventy-seven of his followers was killed by the young hero with a club or *gadā* (Droṇaparva, 48, 7). Next, when the Kurus were making every effort to save the life of Jayadratha from the wrath of Arjuna who had taken up the dreadful resolve of killing him, on the Gāndhāras was laid the duty of being his immediate guards; they were decked with all sorts of defensive armour and mounted on their horses. *(Ibid.,* Ch. 85, 16-17). Evidently great trust was placed on their prowess and perhaps specially on their fast horses.

When Karṇa abusing Śalya was enumerating the evil practices of the Madras, he included the Gāndhāras also in the same category and said that the Gāndhāras along with the other races on the north-western frontier were men of disgusting practices and customs (Karṇaparva, 44, 46 and 45, 8). When at last Karṇa lay dead on the field, then it is said that cowardly Śakuni precipitately filed from the battle to the camp, surrounded by thousands of the Gāndhāras *(Ibid.,* 95, 6). The Gāndhāra cavalry had not yet come to an end and when Śalya rallied the Kuru forces, we hear of Śakuni joining the Kuru army with a large battalion of his mounted troops (Śalyaparva, 8, 26). It appears that like the Kāmbojas in their neighbourhood, the Gāndhāras also reared a large number of horses in their country and that their troops mostly fought on horseback.

Gāndhāra in the Purāṇas

Gāndhāra is also found in the Purāṇas. According to the Matsya Purāṇa, in the family of Druhyu, one of the sons of Yayāti, Gāndhāra was born and the kingdom of Gāndhāra was named after him.[1] In the Bhāgavata Purāṇa[2] Gāndhāra was the fourth in line of descent from Druhyu. The Viṣṇupurāṇa[3] also agrees with the Matsya, in stating that Gāndhāra, the eponymous founder of the country, was born in the family of Druhyu. Gāndhāra had the following descendants, namely, Dharma. Dhṛti, Durgam and Pracetā. Pracetā had one hundred sons who being the kings of the Mleccha country, conquered[4] the north. In the Matsya Purāṇa, we find that Druhyu had two sons, Setu and Ketu. Setu had a son named Saradvana, who had a son named Gāndhāra. The kingdom of Gāndhāra was named after Gāndhāra who had the following descendants—Dharma, Vidusa and Pracetā. Pracetā had one hundred sons and all of them became kings of the Mleccha kingdom after conquering the north. (Ch. 48.) In the Brahmapurāṇa (Ch. 13), Gāndhāra was the great grandson of Druhyu, whose son was Setu who had a son named Aṅgārasetu. It is also stated there that the kingdom of Gāndhāra was named after Gāndhāra. Mention is made of the Gāndhāra people in the Bṛhatsaṁhitā of Varāhamihira (Kern's Edition, p. 92). In spite of slight differences, it is evident that the Epic and Pauranic accounts agree in making the Gāndhāras descend from the great kṣatriya family of the lunar dynasty.

Description of Chinese Pilgrims

Fā-Hien, who visited India at the beginning of the fifth century A.D., narrates that Gāndhāra was the place where Dharmavivardhana son of Aśoka, ruled. When the Buddha was a Bodhisattva, he gave his eyes for another man here; there was a large stūpa adorned with layers of gold and silver plates. The people of the country were mostly students of the Hīnayāna School (Legge, Travels of Fa-Hien, pp. 31-32).

Hiuen Tsang who visited India in the seventh century A.D., has left for us an interesting account of Gāndhāra. He records the ruined state of monasteries and shrines which two centuries before showed no traces of decay. Kern cites the example of Gāndhāra where such a state of things happened. Hiuen Tsang further says that the great stūpa of Peshawar which on account of its height of more than four hundred cubits, must have been a stūpa of the more composite type, had already thrice been damaged by fire before the pilgrim visited the country. The foundation of the great stūpa at Peshawar dates from Kaniṣka's time (Kern, Indian Buddhism, p. 93 and p. 93 f.n.). The kingdom of Gāndhāra is about one thousand li from east to west, and about eight hundred li from north to south. On the east, it borders on the river Sin (Sindhu). The capital of the country is called Po-lu-sha-pu-lo *i.e.,* Puruṣapura; it is about forty li in circuit. The royal family is extinct and the kingdom is governed by deputies from Kāpiśa. The towns and villages are deserted and there are but few inhabitants. At one corner of the royal residence, there are about one thousand families. The country is rich in cereals and produces a variety of flowers and fruits; it abounds also in sugarcane. The climate is warm and moist, and in general without ice or snow. The disposition of the people is timid and soft: they love literature. Most of them belong to heretical schools, a few believe in the true law. From old time till now this border-land of India has produced many authors of Śāstras, *e.g.,* Nārāyaṇadeva, Asaṅga, Vasubandhu, Dharmatrāta, Manorhita, Pārśva the noble; and so on. There are one thousand Saṅghārāmas which are deserted and in ruins. They are filled with wild shrubs, and solitary to the last degree. The stūpas are mostly decayed. The heretical temples, to the number of about one hundred, are occupied pell-mell by heretics (Buddhist Records of the W.W., Vol. I, pp. 97-98). In the town of P'o-lo-tu-lo, *i.e.*, the town of Salātula, Pāṇini was born who composed his Vyākaraṇa (p. 114).

Capital Cities

The early capital cities of Gāndhāra were Puṣkalāvatī or Puṣkarāvatī and Takṣaśilā (Taxila). The former is situated to the west and the latter to the east of the Indus. It would appear that in early times the Gāndhāra territory lay on both sides of that river though in subsequent times it was confined to the western side. (Ancient India, Ptolemy, McCrindle, p. 115.)

Puṣkarāvatī

According to Cunningham, the ancient capital of Gāndhāra was Puṣkarāvatī which is said to have been founded by Puṣkara, son ot Bharata and nephew of Rāmā. (Viṣṇupurāṇa, Wilson's Edition, Vol. IV, p. 4.)

In the Cambridge History of India, we read that Puṣ hkalāvatī was to the west of the Indus and it together with Taxila came under the Śaka rule during the reign of Maues (p. 560). Mr. Brown says that the chief of the Śakas, Maues captured Puṣhkalāvatī (Peshawar). (Brown's Coins of India, p. 24.) Its antiquity is undoubted as it was the capital of an Indian Prince named Astes at the time of Alexanders expedition. Puṣhkalāvatī is called Peukelas by Arrian and Peukalei by Dionysius Periegetes (see Cunningham's Ancient Geography of India, p. 49). It was famous for a large stūpa *(Ibid.*, p. 51). Tārānāth mentions the town of Puṣhkalāvatī as a royal residence of Kaniṣka's sea (Vincent Smith, Early History of India, p. 261, n.).

Takṣaśilā

Another capital city of Gāndhāra was Takṣaśilā (Shi-shi-Ch'eng).[5]

Taxila, the eastern capital of Gāndhāra, means severed head in the language of China. Here, when the Buddha was a Bodhisatta, he is said to have given away his head to a man and from this circumstance, the kingdom got its name (Legge, Fā-Hien, p. 32.) The city was great, wealthy and most populous as described by Arrian. Strabo and Hiuen Tsiang praise the fertility of the soil. Pliny calls it a famous city and states that it was situated on a level where the hills sank down into the plains. In the early part of the second century B.C., it became a province of the Graeco-Bactrian monarchy and then it was occupied by the Indo-Scythians. Near the middle of the first century A.D., it was visited by Apollonius of Tyana and his companion Damis, who described it as being about the size of Nineveh, walled like a Greek city. Streets were narrow but well-arranged. To all Buddhists, Taxila is a very interesting place as it was the scene of one of the Buddha's most meritorious acts of alms-giving, when he bestowed his head in charity. It was not mentioned by Alberuni. (Ancient India as described by Ptolemy, pp. 119, foll.)

Its Site

Cunningham says that the site of Takṣaśilā is found near Shah-Dheri just one mile to the north-east of Kala-ka-sarāi, in the extensive ruins of a fortified city around which he was able to trace no less than fifty-five stūpas, of which two are as large as the great Mānikyāla tope, twenty-eight monasteries and nine temples. Now the distance from Shah-Dheri to Ohind is thirty-six miles, and from Ohind to Hashtnagar is thirty-eight more or altogether seventy-four miles, which is nineteen in excess of the distance recorded by Pliny between Taxila and Peukelaotis. To reconcile these discrepant numbers Cunningham suggests that Pliny's sixty miles or LX, should be read as eighty miles or LXXX, which are equivalent to seventy-three and half English miles or within half a mile of the actual distance between the two places. (Cunningham, Ancient Geography, p. 105.) Dr. Bhāndārkar says that in Aśoka's time Takṣaśilā does not appear to have been the capital of Gāndhāra, for from his Rock Edict, XIII, we see that Gāndhāra was not in his dominions proper, but was feudatory to him. From the separate Orissa Edict I, We learn that Takkasilā was directly under him as one of his sons was stationed there. Evidently Takkasilā was not the capital of Gāndhāra in Aśoka's time. This agrees with the statement of Ptolemy that the Gandarai (Gandhāra) country was to the west of the Indus with its city Proklais, *i.e.* Puṣkarāvatī, (Carmichael Lectures, 1918, p. 54 f.n.).

Takkhaśilā was visited by Hiuen Tsiang in the seventh century A.D. It was above two thousand li in circuit. Its capital was above ten li in circuit. Its soil was fertile and the crops good, with flowing streams and luxuriant vegetables. The climate was genial, and the people being plucky were adherents of Buddhism. Although there were many monasteries, some of them were desolate and the monks who were very few were all Mahāyānists (Watters on Yuan Chwang, Vol. I, p, 240). There were stupas, *e.g.*, the Kunāla stūpa, the Dharmarājika stūpa.

Jaina and Buddhist Legends about Taxila

Taxila figures prominently in Jaina and Buddhist stories. There was a plague that raged in Taxila when Mahāvīra, the head of the Jaina community, composed many mantras (Śānti-stotras) (Heart of Jainism by Mrs. Sinclair Stevenson, p. 80, f.n.).

In the Psalms of the Brethren we find that Bhāradvāja was born in a Brahmin family at the time of the Buddha at Rājagaha. A son was born to him and when the son grew up, Bhāradvāja sent him to Takkasilā. On his way to Taxila, he made friends with a thera, a disciple of the Master, took orders and on Arahatship. (Psalms of the Brethren, p. 136.)

It is stated in the Dīpavaṁsa that a kṣatriya prince named Dīpaṁkara, and his sons and grandsons, twelve royal princes, governed their great kingdom in Taxila. (Dīpavaṁsa by Oldenberg, p. 28.) In the Dutiyapalāyi Jātaka we find that King

Gāndhāra of Taxila attacked and surrounded Benares with his four-fold army and boasted that nobody would be able to defeat his unconquerable army consisting of innumerable horses, elephants, and chariots decorated with flags. The king of Benares told him thus : "Don't talk nonsense, I shall soon destroy your army like mad elephants destroying nalavana. Thus shouted the king of Benares and King Gāndhāra seeing his forehead shining like a gold plate was terrified and fled to his own kingdom. (Fausboll, Jātaka, Vol. II, pp. 219-221). In the Palāyi Jātaka we find that in the kingdom of Gāndhāra, in the city of Taxila, the Bodhisatta was the king and Brahmādatta was the king of Benares. Brahmādatta surrounded the city of Taxila with a large array and he was giving instructions to his army thus:—"Send elephants, horses, chariots, and foot soldiers in the manner stated by me to attack forcibly and strike weapons and shoot arrows like heavy showers of rain." Thus, he led his army to the gate of the city of Taxila and enquired whether the (city-gate) was the king's palace and was informed that it was the city-gate and the king lived in a palace like that of Inda. He then thought that it was not proper to fight with such a mighty king and then he went back to Benares. (Fausboll, Jātaka, Vol. II, pp. 217-218.)

Takkhaśilā Seat of Learning

Takkhaśilā was a great seat of learning in Ancient India. Various arts and sciences were taught here and Pupils from different parts of India used to visit this place for learning them. In Taxila, magic charms were taught (Jātaka, II No. 185, p. 69). Here spells for understanding cries of animals were taught (Jātaka, Vol. III, No. 416, p. 249). Among the celebrated Buddhist scholars who made the name of Taxila and its janapada, Gāndhāra, famous all over India were Dhammapāla (Psalms of the Brethren, p. 149), Yasadatta *(Ibid.,* p. 201), Aṅgulimāla *(Ibid.,* p. 319, foil.), Asaṅga, a great teacher of Yogācāra and Vasuvandhu, the celebrated author of the Abhidharmakosa. The details about Taxila's importance as a seat of learning have been given by me elsewhere[6] and a brief notice is all that is necessary here.

Political History

In the Kumbhakāra Jātaka we read that there was a king named Naggaji who ruled both the kingdoms of Kashmere and Gāndhāra. He afterwards obtained paccekabodhi (Jātaka, Vol. III, pp. 377-378). Naggaji left the kingdom and became a monk *(Ibid.*, p. 381). In the Buddha's time Pukkusāti, king of Gāndhāra, is said to have sent an embassy and a letter to King Bimbisāra of Magadha (Buddhist India, p. 28). Mr. Rapson says that it was a Persian province for about two centuries ; and after the downfall of the empire in 331 B.C. it together with the Persian province of 'India' or 'the country of the Indus,' which had been added to the empire by Darius not long after 516 B.C. came under the sway of Alexander the Great. Through Gāndhāra and the Indian province was exercised the Persian influence which so greatly modified the civilisation of North-Western India (Ancient India, pp. 81-82). Shortly after the death of Aśoka, Gāndhāra declared independence (R.D. Banerjee, Vāṅgālār Itihāsa, p. 31). It was brought under the sway of the Greek kings shortly after Aśoka's death *(Ibid.*, p. 32). Apparently near the 5th century A.D. Gāndhāra was conquered by the Ye-ta, *i.e.*, the Yets or Jats. Mr. R.D. Banerjee presumes that Diyadāta II conquered Gāndhāra because some gold coins of Diyadāta II have been discovered by Sir John Marshall in the ruins of the city of Takṣaśilā (R.D. Banerjee, Prācīna Mudrā, p. 27). Whitehead presumes that Euthydemus conquered Gāndhāra (Catalogue of coins in the Punjab Museum, Lahore, Vol. I, p. 4). The fourth Bactriatt king Demetrios was confronted with a rival, Eucratides (c. 175-155 B.C.) who deprived him of his Bactrian dominions and even of a portion of Gāndhāṛa (the present districts of Peshawar and Rawalpindi). Henceforward there were two rival Greek dynasties, the house of Eucratides including the princes Heliokles, Antialkidas and Hermaios ruling in Kabul, Kandahar and Gāndhāra. (The Coins of India, by Brown, pp. 23-24). The Hūṇs first of all defeated the kings of the Kidāra Kuṣaṇa dynasty and then entered India (Prācīna Mudrā, p. 188). The Hūṇs occupied Gāndhāra (V.A. Smith, Early History of India, p. 310).

Dharmapāla of the Pāla Dynasty dethroned Indrāyudha or Indrarāja, king of Pañcāla, whose capital was Kanauj, and installed in his stead Chakrayudha, with the assent of the neighbouring northern powers enumerated as the Bhoja, Matsya, Gāndhāra, Avanti and so forth (V.A. Smith, Early History of India, p. 398)

Trilochanapāla was the last king of the Shahi dynasty. During his reign the Hindu rule was lost in Gāndhāra. In the eleventh century, Trilochanapāla was defeated on the bank of river Toṣi by Sultan Mahmud of Ghajni. Trilochan's son Bhīmapāla became independent for five years. After him no account is available of the Hindu rule in Gāndhāra (R.D. Banerjee, Prācīna Mudrā, p.198).

Legendary Accounts

In the Gāndhāra Jātaka we find that Bodhisatta who was at the time the king of Gāndhāra, ruled his kingdom righteously. In the middle country, King Videha ruled in Videhanagara. They were friends though they never met each other. On the first day of the full moon, the king of Gāndhāra saw the moon swallowed up by Rāhu. The king observing this phenomenon thought that the trouble came from outside, his royal retinue was nothing but a trouble and that it was not proper that he should lose his light like the moon swallowed up by Rāhu. He then gave up his kingdom, became a ṛṣi and dwelt in the Himavantapadesa by practising Jhāna. His friend, the king of Videha followed his example. After wandering through various places they met each other at a certain place, but could not recognise each other. They saw the moon's orb seized by Rāhu. The king of Gāndhāra informed the king of Videha of the cause of his giving up his kingdom. The Videhan king recognised him and told him the cause of his giving up the kingdom. After staying in the Himālayan region for a long time, they came down to the frontier village for sour and salty food (cooked food). It happened that one day the Videhan ascetic stored up some salt to be taken when wanting. The Gāndhāra ascetic knew about it and told him, "You (the Videha ascetic) have given up your kingdom consisting of 16,000 villages, with store-houses filled, but now you are storing a small quantity of salt." The Videha ascetic grew angry and told him, "You are blaming me, you are not looking to your own defect. You are now ruling me after giving up the rule of the kingdom of Gāndhāra which is full of wealth." The king of Gāndhāra replied,"I am speaking dharma, there is no wrong in giving instructions on Dharma." Both of them returned to the Himālayan region to dwell in peace and happiness. The Gāndhāra ascetic instructed the Videha ascetic.

The Sāsanavaṁsa tells us that the thera Majjhantika was sent to Kashmir and Gāndhāra to preach Buddha-sāsana.[7] The Dīpavaṁsa also supports the statement that the great sage Majjhantika went to the country of the Gāndhāras and there he appeased an enraged nāga and freed many people from the fetters of sin.[8]

In the Divyāvadāna we find that a Yūpa or sacrificial wood thrown into the Ganges by Mahāpanāda will be taken up by the four great kings, one of whom was Elāpatra of Gāndhāra who would hand it over to Saṁkha (Cowell and Neil, pp. 60-61).

Spread of Buddhism in Gāndhāra

The Rock Edict V. of Aśoka points out that for the welfare and happiness of the Gāndhāras, Dharmamahāmātras (high officers in the department of dharma) were appointed by Aśoka. (Vincent Smith, Aśoka, p. 168.)

Celebrities of Gāndhāra

In the fifth century A.D. Buddhist scholastic philosophy

reached its culmination. About that time two famous Gāndhārians flourished, *viz.*, Asaṅga and Vasuvandhu. Asaṅga at first an adherent of the semi-orthodox Mahīsāsakas afterwards became a convert to Mahāyānism. He was a great teacher of Yogācāra. He lived for some time in a monastery in Oudh and afterwards in Magadha. He died at Rājagaha.

Vasuvandhu was a disciple of Sanghabhadra. From Kashmir he went to Oudh where he lived for many years. At first a staunch adherent of the Sarvāstivādins, he disapproved of Asaṅga's Yogaśāstra but afterwards became a convert to Mahāyānism. After his conversion, he is said to have been a teacher at Nālandā College. He was celebrated as the author of the Abhidharmakoṣa. Besides this, he wrote many commentaries on Mahāyāna texts. He died at an advanced age. Some say he died in Nepal, others say in Oudh.

Trade Relations

The Jātakas testify to the existence of trade relations between the Kashmir-Gāndhāra kingdom on one side and the Videha land on the other. We learn from the Gāndhāra Jātaka that the king of Videha enquires of the tradesmen about the health of his friend, the king of Kashmir and Gāndhāra (Pick, The Social Organisation in North-east India in Buddha's time, p. 272). Horse-dealers figure prominently amongst the Gāndhāra traders. We learn from the Vāyupurāṇa that the Gāndhārian horses were the best of all (Chap. 99th). In Taxila, people used to flock together to earn money (Niddesa, P.T.S., Vol. I, p. 154). In the Vessantara Jātaka we read that in the kingdom of Gāndhāra, red blankets worth one hundred thousand coins were produced and the soldiers of Gāndhāra dressed up with red blankets used to follow King Vessantara of the kingdom of Jetuttara. (Fausboll, Jātaka, Vol. VI, pp. 500-501.)

REFERENCES

1. Matsya Purāṇa, 48, Vāyu Purāṇa, 99.
2. Bhāgavata Purāṇa, 9th Skandha. Chtp. 23.

3. Visṇupurāṇa, 4th Anka, 17th Chap.
4. *Ibid.*
5. Watters on Yuan Chwang, Vol. I, p. 200.
6. See my work, 'Historical Gleanings,' Chapter I, pp. 1-8.
7. Sāsanavaṁsa, P.T.S., p. 12.
8. Dīpavaṁsa, Oldenberg, p. 53.

APPENDIX - A

GĀNDHĀRA ART

A celebrated school of art developed and nourished in Gāndhāra. The reigns of Kaniṣhka and Huviṣhka coincide with the most flourishing period of the great Gāndhāran school of sculpture which had arisen during the rule of the Śaka princes. Hellenistic influence is very great in this art. A careful inspection of the successive coinages of the Indo-Greeks, the Śakas, and the Kuṣāṇs will show that the strongest influences of pure Greek Art had passed away before the reign of Kaniṣka. With the establishment of Greek rule, south, of the Hindukush, traces of the Indian craftsman's hand begin to appear. As time goes on these become more apparent, until, in the Kuṣāṇ period the whole fabric of the coins, if not entirely Indian, is far more oriental than Greek. That purely Indian influences were strongly at work is very evident in the cult of Śiva as expressed on the coins of Vima Kadphises and Vāsudeva for instance; in the Buddha coins of Kadaphes and Kaniṣka and in the typical Indian cross-legged attitude in which Kadphises II and Huviṣka are depicted; and, after all is said, the art was produced in India and must have been largely, if not entirely, the work of Indian craftsmen. It was at the time of Kaniṣka that Indian mysticism allowed itself to be clad in Greek beauty of form. Eastern feeling ran as it were into Western moulds to create this wonderful aftermath of Hellenic art, which left an indelible mark upon every country ot the Orient where the cult of the Buddha penetrated (The Coins of India by Brown, pp. 38-39). The above observation of Mr. Brown seems to be just and accurate on the subject. But Prof. Foucher, the great authority on Gāndhāran art, has made the following observations. It has long been ascertained that the art of Gāndhāra borrowed its technique from the Hellenistic art. It is impossible then that it should not have features in common with Greco-Roman and consequently with the Gallo-Roman art. The degree of this relationship may be distant, yet it can be justified with the help of archaeology and linguistics. It might be held that the sculptors of these countries had each learnt the art at the school of the Greeks. (A. Foucher, Beginnings of the Buddhist Art, p. 145.) The bas-reliefs of Gāndhāra and Amarāvatī are by common accord attributed to the first or second century B.C. *(Ibia.,* p. 190).

Prof. Foucher points out that in Gāndhāra existed columns in Corinthian or Persepolitan style. (Plate XXV.) The image of the Buddha is like a trade mark of the workshops of Gāndhāra *(Ibid.,* p. 130).

During the reign of Menander (150-100 B.C.), circumstances were favourable for planting the germ of the subsequent development of Greco-Buddhist Art by the creation of the Indo-Greek type of the Buddha. Prof. Foucher says that it is for the first time in the annals of Gāndhāra that we find the Indian statue of the Buddha in an European style (pp. 125-128). With the fruitless entrance of Alexander into India. (326 B.C.) we find that Gāndhāra had been the centre of attraction for Greek adventure of all kinds. From the sculptures, *e.g.*, types of Bodhisattva, Greco-Buddhist Buddha, tutelary pair, the great miracle of Śrāvastī in Gāndhāra, the six tusked elephant, Buddhist Madonna, the Indo-Greek image of Hāritī, it is evident that Hellenistic art played an important part in the development of the fine art of sculpture in Gāndhāra.

Vincent Smith in his Aśoka, says that the Persepolitan capital long continued to be used as a decorative element in Indian sculpture and is common in the reliefs from Gāndhāra, the so-called Graeco-Buddhist school, (p. 141.)

The Hellenistic influence on Indian art which is most plainly manifested in the Gāndhāra sculptures dating from the early centuries of the Christian era, may be traced less conspicuously in other directions. There is good reason to believe that Buddhist teaching was considerably modified by contact with the Greek gods, and that the use of images in particular as an essential element in the Buddhist cult was mainly due to Greek example. Whatever Hellenistic elements in Indian civilisation can be detected, they were all indirect consequences of Alexander's invasion. The Greek influence never penetrated deeply. Indian polity and the structure of society resting on the caste basis remained substantially unchanged, and even in military science India showed no disposition to learn the lessons taught by the sharp sword of Alexander (Vincent Smith, Ancient and Hindu India, p. 67). Then the learned author says that much of the Buddhist sculpture at the time of Kaniṣka and his successors is executed in the style of Gāndhāra, the frontier province which included both Peshawar and Taxila. This style is called the Graeco Buddhist style because the forms of Greek art were applied to Buddhist subjects with considerable artistic success in many cases. Images of the Buddha appear in the likeness of Apollo, the Yakkha Kuvera is posed in the fashion of the Phidian Zeus and so on. The drapery follows Hellenistic models. The style was transmitted to the far east through Chinese Turkistan and the figures of the Buddha now made in China and Japan exhibit distinct traces of the Hellenistic modes in vogue at the court of Kaniṣka. Sir A. Stein and other archaeologists have proved that the Khotan region in Chinese Turkistan was the meeting place of four civilisations, Greek, Indian, Iranian and Chinese, during the early centuries of the Christian era, including the reign of Kaniṣka. Gāndhāras. style is Graeco-Roman, based on the Cosmopolitan art of Asia Minor and the Roman Empire as practised in the first three centuries of the Christian era. Much of the best work in that style was executed during the second century A.D., in the reigns of Kaniṣhka and Huviṣka (Vincent Smith, Ancient and Hindu India, p. 136).

In the later school of Gāndhāra or Graeco-Buddhist sculpture, the Buddha is frequently shown in full length (Sir Charles Eliot, Hinduism and Buddhism. Vol. II, 172). Sir Charles says on the authority of Foucher that Aśvaghoṣa's treatment of legends is in remarkable accord with their artistic presentation in the Gāndhāra sculpture. He further holds that the prevalence of Gāndhāra art in the cities of the Tarim basin makes it likely that their efflorescence was not far removed in time from the Gāndhāran epoch of India. *(Ibid.,* Vol. Ill, p. 7.) V.A. Smith is of opinion that the well-known sculptures of Gāndhāra are much later in date and are the offspring of Cosmopolitan Graeco-Roman art. (Early History of India, p. 241.) The celebrated Gāndhāra sculptures, found abundantly in the Peshawar district and neighbouring regions, the ancient Gāndhāra, of which marry excellent examples date from the time of Kaniṣka and his proximate successors, give vivid expression in classical forms of considerable artistic merit to modified Buddhism, a religion with a complicated mythology and well-filled pantheon. *(Ibid.,* pp. 266-267.) Sir Charles Eliot says that the Buddha appears to be represented in the earliest Gāndhāra sculptures and there was a famous image of him in Udyāna of which Fā-Hien speaks as if it were already ancient. (Hinduism and Buddhism, Vol. II, p. 22.) The Yueh-chih who invaded India, were intimately connected with the Gāndhāran Art and the form of Baddhism which finds expression in it (Eliot, Hinduism and Buddhism, Vol. III, p. 213).

The Art of Painting in Gāndhāra

No specimen of painting of the Gāndhāra school has come down to our times, but in a technical book on painting, Chitralakṣaṇa to which we have already referred, a Gāndhāra King Nagnajit is credited with having originated the art and the book itself is said to have been written by that Nagnajit. This book is included in the Tibetan Tangyur and is one of four works on Śilpaśāstra found in Section 123 of the Sūtra portion of that great compilation. It purports to be a Tibetan translation of a Sanskrit book which, however, has not been discovered yet. The Tibetan text has recently been edited by Berthold Laufer and is highly interesting as establishing a connection between Gāndhāra and the art of painting. It gives a story of the origin of the art which runs as follows:—There was once a monarch of the name of Bhagajit who had acquired great fame and renown by his prowess and his pure life and austerities. One day a Brahmin came to him weeping for the death of his young son and charged him with the responsibility for that untimely death; there must have been, he said, in his kingdom some serious breach of Dharma which the king did not take care to suppress. The king roused by the words of the Brahmin sought for the cause of this irregularity and by the power of his penances brought down Yama, the god of death and fought a severe duel with him. When Yama was on the point of defeat, the great God, Brahmā came down, and settled the dispute. He explained to the king that life and death were but the fruition of the results of Karma and it was not possible for Yama to undo or change this law. But to satisfy the king he told him to paint with the proper colours a likeness of the Brahmin boy and when Bhagajit had done so, Brahmā infused life into it and the king made it over to the Brahmin. Brahmā then told the king, "You have conquered to-day the Nagna Pretas *(i.e.,* the naked spirits), therefore shall you be called Nagnajit henceforward," and he further added, "With my help you have painted a likeness of the Brahmin boy. This is the first of its kind down below here among men." The god also advised the king to perfect his education in the art of painting by taking some lessons from Viśvakarmā, the artist of the gods and to learn from him the details about exact measurement and other rules. Moreover, the introduction to the book avers that the Citralakṣaṇa was composed by bringing together the lessons given by Viśvakarmā, Prahlād and Nagnajit.

Now in the Mahābhārata we meet with Nagnajit, the king of Gāndhāra, who is also referred to in the Aitareya and Śatapatha Brāhmaṇas, as we have already shown before. In the Mahābhārata Nagnajit is called *Prahlāda-śiṣya,* "the disciple of Prahlāda," and as we have seen from the Citralakṣaṇa, Prahlāda is considered as an authority of painting after Viśvakarmā, connecting these two together, there remains hardly any doubt that Nagnajit of the Citralakṣaṇa is none else than the Gāndhāra King Nagnajit of the Brāhmaṇas and the great Epic. In the Jaina literature also a Gāndhāra sovereign Naggati or Nagnajit is referred to as one of the kings who left their kingdoms to embrace an ascetic life, but in the Citralakṣaṇa there is no trace of Jaina influence but the entire work is evidently Brāhmanical.

Putting together all the facts about Gāndhāra and Nagnajit it appears that the Chitralakṣaṇa is a text book of Gāndhāran art and it is highly probable, as Laufer suggests, that there must have been an ancient indigenous school of Gāndhāra art. This was influenced by the Hellenic art and produced the numerous sculptures that have come down to our times. Prof. Grünwedel also came to a similar conclusion from a study of certain peculiarities of the Gāndhāra style. He says: "In many sculptures of the Gāndhāra school, the pictorial element is so strongly in evidence that one might imagine that an early school of painting had existed in Gāndhāra whose extreme offshoot is represented to some extent in the Tibetan ecclesiastical painting; for example, the nimbus, and the reliefs of 'the flight of the Bodhisattva,' 'the birth of Gautama,' etc."

The paintings discovered by Sir Aurel Stein in Khotan and Central Asia show some influence of Gāndhāra art and Chinese tradition also narrates that two Khotanese painters, Wajna and Wei-chi-i-Song, introduced the Indian ideals and methods of painting in China and Korea. This makes it not unreasonable to surmise that it was the ancient pre-Hellenic Gāndhāra school of painting that influenced the art of Central Asia and the Far East.[1]

REFERENCE

1. See an article by Prof. Rabindra Narayan Ghosh in the Sāhitya-Pariṣat Patrikā, Vol. 29, pt. II, pp. 55-65.

APPENDIX - B

COINS

It was in Gāndhāra that the finest "double-die" (impressed on both sides of the coin) coins were struck. Among these, one of the commonest, bearing a lion on the obverse, and an elephant on the reverse, is of special importance, since an approximate date can be assigned to it, for it was imitated by the Greek princes, Pantaleon and Agathokles (Brown's Coins of India, p. 19). The seated bull and horseman, the almost invariable devices on Rajput copper and billon coins, were introduced by the Brāhmaṇa kings of Gāndhāra or Ohind (Circa. 860-950), who first used them on silver ; the commonest of these are the issues of Spalapatideva and Samantadeva. (The Coins of India by Brown, p. 53.)

It is interesting to note that Pantaleon and Agathokles were undoubtedly closely connected, since they struck coins which were identical in type and form. These were borrowed from the earlier native currency which prevailed generally in the Paropanisadae and Gāndhāra (Cambridge History of India, p. 546). The passing of Pahlava rule in Eastern Gāndhāra is illustrated by the remarkable hoard of 21 small silver coins, which was found by Sir John Marshall in an earthen jar on the ancient site of Sirkap. (Cambridge History of India, p. 580.)

Dr. D.R. Bhāndārkar while speaking of the Kārṣāpaṇas holds that sometimes a coin which was even fifteen grains lighter was pronounced to be the heavier of the two. The ordinary human hand cannot unaided detect a difference of even fifteen grains. No wonder therefore if the Purāṇas of the Peshawar hoard were debased to the extent of 14.66 grs. The people of Gāndhāra, says Dr. Bhāndārkar, could not possibly have detected this reduction of weight by the mere touch of their hand, and the debasement of the coin, necessitated perhaps by political exigencies, could thus have been safely practised on them. (Carmichsel Lectures, 1921, p. 116.)

Coins of the Kidāra-Kuṣāṇas have been found in Kashmir and some parts of Gāndhāra. All the coins have the name of Kidāra on the obverse. This Kidāra has been identified by Cunningham with Ki-to-lo, the leader of the great Yuch-ti, known from Chinese sources. (Carmichasl Lectures, 1921, p. 205.)

The territories on the extreme north-western frontier of India, *i,e.,* the Kābul valley and Gāndhāra (including Taxila) which were originally conquered by Euthydemus or by Demetrius were wrested from the family of Greek princes by Eucratides. Coins originally issued by Apollodotus and re-struck by Eucratides bear the image and superscription of the tutelary deity of Kāpiśa, the capital city of Gāndhāra, they testify to the change of government which had taken place in this province. Rapson says that coins and inscriptions show that the family of Eucratides was supplanted by Śaka Satraps in both Kāpiśa and Taxila (Rapson, Ancient India, p. 133). Rapson points out that an inscription affords the bare mention of a satrap of Kāpiśa, the capital of Gāndhāra. which as we know from coins had passed from the family of Euthydemus (Apollodotus) into the power of Eucratides. There is a copper-plate inscription of a satrap at Taxila, one of the capitals of Gāndhāra, named Pātika which records the deposit of relics of the Buddha and a donation made in the seventy-eighth year of an unknown era. (Rapson's Ancient India, p. 141.)

OPINIONS

Dr. Sten Konow of Norway:—It is a very useful work you have undertaken to put together all the references available from literature about the Kṣatriya clans. I wish that we had more books of the same kind, not only about tribes and clans but also about geographical designations. The great merit of such books is that they allow you to judge for yourself without simply accepting the opinion of the author. I am very thankful to you for your careful piecing together of such evidence as is available and I look forward to further important contributions from you in elucidation of ancient Indian history.

Mrs. C. A.F. Rhys Davids of England:—Thank you much for the gift of your very readable and clear-written work. You give us many apercus of what seems to have been a simple folk of a crude stage of civilisation, when we get light upon them. Your book is a more ample and detailed monograph than what I had expected.

Dr. A. Berriedale Keith of Scotland, writes in his foreword to the above book:—The most pressing need at the present day is a detailed investigation of carefully chosen aspects of Indian history, and it was a happy thought of Dr. Bimala Charan Law to select for investigation the history of certain Kṣatriya clans of ancient India. Careful collections of facts such as are contained in this work form the only sound basis of further research and the future historian of India will find his task substantially furthered both by the wide knowledge and by the sound judgment of the author. Many things are obscure in the history of these clans and it is of special value to have the whole of the facts regarding them set out without *parti pris* in a spirit of scientific research.

Dr. F.O. Schrader of Germany:—There is so much interesting material in it and your way of dealing with it is attractive throughout.

Dr. E. W. Hopkins of America:—I was much pleased with your volume on Kṣatriya Tribes of Ancient India, which I have read with much historical profit. Please accept my thanks for the very useful work.

Dr. Jarl Charpentier of Upsala:—Your valuable book on "Kṣatriya Tribes in Ancient India." I have found it a very valuable contribution to the history of ancient India. The subject has not, to my knowledge, been dealt with properly in any previous work, and I am astonished at the vast and, as far as I can judge, exhaustive collections of materials that you have succeeded in bringing together. I shall certainly recommend the book to those of my students who are concerned with similar topics.

Dr. W. Geiger of Germany:—Valuable present... .It was a happy idea, I think, to collect all the notices to be found in Indian sources about the Kṣatriya clans in India in the Buddhist period. For this is of special importance for our knowledge of Indian life during those centuries. You have splendidly enlarged and supplied the materials shortly dealt with by Prof. Rhys Davids in his well-known book on Buddhist India. I see with special interest that you have even utilised for your work the Mahāvaṁsa Ṭīkā.

Dr. L.D. Barnett of England:—The additions that you have made increase the usefulness of the work.

Sir charles eliot, British Ambassador, Japan:—In looking through the Kṣatriya tribes, I found the chapters on the Licchavis and Śākyas particularly interesting and I am confident that the book will prove of real value to students.

Dr. Louis de la Vallee Poussin of Belgium:—... .Unfortunately your book on Kṣatriyas conies when I am dispatching the last proofs of a *Histoire de I Inde,* and I can only add in a footnote that I have not been able to draw from it a number of details and observations worthy of notice. But when I shall come to the Guptas, your remarks on the Licchavis will be discussed.

The Times literary supplement :—In his search for material for the history of Kṣatriya clans in early India Mr. Law has, one would think, very nearly exhausted all the available records. He claims to have studied not only the European and Indian scholars who have made researches, but also to have ransacked an immense quantity of Hindu and Buddhist literature........To collect every possible reference to a particular tribe or to any individual of eminence belonging to that tribe is undoubtedly useful..........Mr. Law has, however, succeeded in showing that many of these ancient clans were exceedingly prosperous, and that they were for the most part a cultivated and a manly race. The section on the Licchavis, which occupies more than a third of the book, is very well done, and Mr. Law claims, no doubt rightly, that he has added much to the information already available, especially as regards matrimonial practices and the condition of Vaiśālī, the capital city. The description, too of Gāndhāra is particularly interesting to European scholars because of its connexion with Alexander and because archaeological research has enabled us to supplement literary remains.

BIBLIOGRAPHY

1. Aitareya Brāhmaṇa.
2. Altndisches Leben.
3. Anargharāghava (Nirṇaya Sāgara's Edition).
4. Ancient Geography of India (Cunningham).
5. Ancient India (E.J. Rapson).
6. Ancient India (S.K. Aiyangar).
7. Ancient and Hindu India (Vincent Smith).
8. Ancient India as described by Ptolemy (McCrindle).
9. Aṅguttara Nikāya (P.T.S.).
10. Archaeological Survey of India, Annual Report, 1903-04.
11. Archaeological Survey Reports, Vols. I and XVI.
12. Arthaśāstra of Kauṭilya (Text).
13. Aśoka (Vincent Smith).
14. Atharvasaṁhitā (Whitney and Lanman).
15. Atharvavedasaṁhitā (Roth and Whitney).
16. Avadānakalpalatā (Bibliotheca Indica Series).
17. Beginnings of the Buddhist Art (Foucher).
18. Bhaviṣyapurāṇa (Vaṅgavāsī Edition).
19. Book of the Kindred Sayings (P.T.S.).
20. Bṛhatsaṁhitā (Kern).
21. Buddhacarita (Text).
22. Buddhism.

23. Buddhist Conception of Spirits (B.C. Law).
24. Buddhist India (Rhys Davids).
25. Buddhist Records of the Western World (S. Beal).
26. Buddhist Suttas (S.B.E., Vol. XI).
27. Cambridge History of India, Vol. I. (Rapson).
28. Carmichae Lectures, 1918 (D.R. Bhandarkar).
29 Cārudatta.
30. Coins of India (Brown).
31. Corporate Life in Ancient India (R.C. Mazumdar).
32. Corpus Inscriptionum Indicarum (Fleet).
33. Dhammapadam (Fausboll).
34. Dialogues of the Buddha (T.W. and C.A.F. Rhys Davids).
35. Dīgha-Nikāya (P.T.S.).
36. Dīpavaṁsa (Oldenberg).
37. Divyāvadāna (Cowell & Neil).
38. Early History of India (Vincent Smith).
39. Fa-Hien (Legge).
40. Fick's Social Organisation in North-East India in Buddha's time (S.K. Maitra).
41. Gaina Sūtras (S.B.E.).
42. Gautama, Āpastamba, Vaśiṣṭha and Baudhāyana.
43. Geographical Dictionary (N.L. Dey).
44. Geschichte der Indischen Litteratur (Winternitz),
45. Gupta Coins (J. Allan).
46. Heart of Jainism (S. Stevenson).
47. Hinduism and Buddhism (Charles Eliot).
48. Historical Gleanings (B.C. Law).
49. History of Ancient Sanskrit Literature (Max Müller).
50. Indian Antiquary.
51. Indian Coins (Rapson).

52. Indische Studien (Weber).
53. Jātaka (Cowell).
54. Jātaka (Fausboll).
55. Journals of Bihar and Orissa Research Society.
56. Journals of the Department of Letters (Calcutta University).
57. Journals of the Pāli Text Society.
58. Journals of the Royal Asiatic Society.
59. Journals and Proceedings of the Asiatic Society of Bengal.
60. Kalpasūtra (Dhanpat Singh's Edition).
61. Karmaśaṭaka (M.L. Feer).
62. Lalitavistara (Bibliotheca Indica Series).
63. Lalitavistara (E. Lefmann).
64. Laws of Manu (Bühler).
65. Le Mahāvastu (E. Senart).
66. Life of Hiuen-Tsiang (Beal).
67. Life of the Buddha (Rockhill).
68. Mahābhārata (Vaṅgavāsī Edition).
69. Mahābhārata (M.N. Dutt).
70. Mahāvaṁsa (Geiger).
71. Mahāvaṁsa Ṭīkā (Sinhalese Edition).
72. Majjhima Nikāya (P.T.S.).
73. Mānavadharmaśāstra (Jolly).
74. Manual of Buddhism (Speuce Hardy).
75. Manual of Indian Buddhism (Kern).
76. Mṛcchakaṭika (Jīvānanda Vidyāsāgara).
77. Mudrārākṣasa (Text).
78. Nirukta (Text).
79. Origin of the Bengali Script (R.D. Banerjee).
80. Paramatthadīpanī on the Petavatthu (P.T.S.).

81. Paramatthadīpanī on the Theragāthā (Sinhalese Edition).
82. Paramatthajotikā on the Khuddakapāṭha (P.T.S.)
83. Petavatthu (P.T.S.).
84. Petavatthu-aṭṭhakathā (Sinhalese Edition).
85. Political History of India (H.C. Rai Chaudhuri).
86. Prācīna Mudrā (R.D. Banerjee).
87. Psalms of the Brethren (Mrs. Rhys Davids).
88. Psalms of the Sisters (Mrs. Rhys Davids.)
89. Public Administration in Ancient India (P.N. Banerjee).
90. Questions of Milinda (S.B.E.).
91. Raghuvaṁśa (Text).
92. Rāmāyaṇa (Bombay Edition).
93. Rāmāyaṇa (Griffith's Translation).
94. Romantic Legend of Śākya Buddha (S. Beal).
95. Sanskrit Dictionary (Monier Williams).
96. Saṁyutta Nikāya (P.T.S.).
97. Sāsanavaṁsa.
98. Śatapatha Brāhmaṇa (S.B.E.).
99. Sīrīkalpasūtraṁ (Bhavnagar Edition).
100. Sumaṅgalavilāsinī (Burmese Edition).
101. Sumaṅgalavilāsinī (P.T.S.).
102. Sutta Nipāta (P.T.S.)
103. Sutta Nipāta Commentary (P.T.S.).
104. Svapnavāsavadattā (Gaṇapati Śāstrī's Edition).
105. Tārānāth's Geschichte des Buddhismus in India (Tr. by Anton Schiefner).
106. Thera-Therī gāthā (P.T.S.).
107. Travels of Fā-Hien (Beal).
108. Travels of Fā-Hien (Legge).
109. Travels of Fā-Hien and Sung-yun (S. Beal).

110. Uvāsagadasāo (Bibliotheca Indica Series).
111. Vaijayantī (Gustav Oppert).
112. Vaiṣṇavism, Śaivism and minor religious systems (R.G. Bhāndārkar)
113. Vaṁśabrāhmaṇa (Satyavrata Śāmasramī's Edition).
114. Vaṅgīya Sāhitya Pariṣad Patrikā.
115. Vāṅgālār Itihāsa (R.D. Banerjee).
116. Vedic Index (Macdonell and Keith).
117. Vinaya Piṭaka (Oldenberg).
118. Vinaya Texts (S.B.E.).
119. Viṣṇupurāṇa (Vaṅgavāsī Edition).
120. Viṣṇupurāṇa (Wilson).
121. Watters on Yuan Chwang.

INDEX

★★★